Why Americans Still Don't Vote

Frances Fox Piven
and Richard A. Cloward

Why Americans
Still Don't Vote

And Why Politicians
Want It That Way

Beacon Press BOSTON

Beacon Press
25 Beacon Street
Boston, Massachusetts 02108-2892
www.beacon.org

Beacon Press books
are published under the auspices of
the Unitarian Universalist Association of Congregations.

05 04 03 02 01 00   8 7 6 5 4 3 2 1

This book is printed on acid-free paper that meets the uncoated
paper ANSI/NISO specifications for permanence as revised in 1992.

Composition by Wilsted & Taylor Publishing Services

LIBRARY OF CONGRESS CATALOGING-IN-PUBLICATION DATA
Piven, Frances Fox.
Why Americans still don't vote : and why politicians want it that way / Frances Fox
Piven and Richard A. Cloward.—[Rev. and updated ed.].
p. cm.
Includes bibliographical references and index.
ISBN 0-8070-0449-9 (pa)
1. Voting—United States—Abstention.   2. Poor—United States—Political activity.
3. Voter registration—United States.   I. Cloward, Richard A.   II. Title.
JK 1987 .P58   2000
324.973—dc21   00-039770

Contents

Introduction

*T*his revised and updated edition of *Why Americans Don't Vote* completes the account of the events beginning in the early 1980s that led to the passage of the National Voter Registration Act of 1993. That story was broken off in 1987 when the first edition went to press. This fuller account includes an analysis of the role of reform groups in winning the legislation, overcoming congressional resistance to making voter registration available not only in driver's license agencies but in agencies dispensing public welfare benefits, food stamps, and Medicaid, and helping finally to override four Republican filibusters and to persist in the face of a veto by a Republican president.

We also tell the troubled story of the implementation of the Act. A "states' rights" revolt was led by Republican governors in the large northern states who went to court claiming that the Congress lacked the authority under the Tenth Amendment to usurp the historic power of states to fashion voter registration arrangements as they saw fit. In effect, the old southern Bourbons had reappeared as northern Republican governors.

Once the federal courts had put down the states' rights challenge, the task was to force the states to implement the new voter registration system effectively by the 1995 startup date. Not surprisingly, implementation in driver's license agencies was far smoother and more effective than in state public assistance agencies.

Still, resistance and procedural gaps notwithstanding, the system did get implemented, and more people registered between 1995 and 1998, the first four years, than ever before in American history. However, turnout did not rise in the 1996 and 1998 elections. Higher registration and lower turnout have large implications, both for American politics and for academic theories about low voting, which we discuss in the final chapter.

We have also made some revisions, largely for clarification, in the early chapters of the book, which deal both with the history of low voting in the United States during the twentieth century and with academic explanations of it. This analysis influenced the strategy we followed—through a voter registration reform organization we formed in 1983 called Human SERVE—to promote congressional action to reform voter registration, and to promote effective implementation of the new system.

CHAPTER ONE

Does Voting Matter?

*T*his book is about an electoral reform project called Human
SERVE (Human Service Employees Registration and Voter Education), which we initiated in 1983. Our purpose was to make voter
registration available in welfare and unemployment offices, and in
private sector agencies such as day care and family planning. The book
discusses the ideas that informed the project, the complex dynamics
of the reform effort itself, and the outcome.

We undertook the project because it was clear by 1980 that a Re-
publican/business/Christian Right coalition was coming to power
and that the New Deal and Great Society programs—which have always been of central interest to us—were seriously threatened. At the
same time, registration and voting levels among the recipient constituencies of these programs were low and falling. We thought it might
be possible to raise voting levels through registration reform and thus
strengthen resistance to the attack on entitlements.

In the late 1980s, a national voting rights coalition of civil rights,
good government, labor, and religious groups took up this strategy of
registration reform, and persuaded Democrats in Congress (joined by
several Republicans) to pass the National Voter Registration Act of
1993, which a Democratic president signed in May of that year. The Act

required that, beginning in 1995, voter registration be made available in AFDC, Food Stamps, Medicaid, and WIC agencies and in agencies serving disabled Americans. It also required that people be allowed to register when they get or renew driver's licenses. It was this last provision that gave the Act its tag name "motor voter." The states were also required to permit people to register by mail, and the Federal Election Commission was ordered to design a mail form that the states were required to use if they failed to design their own. With this reform, historic barriers to voter registration that had kept voting down among blacks and many poor whites in the South and among many in the northern industrial working class were largely abolished.

The first part of the book (chapters 1 through 6) sets out the history of low voting by poorer and minority people and the competing theoretical explanations for it. This history and the debates it generated greatly influenced our decision to undertake an electoral reform project, as well as the strategy of reform that we pursued. In chapters 7 through 12 we describe the reform efforts that led to the National Voter Registration Act of 1993. Finally, we assess the impact of the new system on voter registration and turnout. We begin in this chapter with a discussion of why we think the shrunken and skewed nature of the American electorate has been and is important.

Has Nonvoting Mattered?

The right to vote is the core symbol of democratic politics. Of course, the vote itself is meaningless unless citizens have other rights, such as the right to speak, write, and assemble; unless opposition parties can compete for power by offering alternative programs, cultural appeals, and leaders; and unless diverse popular groupings can gain some recognition by the parties. And democratic arrangements that guarantee formal equality through the universal franchise are inevitably compromised by sharp social and economic inequalities. Nevertheless, the right to vote is the feature of the democratic polity that makes all other political rights significant. "The electorate occupies, at least in the mystique of [democratic] orders, the position of the principal organ of governance."[1]

Americans generally take for granted that ours is the very model of a democracy. Our leaders regularly proclaim the United States to be the world's leading democracy and assert that other nations should measure their progress by the extent to which they develop electoral arrangements that match our own. At the core of this self-congratulation is the belief that the right to vote is firmly established here. But in fact the United States is the only major democratic nation in which the less-well-off, as well as the young and minorities, are substantially underrepresented in the electorate. Only about half of the eligible population votes in presidential elections, and far fewer vote in off-year elections. As a result, the United States ranks at the bottom in turnout compared with other major democracies.[2] Moreover, those who vote are different in politically important respects from those who do not. Voters are better off and better educated, and nonvoters are poorer and less well educated. Modest shifts from time to time notwithstanding, this has been true for most of the twentieth century and has actually worsened in the last three decades. In sum, the active American electorate overrepresents those who have more and underrepresents those who have less.[3]

Despite the central role that political scientists typically assign to electoral processes in shaping politics, some scholars deny that important political consequences follow from the constriction of the electorate. In one variant of this argument, nonvoting is defined as a kind of voting, a tacit expression of satisfaction with the political status quo. Since many people abstain and are apparently satisfied, the size of the nonvoting population actually demonstrates the strength of the American democracy. Of course, no one has offered an adequate explanation of why this "politics of happiness"[4] is consistently concentrated among the least well-off.

Another variant of the no-problem position asserts that mass abstention contributes to the health of a democratic polity not because it is a mark of satisfaction but because it reduces conflict and provides political leaders with the latitude they require for responsible governance. A functioning democracy, the argument goes, requires a balance between participation and nonparticipation, between involvement and noninvolvement.[5] The "crisis of democracy" theorists of the 1970s, for example, reasoned that an "excess" of participation endangered democratic institutions by "overloading" them with demands, especially economic demands.[6] This rather Olympian view of the democratic "functions" of nonvoting fails, of course, to deal with the decidedly undemocratic consequences of muffling the demands of some groups in the polity and not others.

A bolder but kindred argument fastens on the characteristics of nonvoters—especially their presumed extremism and volatility—to explain why their abstention is healthy for the polity. To cite a classic example, Lipset (1960) points to evidence that nonvoters are more likely to have antidemocratic attitudes.[7] Similarly, George Will, writing "In Defense of Nonvoting," says that "the fundamental human right" is not to the franchise but "to good government"; he points to the high turnouts in the late Weimar Republic as evidence of the dangers of increased voter participation, an example often favored by those who make this argument.[8] Will's point of view is reminiscent of the arguments of nineteenth-century reformers who proposed various methods of *reducing* turnout—by introducing property qualifications on the vote, for example—in order to improve the quality of the electorate. Consider, for example, the *New York Times* in 1878: "It would be a great gain if people could be made to understand distinctly that the right to life, liberty, and the pursuit of happiness involves, to be sure, the right to good government, but not the right to take part, either immediately or indirectly, in the management of the state."[9]

The Contested Vote

American history has been marked by sharp contests over the question of who may vote, the conditions under which they may vote, or just which state offices they may vote for, and how much some votes will weigh in relation to other votes. These questions were hard fought because they were a crucial dimension of struggles for political advantage, as the chapters which follow will show.

The United States was the first nation in the world in which the franchise began to be widely distributed,[10] a historical achievement that helps to explain the democratic hubris we display to this day. That achievement occurred at a time when the hopes of peasants, artisans, and the urban poor everywhere in the West were fired by the essential democratic idea, the idea that if ordinary people had the right to participate in the selection of state leaders, their grievances would be acted upon.[11] That hope was surely overstated, as were the fears of the propertied classes that the extension of the vote would give the "poor and ignorant majority" the power to "bring about a more equitable distribution of the good things of this world."[12] Nevertheless, the large possibilities associated with democracy help to explain why the right of ordinary people to vote was sharply contested. And if the franchise was ceded earlier in the United States, it was because post-Revolutionary elites had less ability to resist popular demands. The common men who had fought the Revolution were still armed and still insurgent. Moreover, having severed their connection with England, American men of property were unprotected by the majesty and military forces of a traditional state apparatus.

The political institutions that developed in the context of an expanded suffrage did not remedy many popular grievances. Still, a state influenced by political parties and elections did not merely replicate traditional patterns of class domination either. It also reflected in some measure the new social compact embodied in the franchise. Contenders for rulership now needed votes, and that fact altered the dynamics of power, modestly most of the time, more sharply some of the time, as we will point out in the pages that follow. In the early nineteenth century, the electoral arrangements that forced leaders to bid for popular support led to the gradual elimination of property, religious, and literacy qualifications on the franchise and to the expansion of the number of government posts whose occupants had to stand for election. By the 1830s, virtually all white men could vote. And, for a brief period after the Civil War, black men could as well. As the century wore on and the political parties developed systematic patronage operations to win elections, wide voting rights meant that common people received at least a share of the largesse, distributed in the form of Civil War pensions, friendly interventions with the courts or city agencies, and sometimes county or municipal poor relief—a reflection, if somewhat dim, of the electoral compact.

But at the beginning of the twentieth century, a series of changes in American electoral arrangements—such as the reintroduction of literacy tests and poll taxes, the invention of cumbersome voter registration requirements, and the subsequent withering of party efforts to mobilize those who were confronted by these barriers—sharply reduced voting by the northern immigrant working class and virtually eliminated voting by blacks and poor whites in the South. By World War I, turnout rates had fallen to half the eligible electorate and, despite some rises and dips, they have never recovered.

The purging of lower-strata voters from the electorate occurred at precisely that time in our history when the possibilities of democratic electoral politics had begun to enlarge. Indeed, we think it occurred *because* the possibilities of popular influence were expanding. First, as the economy industrialized and nationalized, government intervened more, so that at least in principle, the vote bore on a wide range of issues that were crucial to economic elites. Of course, government policies had always played a pivotal role in economic development: policies on tariffs and currency, slavery, immigration and welfare, internal improvements, and the subsidization of the railroads had all shaped the course of American development. But as the twentieth century began, the scale and penetration of government activity, especially regulatory activity, grew rapidly. It grew even more rapidly during the Great Depression.

Second, government's expanding role in the economy came to influence popular political ideas, and popular organizational capacities, in ways that suggested a new potential for popular struggle and electoral mobilization. Thus, a more pervasively and transparently interventionist state undermined the old laissez-faire idea that economy and polity necessarily belonged to separate spheres[13] and encouraged the twentieth-century idea that political rights include economic rights, particularly the right to protection by government from the worst instabilities and predations of the market.

Expanded state activities created new solidarities that became the basis for political action, including action in electoral politics. For example, government protection of the right to collective bargaining, ceded in response to mass strikes, reinforced the idea that workers had rights, promoted the unionization of millions of industrial workers, and made possible a large role for unions in electoral politics; Social Security reinforced the idea that government was responsible for economic well-being and promoted the organization of millions of "seniors" and the disabled; increased expenditures on social services nourished the growth of a voluntary sector that contracted to provide these services; and the enormous expansion of public programs gave rise to a vast network of public employee organizations, which were naturally keenly interested in electoral politics and had the organizational capacity to express that interest. In other words, new and expanded state activities gave rise to new political understandings and new political forces, and to the possibility that these new understandings and forces would become an influence in electoral politics.[14]

But while the enlarged role of government and the new popular ideas and solidarities that resulted created the possibility that electoral politics would become a major arena for the expression of working- and lower-class interests, that possibility was only partly realized. One reason was that vast numbers of those who might have been at the vortex of electoral discontents were, for all practical purposes, effectively disenfranchised at the beginning of the twentieth century. In Western Europe, the pattern was virtually reversed. There working-class men were enfranchised at the beginning of the twentieth century, and their enfranchisement led to the emergence of labor or socialist or social democratic parties that articulated working class interests and ultimately exerted considerable influence on the policies and political culture of their nations. In the United States, by contrast, the partial disfranchisement of working people during the same period helps explain why no comparable labor-based political party developed here, and why public policy and political culture remained more narrowly individualistic and property-oriented.[15]

The costs of exclusion were also indirect, for exclusion helped to sustain the distinctive southern system. Southern states had been especially aggressive in promulgating legal and administrative barriers to the vote, arrangements that of course disfranchised blacks, and most poor whites as well, and ensured that the quasi-feudal plantation system and the regular use of terror on which it depended would remain unchallenged within the South. But the consequences went beyond the South to the nation as a whole. Southern representatives always wielded great influence in national politics, largely as a result of the terms of the sectional compromise through which a nation had been formed in 1789. The compromise not only guaranteed the "states' rights" through which the southern section managed their own affairs before the Civil War, and afterward as well. It also laid out the several arrangements that guaranteed the South enduring predominance in national politics, including the three-fifths rule, which weighted slaves, a form of property, in allocating representation in the Congress, and a system of allocating representation to the states in the electoral college and in the Senate without regard to population. After the Civil War, and especially after the election of 1896, party competition disappeared from the South, and the subsequent disfranchisement of blacks and poor whites made its reemergence unlikely, with the consequence that unfailingly reelected southern congressmen gained the seniority that permitted them to dominate congressional committees.

If the peculiar development of the South was made possible by disfranchisement, southern representatives used their large influence in national government to steadfastly resist any federal policies that threatened the southern system. In particular, they vigorously resisted the labor and welfare policies that might have nourished the development of working-class politics during the New Deal and thereafter, as a matter of sectional and class interest and also as a matter of ideology. National welfare and labor policies were weakened as a result, and, even then, southern states were often granted exemption from coverage, with the further consequence that the South with its low wages and draconian labor discipline became—and remains today—a haven for industries eager to escape from the unionized workforces and more liberal state policies in the non-South.[16]

The South also illustrates the important political consequences that followed from the expansion of the franchise. Consider, for example, the impact of the Twenty-fourth Amendment of 1964 and the Voting Rights Act of 1965, which together eliminated poll taxes, literacy tests, and voter-registration obstructions that had kept blacks and many poor whites from the polls. In the aftermath of these reforms, both black and white voter participation rose sharply, and as it did, state and local policies became less discriminatory. More important, once politicians had to face blacks at the polls, the age-old use of violence against blacks, which had been the linchpin of southern apartheid, declined sharply, signaling the inevitable transformation of the southern system.[17]

We do not mean by these comments to overstate the importance of the ballot. Voters have limited ability to affect policy, and that limited influence is tempered by other influences. In the United States, a weak party system penetrated by moneyed interest groups and a strong laissez-faire culture were and are constraints on the political influence of the less-well-off, no matter the shape of the electorate.[18] Nevertheless, a full complement of lower-strata voters would have at least moderated the distinctively harsh features of American capitalist development in the twentieth century. Corporate predations against workers and consumers probably would have been curbed more effectively. Enlarged electoral influence from the bottom might have blocked public policies that weakened unions and inhibited their ability to organize. And an effectively enfranchised working class almost surely would have prodded political leaders to initiate social welfare protections earlier and to provide more comprehensive coverage in a pattern more nearly resembling that of Western Europe. Not least important, the enfranchisement of blacks and poor whites would have prevented the restoration of the caste labor system in the South after Reconstruction and the development of a one-party system whose oligarchical leaders wielded enormous power in national politics for most of the twentieth century. The influence of the South, in turn, effectively countered what influence the working-class electorate in the North, its strength reduced by disfranchisement, was able to exert. And finally, the exclusion from electoral politics of large sectors of the working class, as well as the rural poor of the South, precluded the emergence of a political party that could have stimulated greater class consciousness among American workers and the poor by articulating their interests and cultural orientations.[19] In other words, the distinctive pattern of American political development at least partly stems from the fact that the United States was not a democracy, in the elementary sense of an effective universal suffrage, during the twentieth century.

The politics of the closing decades of the twentieth century also illustrate the pivotal role of a skewed electorate. Numerous commentators have pointed out that beginning in the 1970s and continuing through the 1980s and 1990s, American corporations mobilized for politics with a focus and determination rare in the American experience. True, large corporations had always maintained a political presence to guard their particular firm and sector interests in legislative and bureaucratic spheres. However, the economic instabilities of the 1970s and the sagging and uncertain profits that resulted spurred business leaders to coordinate their efforts and to develop a broad legislative program calling for tax and regulatory rollbacks, cuts in spending on social programs, a tougher stance toward unions, and increases in military spending. The scale of this agenda demanded a new and broad-ranging political mobilization, including the creation of an extensive infrastructure of business associations, policy institutes, and think tanks that functioned as lobbying and public relations organizations.[20]

During the same years that business leaders were organizing to break the constraints of post–World War II public policies, and especially the constraints of the regulatory and social policy expansion of the 1960s, the Christian Right movement was emerging. The movement was also a reaction to the politics of the 1960s, albeit less to the public policies of the decade than to the cultural assaults on traditional sexual and family mores with which the sixties movements were associated. This late-twentieth-century revival movement turned out to be, at least during the 1970s and 1980s, an opportunity for newly politicized corporate leaders. Business organization and money are of course themselves formidable political resources, especially when campaign contributions are coordinated to achieve party influence as they began to be in the 1970s.[21] But elections are ultimately won by voters at the polls, and the Christian Right provided the foot soldiers— the activists and many of the voters—who brought a business-backed Republican party to power.

These several developments came together in the election of 1980, shortly before the reform efforts recounted here began. Reagan's victory was made possible by the coordination of business campaign contributions on the one hand, and on the other the voter registration and mobilization efforts of the growing Christian Right with a network of fundamentalist churches at its base. However achieved, the election made it possible for the new Republican-business-fundamentalist alliance to claim that their agenda was in fact demanded by the American people. Among other things, Reagan was said to have tapped deep popular resentments against the public policies that were singled out for attack, as well as vast popular support for tax cuts and a military buildup. In fact, postelection polls showed that Reagan won not because of his campaign broadsides against big government[22] but because of popular discontent with the Carter administration's policies, especially anger over high unemployment.[23] Americans believe that presidents are responsible for the state of the economy, and by that criterion, Carter had failed.[24]

But the truncated electorate may have mattered even more than the formidable corporate campaign mobilization, the surge of activism among Christian fundamentalists, and Carter's failure to manage the "political business" cycle.[25] The underrepresentation of working and poor people, whose living standards were the target of much of the business program, helped to explain the weakness of political opposition to the Reagan administration's agenda during the 1980 campaign and thereafter. Elections were being won in the teeth of public opposition to the programmatic goals of the victors, and one reason was simply that the electorate did not represent the public.[26] The 1980 evidence was clearcut. Polls showed that voters tilted toward Reagan by 52 percent over Carter's 38 percent. But nonvoters, who were nearly as numerous, tilted toward Carter by 51 percent over 37 percent. In a close study of that election, Petrocik concluded that the "margin for Ronald Reagan in 1980 was made possible by a failure of prospective Carter voters to turn out on election day."[27]

To be sure, over the course of the next decade and more, a dominant conservative regime did succeed in promoting a conservative swing in public opinion and in the Democratic party. Nevertheless, fast-forward to 1994, the year of another historic victory, the takeover of the House of Representatives by the same Republican-business-fundamentalist coalition, with the fundamentalists now even more prominent and more assertive. The data repeat the pattern of 1980: while the Democrats won only 47 percent of the actual vote, they scored 58 percent among nonvoters, according to the National Election Studies, a percentage-point spread sufficient to throw the election to them. In a definitive study of that election, Joel Lefkowitz (1999) concludes that "Republicans won, then, not because more potential voters preferred their party, but because more of those who preferred Republicans voted."[28] In sum, nonvoting is important not merely for the intellectual queries it suggests but for its role in patterning American politics.

Movements and Electoral Participation

With their voting numbers depleted and without a labor party, whatever influence poor and working-class people have exerted in American politics has depended mainly on the emergence of mass insurgency. Protest movements dramatized the issues that parties detached from a lower class base could ignore, galvanized broad public attention to those issues, and threatened to cause the dissensus that parties dependent on broad coalitions feared. In *Poor People's Movements* (1977), we argued that it was when political discontent among the lower classes "breaks out of the confines of electoral procedures that the poor may have some influence."[29] Our view, in brief, was that poor and working-class people sometimes exercised power when they mobilized in mass defiance, breaking the rules that governed their participation in the institutions of a densely interdependent society. As evidence for this thesis, we summoned our studies of the role of protest movements of the 1930s and 1960s in winning major reforms. Consistently, the virtual absence of large-scale protest during the 1980s made it possible to initiate domestic policies that dramatically increased the bias of public policy against working-class and lower-class groups.

But the electoral context matters, nevertheless, for it is a crucial influence on the emergence and success of movements in contemporary democracies. This point needs a little explaining, because movements and voting are sometimes treated simply as conflicting and alternative forms of political expression. The bearing of each on the other is, however, multifaceted; some aspects of electoral politics undermine movements, as many observers have emphasized. But other aspects of electoral politics are crucial to the growth and success of movements.

On the one hand, there are features of a vigorous and inclusive electoral politics that tend to suppress collective protest. Electoral arrangements promulgate powerful meanings and rituals which define and limit the appropriate forms of political action. The very availability of the vote and the ritual of the periodic election are like magnets attracting and channeling popular political impulses. Other forms of collective action, and especially defiant collective action, are discredited precisely because voting and electioneering are presumably available as the normative ways to act on political discontent. In addition to constraining the forms of popular political action, the electoral system tends to restrict the goals of popular politics, and even the orientations of popular political culture, to the political alternatives generated by the dominant parties. Further, involvement in electoral politics can weaken the solidarities which undergird political movements, a development which takes its most extreme form under clientelist or machine modes of appealing to voters. And finally, electoral political institutions can seduce people away from any kind of oppositional politics. People are hypnotized by the circuses of election campaigns, while their leaders are enticed by the multiple opportunities to gain positions in the electoral representative system. In short, involvement in electoral politics can channel people away from movement politics.

Despite the hyperbole with which this sort of view is sometimes expressed, it is supported by a long and serious intellectual tradition. Reinhard Bendix (1968), for example, argued that the class consciousness of European workers was enhanced precisely because they were barred from electoral participation during most of the nineteenth century; Ted Robert Gurr (1968) and other movement analysts explicitly posited that electoral institutions channel people away from protest; and Murray Edelman (1971) stressed the symbolic manipulation associated with electoral participation. And there is clearly some broad historical fit between the idea that electoral arrangements constrain protest movements and the actual course of movements in American history. For example, as electoral participation expanded in the first third of the nineteenth century, particularly with the emergence of machine-style political organization, early workingmen's insurgencies did in fact tend to become absorbed in regular party politics. At the end of the nineteenth century, the Populist movement was fragmented, diminished, and ultimately destroyed by its venture into national electoral politics. Much of the momentum of the labor movement of the 1930s was lost as it became absorbed in Democratic party politics. Similarly, the black movement dissipated as it turned

from protest to politics in the 1970s. And historical trends in European politics also suggest that strong electoral organization tends to
supplant mass protest.

However, we think the bearing of electoral politics on movement
politics is more complex and multifaceted than these simple opposi-
tions suggest. Electoral politics also constitutes the principal environment of contemporary movements, and aspects of that environment
nurture rather than suppress movements. After all, the idea of popular rights associated with democratic electoral arrangements encourages the belief that change is possible, and by the efforts of ordinary
people. This is the implication of the very core democratic idea, the
idea that ordinary people have the right to participate in governance
by choosing their rulers. Furthermore, movements may also gain protection from electoral politics, since the anticipation of adverse voter
reactions oftens restrains state leaders from resorting to repression as
a way of dealing with political defiance.

Some electoral conditions are more conducive to movements than
others. Movements tend to arise when electoral alignments become
unstable, usually as a result of changes in the larger society that generate new discontents or stimulate new aspirations and thus undermine
established party allegiances. Electoral volatility is particularly associated with large-scale economic change, especially change that gener-
ates widespread hardship. When the allegiance of key voter blocs can
no longer be taken for granted, contenders are likely to raise the stakes
in electoral contests by employing campaign rhetoric that acknowledges grievances and gives voice to demands as a way of building majorities. In other words, movements are more likely to emerge when a
climate of political possibility has been created and communicated
through the electoral system.

Movements also win what they win largely as a result of their impact on electoral politics. The issues raised when masses of people become defiant sometimes break the grip of ruling groups on political
interpretations so that new definitions of social reality, and new definitions of the possible and just, can be advanced. In turn, these issues
and understandings, raised and communicated by masses of defiant
people, activate and politicize voters and sometimes attract new voters to the polls who alter electoral calculations. It is in fact mainly by

their ability to galvanize and polarize voters, with the result that electoral coalitions fragment or threaten to fragment, that protest movements score gains in electoral-representative systems.[30] When political leaders issue new rhetorical appeals to attract or hold voters or go on to make policy concessions, it is to cope with threats of electoral defection and cleavage or to rebuild coalitions when faced with the threat or reality of electoral defections. In this way, the electoral system not only protects and nourishes movements but also yields them leverage on state leaders. The influence of voters is also enhanced, for movements activate electoral constituencies and make their allegiance conditional on policy responses. In short, the life course of contemporary movements can be understood only in relation to the electoral environment in which they emerge and on which they have an impact.

There is broad historical confirmation for this aspect of the relationship between movements and electoral politics. In the 1930s, striking industrial workers were able to force a wavering New Deal administration to support government protection for collective bargaining. The strike movement had so antagonized business groups as to eliminate any possibility that the New Deal could recover their support, and it also threatened to put at risk the votes of the working class, on which the New Deal depended. Similarly, in the 1950s and 1960s, the southern civil rights movement forced national Democratic leaders to throw their weight behind legislation that would dismantle the southern caste system and strike down the procedures by which blacks and most poor whites had been disfranchised. The reason is that the civil rights movement simultaneously precipitated defections among southern whites to the Republican party and jeopardized the votes of growing numbers of blacks in the cities of the border states and the North.

Thus, while a vigorous electoral politics probably dampens the tendency to protest, electoral politics is nevertheless also critical to movement success. When we wrote *Poor People's Movements* (1977) it was in part to specify some of the ways in which this was so, if only because earlier analyses of protest movements tended to ignore their electoral environment. But there was one major feature of the American electoral system with which we did not deal. We did not call attention to the distinctive pattern of lower-strata exclusion in the United States or explore its implications for the emergence and evolution of protest movements.

How, then, did the twentieth-century history of massive nonvoting by poorer and minority people bear on the fate of movements in American politics? At first glance, one might expect large-scale non-voting to reduce the effectiveness of the electoral system in absorbing discontent and suppressing movements. However, the methods by which people are made into nonvoters matter. When whole categories of people are denied the vote as a matter of acknowledged state policy—as southern blacks were—their exclusion may well strengthen their collective identity, provoke their indignation, and legitimate defiant forms of political action. But in the United States, the formal right to the franchise has been virtually universal, a condition much celebrated in the political culture. Only those who are aliens, felons, not yet of age, or undomiciled are denied the vote as a matter of acknowledged policy. At the same time, the effectiveness of the franchise for the bottom strata has been reduced by the failure of the parties to make the appeals and deploy the outreach strategies that would mobilize these voters and by residual procedural obstructions embedded in the voting process. This pattern of demobilization and obstruction was selective in that it was more likely to reduce voting by the poor and unlettered than by the better-off and educated. Still, entire categories of the population were not legally denied the franchise, and the administrative methods by which the exercise of the franchise is impeded remained obscure and indeed seemed to be the fault of the nonvoters themselves, of their apathy or poor education. Under these circumstances, the *idea* that voting and elections provided the means for acting on political grievances remained largely intact, even though the means were not in fact available to tens of millions of people. The demobilization of large sectors of the American electorate was thus secured at less cost to the legitimacy of electoral processes as the prescribed avenue for political change than would otherwise have been the case.

At the same time, the constriction of the electorate weakened the complementarities between electoral politics and protest movements.

The interactions between movements and the electoral context that encouraged the growth of movements and sometimes led to movement victories depended on the existence of voter constituencies inclined to be responsive to the appeals of protesters. Thus protests from below were more likely to arise in the first place when contenders for office were forced to employ rhetoric that appealed to less-well-off voters and thus gave courage to the potential protesters. Such movements were more likely to grow when they were at least somewhat safe from the threat of state repression because political leaders were constrained by fear of adverse reactions by working-class or lower-class or minority voters. Finally, protesters were more likely to win when the issues they raised stirred support among significant numbers of these voters, threatening to lead to voter defections. The complementary dynamic between movements and electoral politics thus depended both on the composition and orientation of movements and on the composition and orientation of significant blocs in the electorate. In other words, the sharp underrepresentation of poor and minority people in the American electorate created an electoral environment that also weakened their ability to act politically through movements. This is another important way in which massive nonvoting has shaped American politics.

For a short time in the 1980s, nonvoters became the focus of wide political attention. Pundits buzzed with the possibility that in reaction to the policies of the Reagan administration, millions of nonvoters would surge to the polls, upsetting electoral predictions. For reasons we are at pains to explain in the following chapters, neither of the major parties was at the forefront of this excited talk or of efforts to recruit new voters. Instead, it was social movement organizations on the right and on the left that seized on voter mobilization as the key to political success. On the one side, the Christian Right worked to register and politicize parishioners through its network of churches. On the other side, civil rights and New Politics groups, spurred by the threat of the Reagan program and by evidence of mounting economic grievances, worked to mobilize new voters from the large reservoir of nonvoting poor, especially poor minorities. Both sides saw new voters not only as the key to short-term electoral victory but as a way to force bold new policy commitments on the parties and even to transform them.

We were provoked by these developments to pay renewed attention to historical analyses of the "changing shape of the American electoral universe."[31] In chapter 2 we turn to a critical examination of the academic studies that purport to explain nonvoting. We focus on two debates in the literature. The first is among the theorists who agree that major changes in American political institutions in the late nineteenth and early twentieth centuries account for nonvoting but disagree about just which of these institutional changes were most important. The other debate is between institutional theorists taken as a group and analysts who explain abstention in terms of the social-psychological-cultural attributes of those who don't vote. We propose a more comprehensive model that synthesizes the main institutional interpretations and also goes far toward explaining why people with particular social-psychological-cultural attributes are more likely to be marginalized from the electoral system.

In chapter 3 we begin an account of the history of the constriction of voting rights in the United States, starting with the mid-nineteenth-century era in which voter participation levels soared. We break with the usual celebratory depiction of this period, however, by focusing on the distinctive modes of political incorporation that flourished at the time and made high participation possible, at least among white men, while muting political conflict. We then turn to the period of rapid and disruptive economic and social change in the decades after the Civil War, when dominant modes of political incorporation were strained by rising popular discontent, resulting in a series of radical electoral insurgencies of which the Populist challenge of 1896 was most important. These developments sparked elite-sponsored efforts to regain control of electoral politics, by methods that led to the demobilization of large numbers of the poor farmers and working-class voters.

In chapter 4, we discuss the specific changes in turn-of-the-century electoral politics that drove turnout down. We argue that the decline in party competition associated with the election of 1896 lowered opposition to new rules governing access to the ballot. In the

South, the drop in turnout was dramatic and precipitous. Turnout fell steadily if less dramatically in the North as well, as electoral "reform" (and a parallel assault on the mobilizing capacities of clientelist local parties) took its toll. By the mid-1920s, the skewed and contracted electorate characteristic of the United States in the twentieth century had been constructed.

In chapter 5 we discuss the developments that led to a modest and incomplete remobilization of working-class voters during the New Deal. We argue that the reach of that remobilization was limited, emphasizing especially its failure to touch the South. In chapter 6 we continue this discussion of the fate of the New Deal Democratic party to show how limits on the remobilization of the 1930s had much to do with the conflicts that have since wracked the New Deal coalition. Sectional and class conflict limited the party's ability to develop the allegiance of its older working-class constituency and ultimately also inhibited its ability or motivation to enlist a new working class composed increasingly of women and minorities, with the result that turnout has again declined, especially among the worse-off.

In chapter 7 we begin our account of our reform efforts with an analysis of the intense competition to register new voters that broke out for a period beginning in 1980. It was not the parties that were engaged in this mini-war but rather social movement organizations that saw their own future success as linked to the success of one party or the other. On one side, the Christian Right recruited new voters, largely through its network of fundamentalist churches. On the other side, veterans of civil rights and the New Politics movements also tried to mobilize new voters, largely among the worse-off. We also participated in this campaign by trying to get voter registration incorporated in public and private agencies serving poorer and minority people. We continued this effort after the election, working first with state and local officials, and later with the Congress. In chapters 7 through 11, we give an account of these reform efforts, the strategic thinking that guided them, our mishaps and successes, and the evolution of the National Voter Registration Act of 1993. Finally, in chapter 12, we evaluate the effects of the new law.

Part One

The Demobilization of the American Electorate

CHAPTER TWO

Why Nonvoting?

*W*hy the shrunken and skewed American electorate? Political scientists have been preoccupied with this question, and explanations have multiplied. Very broadly, they fall into three camps. Two camps locate the causes squarely in political institutions, although they differ about which institutional features depress voting. The third camp locates the causes outside of politics, in the social or psychological characteristics, especially poor education, of the individuals who abstain. We consider each of these perspectives in turn, and then argue for a synthesis of the two institutional theories which suggests that the correlations between individual characteristics and nonvoting may well be spurious.

The Debate about the Institutional Causes of Nonvoting

Our answer to the question of why so many Americans don't vote focuses on political institutions. Patterns of electoral participation and nonparticipation are shaped by institutional arrangements, and patterns of participation in turn have consequences that sustain those arrangements. However, there is a good deal of debate and uncertainty about which of the institutional changes that occurred in the late nineteenth and twentieth centuries best account for the decline of voting. The main disagreement has been between analysts who see shrinking electoral participation as a consequence of changes in the political parties and in patterns of party competition, and those who emphasize newly-constructed legal barriers to the suffrage, including particularly the Australian ballot and personal voter registration requirements.[1] Walter Dean Burnham is surely the unchallenged leader of the first school. His work is heavily influenced by E. E. Schattschneider's earlier analysis, which traced diminishing voter involvement to the collapse of party competition in much of the country in 1896, and to the increasingly oligarchical character of the parties that resulted from the decline of competition. For Schattschneider, the expansion of the electorate earlier in the nineteenth century had been "largely a by-product of the system of party conflict." The rise of non-voting at the close of the century, in turn, resulted from "the attempt to make the vote meaningless":

> Abstention reflects the suppression of the options and alternatives that reflect the needs of the nonparticipants. . . . Whoever decides what the game is about decides also who can get into the game.[2]

The significance of the system of 1896, which we discuss in chapters 3 and 4, is thus clear. As party competition disappeared in much of the country, "votes decline in value because the voters no longer have a viable party alternative."[3] A similar interpretation informs Paul Kleppner's authoritative studies of nineteenth and early twentieth century electoral politics.[4]

Analysts who propound what is sometimes called the "legal-institutional" theory attribute turnout decline and volatile voting patterns to changes in laws and administrative procedures.[5] This view is associated with the influential work of Campbell, Converse, Miller, and Stokes, as well as of Kelley, Kousser, Milbraith, Rusk, and Stucker, all of whom emphasize aspects of electoral law and machinery as major determinants of electoral behavior. Thus, Campbell and his colleagues reported in *The American Voter,* on the basis of data from the 1950s, that variations in registration and voting requirements were important determinants of differences in state turnout levels.[6] Earlier, Campbell and Miller had reported that straight ticket or split ticket voting was significantly affected by the type of ballot.[7] And a few years after *The American Voter* was published in 1960, Miller reported that variations in voting rates were strongly associated with residence requirements, registration procedures, closing dates for registration, poll tax requirements, and the ballot form.[8] Subsequently, in 1967, Kelley, Ayres, and Bowen published a study of variations in turnout rates in 1960 in 104 of the largest cities with the stunning conclusion that 78 percent of the variation among cities could be explained by variations in the percentage of citizens who were registered.

Converse and Rusk in particular have vigorously promoted the legal-institutional interpretation as a sweeping alternative to Burnham's political-behavioral interpretation.[9] Much of their debate has been focused on rather narrow empirical questions such as the extent of fraud in nineteenth-century electoral politics. The legal-institutional adherents argue that the voting decline was in substantial part illusory, a result of reforms such as the Australian ballot and voter registration that deflated the voter rolls by reducing the numbers of coerced or fraudulent ballots cast, and that this was in fact what the reformers who promoted the legal reforms were trying to accomplish, much as they claimed. The decline in turnout, in other words, was at least partly an artifact of more honest elections. In addition, these analysts allow that the changes in electoral machinery which reduced fraud, such as the introduction of voter registration, also had the unintended consequence of reducing actual turnout by making it more difficult to vote and more difficult for the parties to enlist voters.

The argument that fraud prompted the reforms, and that lower turnout is in large part evidence of the elimination of fraudulent ballots, depends on the assumption that voter fraud was in fact pervasive in the nineteenth century, as Converse and Rusk insist it was. For their part, Burnham and Kleppner insist that fraud was an episodic rather than an endemic problem, and that the decline in turnout was the real and deliberate outcome of political changes, notably reduced party competition. This dispute is not readily resolved by reference to available facts, since much of what passes for data on fraud consists of anecdotal charges by contemporaries, including the reformers themselves. While such charges cannot be dismissed out of hand, we must regard them as the opinions of highly motivated observers. Moreover, the bearing of fraud on turnout is complicated, as Argersinger points out, by the fact that fraud also took the form of intimidation or of deterring voting, or of stealing ballots, which deflated turnout.[10] It is even possible that these two forms of fraud simply canceled each other out.

The dispute about fraud and turnout only hints at the large differences in interpretations of American political development that animate the debate. In particular, Converse and Rusk oppose the Schattschneider and Burnham thesis that the electoral changes of the late nineteenth century reflected the politics of class conflict. Rusk states the issue forthrightly when he proceeds to attack Burnham as something of an "economic determinist" who accounts for the decline of voting as a response to a "capitalist conspiracy" by businessmen and Republicans whose "capture of the electoral system" in 1896 led to the alienation of voters from the political system.[11] Converse and Rusk retort that "the idealistic forces of reform [were] bent on cleaning up fraud" just as they said they were.[12] Business involvement, Converse asserts, was only "spotty." Instead,

> the forces of good government who as "idea men" generated the proposals, struggled to publicize them, and remained their most energetic and reliable core of support through the process of adoption included mainly intellectuals, journalists, ministers, and other professionals.[13]

In other words, the reformers promoted the legal changes, particularly voter registration, in order to reduce corruption, although the "unintended effect . . . was to put up an additional barrier to the vote, eliminating many honest votes on the part of marginally involved citizens."[14]

However, if the important question that lurks in this debate, about the role of class forces in explaining either political-behavioral or legal-institutional changes, is put aside, the dispute between the schools loses much of its force, and indeed scarcely seems to be a debate at all. The theories, as Kleppner and Baker point out, are "not mutually exclusive, either logically or behaviorally."[15] After all, it is in politics, including party politics, that legal arrangements and administrative procedures are forged. In fact, Burnham and Kleppner have moved part of the way toward such an integration of political changes and rules changes. Burnham's earlier work tended to relegate voter registration to a marginal role, emphasizing instead the narrowing of political options associated with the system of 1896 as the principal explanation of declining turnout.[16] By 1970, however, perhaps in response to the findings reported in the interim by Kelley, Ayres, and Bowen (showing strong correlations between aggregate registration and turnout levels by city), Burnham allowed that voter registration requirements "counted for something," although not for much:

> But putting first things first, one concludes that the systemic forces at work during these periods were far broader in their scope and far heavier in their impact than any single change in the rules of the game or, in all probability, of all such changes put together.[17]

In the years since this was written, Burnham has gradually come to attribute greater statistical weight to personal voter registration requirements in accounting for the drop in turnout. Voter registration requirements not only "count for something," they have become "a highly significant intervening variable,"[18] but a variable that itself can only be understood as a consequence of the political changes associated with the system of 1896. Fair enough. But this elides the possibility and indeed the likelihood that, in the complexly interactive real world of politics, "intervening" variables can become forces in their own right.

It was actually Schattschneider who said that politics is in fact mainly about rules, "about procedure rather than substance."[19] In this sense, political and legal variables are related, but political variables take pride of place; they are the independent variables. However, it was also Schattschneider's point that rules, once institutionalized, change politics—the "rules of the game determine the requirements for success"—which is why they are the focus of so much political contention in the first place.[20]

> One difficulty scholars have experienced in interpreting American politics has always been that the grand strategy of politics has concerned itself first of all with the structure of institutions. The function of institutions is to channel conflict; institutions do not treat all forms of conflict impartially, just as football rules do not treat all forms of violence with indiscriminate equality.[21]

Schattschneider's point about rules and politics clearly applies to the debate about parties and legal barriers. The contraction of electoral participation that began in the twentieth century was the compound consequence of declining party mobilization and the construction of new legal and procedural barriers. Party mobilization efforts diminished partly because party competition—and thus the incentive to recruit voters—diminished. Mobilization also faltered because, as competition declined, the influence of economic elites on the parties increased, and as it did the freedom of party leaders to make appeals that would attract voters, especially lower-strata voters, declined. Moreover, and during the same period, reforms pushed by business-backed reform organizations were reducing the resources of clientelist state and local parties, and especially big-city parties. So, for these several reasons, party efforts at popular mobilization declined. Meanwhile, changes in the rules governing access to the ballot, promoted not only by reformers but by the state parties—Republicans in the North, Bourbon Democrats in the South—placed new obstacles in the path of potential voters that were especially troublesome to lower-class voters. These obstructions made party mobilization efforts all the more essential if turnout was to be sustained.

That local parties were enfeebled during the same period that procedural constraints on voting were introduced is not accidental, since both parties and voters were targeted by business-backed reformers. But the simultaneity has helped to nourish the debate, since empirical complexities yield the data used to justify different points of view. The better way to understand these developments, however, is that each had consequences that reinforced the other. New procedural requirements for voting, especially voter registration requirements, made it less likely that voters with fewer personal resources would vote. And as levels of voter participation among working people gradually eroded, weakened parties were all the more likely to turn away from the issues and campaign stratagems needed to mobilize lower-class support.[22] The resulting marginalization of poor and working people, not only from political influence but from the political culture created by the parties, in turn reinforced their tendency to abstain. Finally, the circle was completed when the local parties that had adapted to this constricted electorate came to rely on and defend the barriers to electoral participation that worked to limit the electorate. In other words, procedural barriers did not simply restrict voting, but by restricting voting, they altered the subsequent campaign calculus of the political parties, with pervasive consequences for American political development. In sum, political and legal-institutional variables are interactive, and they are each both independent and dependent variables.[23]

Just Who Did It, and Why?

The arrangements which created a large stratum of nonvoters were forged over the course of a history of political conflict, including conflict specifically over the question of who should enjoy the right to vote. Those conflicts, in turn, were motivated by the recognition that who votes and who does not has consequences for American political development. But just who was it that was motivated to demobilize portions of the electorate, and exactly why?[24]

Burnham's answer is that demobilization was produced by economic elites represented for him by the national Republican party. The legal-institutionalists emphasize progressive reformers. Political life is complicated, and both economic elites and reformers in fact played a role (and indeed the reformers often were economic elites). But our contention is that the parties themselves were important agents of electoral constriction, and this requires some discussion. Why did mass-based parties collaborate in establishing rules that drove away voters? And why, once the rules were in place, did they not exert themselves to help voters hurdle the new barriers?

Our view, that the parties played an active role in demobilizing the electorate, flies in the face of the usual view that party competition inevitably leads to the expansion of electoral participation. Once again, we turn to Schattschneider as the authority, although this time it is to dispute his argument:

> Once party organization becomes active in the electorate, a vast field for extension and intensification of effort is opened up, the extension of the franchise to new social classes, for example. The natural history of parties is a story of continuous expansion and intensification . . . to a larger and larger electorate.[25]

Schattschneider's reasoning is straightforward. Competitive parties will strive to select candidates and fashion their appeals and strategies so as to win majorities. And, in principle, electoral competition should stimulate contending parties to also mobilize voters, including new voters and, Schattschneider thought, especially new voters:

> What voters can be most profitably solicited by the parties in the expansion of their constituencies? Obviously, new voters who have formed no strong party attachments. In the search for new segments of the populace that might be exploited profitably, the parties have kept the movement to liberalize the franchise well ahead of the demand.[26]

But Schattschneider's thumbnail characterization is wrong, and in fact inconsistent with his own account of the aftermath of the system of 1896. While the active electorate did expand through most of the nineteenth century, it did not through most of the twentieth century, despite the revival of party competition. How do we account for the failure of the parties to do what Schattschneider thought had become a "permanent part of the American political process because it yielded enormous profits for a relatively slight effort"?[27] And relatedly, how do we account for the dramatic contraction of the electorate that occurred at the beginning of the century? Schattschneider thinks competitive parties inevitably have an incentive to mobilize voters, and nonvoting was caused simply by a decline in competition. But are there conditions under which competitive parties might decline to mobilize, and even actively strive to demobilize voters?

Martin Shefter provides the beginning of an answer.[28] He argues in fact that the mobilization of new constituencies by established parties is by no means inevitable. Indeed, he stresses the risks to established political elites of newly activated voters, which leads them to seek to "forestall the emergence of an ever-widening spiral of mobilization and countermobilization, of organization and counterorganization."[29] Indeed, in contradiction to Schattschneider who saw the spiral of mobilization as the inevitable consequence of party competition, Shefter thinks mobilization occurs only under unusual conditions, when the option of repression is not available, for example, or when broad popular cooperation is essential, as in wartime. Absent such conditions, party elites are more likely to seek to collude with each other to prevent the possibility of an enlarging electorate. This is especially the case when the mobilization of new voters from marginal social strata risks splitting established coalitions. In other words, mobilization can be dangerous to established parties, even when it promises short-term electoral advantages. Shefter's observations go a large part of the way to explaining the *failure* of the parties to reach out to new voters over the course of the twentieth century.

Shefter's emphasis on the risks of electoral mobilization also helps make sense of the historic turn toward the demobilization of large sectors of the electorate that marks American political history. The happy notion that competitive parties are inevitably driven to enlarge electoral participation has so captured our fancy that relatively little attention has been given to the *actual role of the parties as demobilizers of participation*. But voters are not singularly determining of party strategies. Other influences matter in the effort to win state office, not least the need to hold elite supporters, to avoid fractious conflict among different constituency groups, and to protect party officeholders from untested voters who might put incumbents at risk. The very campaign calculus that may sometimes prompt electoral mobilization can also turn the parties toward the strategy of demobilization. Not unimportantly, parties can compete not only by enlarging their own following, but by working to shrink the following of the opposition. Changing the rules governing access to the ballot is just such a strategy. And parties may even collaborate in the demobilization of fractious elements of their own constituency, at least when party competition is at an ebb so that demobilization does not put the party at risk at the polls. Once demobilization is recognized as a credible party strategy, we are drawn back to our theoretical emphasis on the interplay of party mobilization and institutional barriers. Demobilizing parties have an incentive to collaborate in the construction of legal and procedural obstructions which narrow the electorate, especially of their opposition, but not necessarily only their opposition. Finally, once demobilization is accomplished, there is the additional advantage to the parties that campaign costs are lowered when the electorate is narrowed.[30]

Thus it is easy to grant Burnham's contention that rule changes originate in politics, that they are "produced by concrete men acting out their ideological biases in concrete legislative form."[31] But which men? The new rules were, to be sure, influenced by the mobilized economic elites represented for Burnham by the national Republican party, "the political vehicle of industrial capitalism."[32] They were influenced by businessmen reformers anxious to weaken big-city clientelist parties. But they were also shaped by state and local political parties competing under specific state and local conditions. Moreover, once rule changes were formally initiated, their implementation was mediated by local political parties in contingent and variable ways, so that the impact of rules on turnout cannot be inferred from their mere existence. And finally, the relationship between the rules and politics also worked the other way. Once the rules were inaugurated and implemented, depending on how they were implemented, they in turn had political consequences.

Thus early voter registration laws emerged out of conflicts in which state and local parties were very active contenders, if not the principal contenders. Converse, notwithstanding his general conviction that idealistic reformers were the main political actors in voter registration reform, describes the "heated political controversy" generated by the registration issue in the period from 1860 to 1900:

> Minority groups in the largest urban centers typically used the Democratic Party as a vehicle to challenge the constitutionality of laws that forced them into an elaborate registration procedure but required nothing of their small-town and rural compatriots. Meanwhile, of course, the Republicans were painfully and often explicitly aware of how sharply their rural vote base might shrink with the extension of controls on voting to the countryside, and fought tooth and nail to preserve their artificial legal advantage. Many of the wanderings into and out of statewide registration laws that occurred in some states were a simple reflection of the momentary ascendancy of one or the other of these competing powers.[33]

The sources of these local partisan conflicts are clear. State Republican parties stood to gain from disfranchising urban and working-class voters, and northern Democratic parties stood to lose, not only because the laws were aimed at the cities where the Democrats were stronger, but because the immigrant and working-class voters who were more likely to be affected were the key to Democratic power in the cities. McCormick makes just this point in describing the legislative battles in New Jersey, where the first registration law was passed in 1866 after the Democrats lost control of both houses of the legislature:

The Democratic press attacked the registry laws on the grounds that they made voting "troublesome, inconvenient and expensive." Too, it was contended that the laws kept from the polls the poor working man who could not afford to take time off from his job to register. Republican spokesmen insisted that the laws had worked well and that the Democrats disliked them because they could no longer flood the polling places with floaters and repeaters.[34]

As it happens, the Democrats regained control of the legislature in 1868 and abolished the new registration law (over the veto by the Republican governor), but when the Republicans returned to power they restored registration.[35]

The first observation to be made about these early battles over registration is how aptly they illustrate Schattschneider's point that the grand strategy of politics concerns itself above all else with the structure of institutions. It follows that the parties themselves always try to shape the rules under which they compete, including the rules governing voter participation, as McCormick says:

Election machinery always has been something more than an instrument through which the will of the voters could be made known. It has been the means of influencing the verdict of the electorate. Any change in the machinery affected the fortunes of the major factions contending for political power.... No factor is more constant in explaining the development of election machinery than this one.[36]

The second observation is that during this early phase in the development of voter registration procedures, the state and local parties were the main actors, and they cannot be understood simply as surrogates for class actors. Of course, there was a good deal of class animus among the promoters of registration reform, especially toward the immigrants who were rapidly becoming majorities in some of the biggest cities and who provided the social base for the political machines that were beginning to provoke business reform campaigns. Nevertheless, the motives of the contenders in these registration battles derived as much from party advantage as class advantage, since economic elites were divided in their partisan allegiances until the elections of 1894 and 1896. In other words, the state legislative battles over voter registration that began in the 1860s were motivated in large part by calculations of party fortune.[37]

However, no matter what the outcome of these legislative conflicts, the impact of early voter registration laws (particularly the weaker forms of registration) was negligible,[38] because the local parties were competitive and vigorous. The legal expansion of the suffrage earlier in the nineteenth century had made high levels of participation possible, and the strong mass parties that developed translated possibility into reality:

> Political parties—as organizations and as objects of habituated loyalties—were critical intermediaries in the process of mobilizing a mass electorate. Party formation in the 1830s and 1840s intersected with a changed legal environment to stimulate electoral participation.[39]

Most historians of the "second party system" agree.[40] But the role readily conceded to the parties in creating and sustaining the mass electorate of the nineteenth century bears on the way voter registration was implemented. So long as the local parties were dependent on voter constituencies at risk of being disfranchised by the new laws, they had ample motive to resist, amend, or circumvent the new registration procedures when they faced electoral challenge. And so long as the local parties were organizationally strong, they also had the capacity to resist, amend, or circumvent them. *In other words, the impact of laws and procedures cannot be assessed without taking into account the motives and capacities of the political parties involved in implementing the new rules.*

The image of machines in American folklore is of all-powerful organizations. The folklore is simply wrong. Clientelist organizations rarely gained undisputed control, and when they did it was usually not for long. In many cities, local bosses competed among themselves. Even the legendary New York Democracy was rent by factionalism for much of its reign, and it was also challenged from without by periodic reform efforts, including, in 1885, a labor mobilization behind the candidacy of Henry George. It was not until the late 1880s that Tammany succeeded in centralizing its control of the local Democratic party.[41] Moreover, from the beginning, the clientelist parties confronted opposition from reformers who also entered the electoral lists and sometimes won, at least for a time. So long as machine control was contested, turnout of working-class voters remained crucial to machine success, and the machines exerted themselves to enlist voters and help them hurdle whatever barriers they confronted.

Accordingly, just how the new requirements worked out in practice depended very much on the vigor of local political parties, and particularly on the clientelist parties that dominated electoral politics in the cities where the immigrant working class was concentrated. Whatever the intentions of the registration reformers, where local parties were strong and closely linked to the immigrant working class, ways were discovered to overcome the new restrictions, just as ways had been found to overcome earlier restrictions, such as naturalization laws.[42] Indeed, the evolution of voter registration requirements, from nonpersonal to personal, from permanent to periodic and even to annual registration, and from local to centralized administration, can be understood as a reflection of the political contest over who could vote. And as particular registration arrangements fell under the control of local party functionaries, efforts were in turn made in the state legislatures to "reform the reforms," so to say, in a continuing struggle for party advantage.

However, after the election of 1896 and the weakening of party competition on the state level throughout most of the country, effective partisan resistance to registration statutes largely dissipated. Registration laws spread rapidly, and became more restrictive. Even so, it was not so simple a matter as enacting restrictive laws. What continued to matter in practice was the motive and capacity of the local parties to shape implementation. When the New York state legislature established an Office of Superintendent of Elections in 1898, the legislature apparently meant to target New York City registration practices. Tammany was still vigorous, however, and managed to dominate the office until it was abolished in 1921.[43] Similarly, a tough Pennsylvania registration statute directed at Philadelphia in 1906 did not affect the city's turnout; "the ring" continued to produce higher turnouts than a majority of the thirty-seven Pennsylvania counties that did not require personal registration.[44] In the 1902 gubernatorial election, eight of the machine-controlled Philadelphia wards produced a turnout rate of 105 percent, with the machine's candidate winning 85 percent.[45]

Still, the tide was turning. The clientelist parties came under assault in this period from both partisan contenders and businessmen reformers. After 1896, the largely Democratic machines lost ground in the state legislatures, and they also lost the protection that once was yielded them by the national power of the Democratic party in an intensely competitive period. As business-backed reform campaigns gained momentum, the local parties were stripped of some of the resources they had used to sustain their cadres, to reach voters, and to overcome registration barriers. Consequently, the gradual weakening of the clientelist parties worked in tandem with more restrictive registration laws to steadily lower turnout, especially among the worse-off.

With these points made, we return to the proposition that rules, once implemented, change politics. As voter registration restrictions took effect, linkages that bound the parties to their working-class and lower-class constituencies weakened. Calculations of electoral advantage turned party strategists away from the worse-off who voted less, and toward the better-off who voted more. This tendency was reinforced by other developments that were changing the local parties, including the contraction of clientelist resources and the rise of business influence. Once this shift in orientation and constituencies had occurred, the parties tried to sustain it in order to avoid the threats to incumbency and to internal stability that new and unpredictable voters entailed. Consequently, *the big-city parties themselves became the defenders of the voter registration procedures which ensured their stability and protected incumbents.* As early as 1917, the machine and the reformers switched sides in Chicago, with the machine defending more cumbersome registration procedures against the Chicago Bureau of Public Efficiency's efforts at simplification.[46] The local parties became the guardians of a contracted electoral universe, using the voter registration restrictions which had helped to create that constricted electorate in the first place. In the late nineteenth century, the local parties had helped voters hurdle electoral barriers because they depended on a broad electorate. But as the parties lost ground to the disenfranchisers, they adapted to a narrow electorate by taking up the defense of electoral barriers.

As the connections between the parties and the electorate were reconstituted so that working-class groups were far less important, party appeals changed. In the mid-nineteenth century, clientelist parties employed the boisterous rhetoric of class in building popular support, along with strident ethnic and religious appeals. And in the decades after the Civil War there were at least some signs of the emergence of appeals based on issues, including economic issues, partly in response to the insurgent third-party challenges which injected broad issue appeals into electoral contests. The campaign of 1896 underlined the possibility of the emergence of issue politics. "Perceptions of 'hard times' dominated ... and strongly influenced the decisionmaking process of large numbers of voters. Older ethnoreligious antagonisms did not suddenly evaporate ... [but] as economic worries came increasingly to the forefront of consciousness, they crosscut the older lines of conflict and decreased their salience."[47] However, as the links between the local parties and the working class became attenuated, party appeals based on class identity and class interests gradually disappeared. Electoral contests were eventually emptied of class rhetoric, with the result that the marginalization of working-class voters from electoral politics, which resulted in the first instance from the combination of registration barriers and the breakdown of clientelist ties, was reinforced.

Under these political conditions, voter registration procedures depressed turnout. Without the parties as intermediaries to help voters complete registration procedures, the "costs" of registration rose. And without appeals that resonated with the identity and interests of working-class groups, the benefits of voting shrank.[48] In short, rules do indeed originate in politics, and their implementation is conditioned by complex features of the political situation, including the new political conditions that the rules themselves help to produce. Voter registration arrangements helped to create a party system severed from the working class. In a politics of weak linkages and hollow appeals, registration became a larger barrier to participation.

Burnham and Schattschneider place a singular emphasis on the crushing of party competition associated with the election of 1896. This ultimately fails, however, as an explanation of the long-term decline in turnout, if only because it cannot explain why low turnout became a permanent feature of twentieth-century political life, persisting throughout the century, long after party competition was restored to most of the country. In our opinion, it was the combined effects of changes in the local parties and the introduction of new rules that marginalized potentially disruptive elements from the electorate. This helped to stabilize the tendency toward one-party sectional domination associated with the election of 1896. Moreover, the changes in the rules and in the parties which secured that result continued to depress turnout, even after party competition intensified in much of the North in the 1930s, and in the South in the 1960s. One-party sectionalism is a thing of the past, to be sure, but aspects of the system of 1896 persist.

One final comment. Schattschneider and Burnham do not rest their case solely on the collapse of party competition. They think the collapse of party competition went hand in glove with the increasing domination of both parties by economic elites, with the consequence that potential voters were alienated because their interests were ignored.[49] There is surely truth in the view that business influence on party programs and symbols dampened political participation by large numbers of minorities, the poor, and blue-collar workers. Still, that was not the whole of it. The singular domination of electoral politics by business was in turn made possible and sustained by institutional barriers that excluded large proportions of the have-nots—of the groups who were made to bear the costs of business policies—and by the weakened local parties who adapted to those constraints. Party organizers turned away from the candidates, the policy appeals, the campaign rhetoric, and the logistics that would reach and appeal to those who are less likely to vote—and in the United States that means the have-nots. As party strategies thus came to reinforce legal encumbrances on the vote, the American political parties became unhinged from large swaths of the potential electorate.

Institutional Versus Social-Psychological Explanations

In the main, however, analysts have not viewed the problem of nonvoting in institutional terms. Rather, to explain the scale and persistence of nonvoting in the twentieth century, scholars fasten on the question of what it is about nonvoters themselves that accounts for their failure to participate. Something approaching a theoretical consensus has developed, albeit a consensus broad enough to permit a flourishing academic debate about a virtually endless number of variations and permutations of the general thesis. Notwithstanding the variety of specific propositions advanced, the overall line of reasoning is simple: the key to the puzzle of why so many people do not vote lies in one or another of their attitudes and preferences, or their lack of necessary resources. Thus people fail to vote because of a sense of political ineffectiveness,[50] or they lack a sense of civic obligation,[51] or they feel little partisan attachment,[52] or they possess few educational resources,[53] or they exhibit some combinations of these factors.[54] Aldrich and Simon speak of this large body of research as having become, by the 1970s, the "normal science" of nonvoting.[55]

Almost half a century ago, Lazarsfeld, Berelson, and Gaudet, writing in *The People's Choice,* set the direction for this sort of interpretation when they concluded that "three quarters of the non-voters stayed away from the polls deliberately because they were unconcerned. . . . A long range program of civic education would be needed to draw such people into the orbit of political life."[56] The assumption underlying these studies is that attitudes determine voting behavior, and that these attitudes are formed by social influences rather than politics.[57] Thus social experience shapes subjective orientations, and shapes orientations differently according to socioeconomic status, or education, or age.[58]

Other analysts treat these demographic characteristics as significant because they are associated with differential access to resources, particularly access to the skills and information that make electoral participation easier and more gratifying. Or in the economistic language of rational choice, people abstain because, given their attitudes, the "costs" of voting outweigh perceived benefits.[59] Perhaps the most influential argument is set out by Wolfinger and Rosenstone, who claim that educational levels exert a stronger influence on voter turnout than either income or occupation because education

> increases cognitive skills, which facilitates learning about politics. . . . Better educated people are likely to get more gratification from political participation. . . . Finally, schooling imparts experience with a variety of bureaucratic relationships: learning requirements, filling out forms, waiting in lines, and meeting deadlines.[60]

Either way, the thrust of this sort of explanation is to locate the causes of nonvoting in the characteristics of the nonvoters, and in the complex of social influences that shape those characteristics. Political arrangements have little to do with it. Berelson, Lazarsfeld, and McPhee called the tune in 1954 when they cautioned against "purely political explanations for non-participation. . . . Nonvoting is related to persistent social conditions having little to do with the candidates or issues of the moment."[61]

There are in fact strong correlations in the United States between a variety of demographic variables and the likelihood of voting. However, the question is whether these correlations illuminate causes. Does something about poorer or younger people lead them to abstain, or do distinctive features of American political institutions selectively deter people with these characteristics from voting? Attributes like low education or low income or youth do not have a comparably depressing impact on voter turnout in the democracies of Western Europe.[62] Nor did education (or income or occupation) much depress turnout in the United States during the nineteenth century. What these correlational analyses cannot explain is why turnout levels reached historic highs in the nineteenth century when educational levels were low, and why they then fell in the twentieth century when educational levels rose.[63]

Of course, everyone would agree that attitudinal or demographic predispositions can be offset by more intense political stimuli.[64] This is why we correctly expect higher turnouts in more important electoral races, or in more closely competitive races, or at moments when group consciousness rises, or when electoral races are associated with sharply divisive issues.[65] It is what Verba and Nie mean when they acknowledge that other forces may moderate the bias toward higher participation by groups with higher socioeconomic status, and with political attitudes that encourage participation:

> If there were more class-based ideologies, more class-based organizations, more explicit class-based appeals by political parties, the participation disparity between upper- and lower-status citizens would very likely be less.[66]

Or, as Teixiera argues in accounting for the new slide in turnout since 1960, political events may breed widespread cynicism with government and politics, and when that occurs, the impact of demographic variables on turnout declines.[67] Rosenstone and Hansen make a similar argument:

> When political leaders offset the costs of political involvement—when they provide information, subsidize participation, occasion the provision of social rewards—they make it possible for people who have few resources of their own to participate. When leaders mobilize extensively, that is, they muster even the disadvantaged into politics.[68]

Similar reasoning is often employed when the supposition that low socioeconomic status depresses political participation is projected backward onto the nineteenth century, as when Chambers and Davis take for granted that high voter participation in the lower social and economic portions of the electorate could only have been made possible by much stronger political stimuli.[69] In these hybrid arguments, a more stimulating and cohesive party culture offsets the effects of the dominant social-psychological model derived from contemporary American data.[70]

This simply is not good enough. It is an effort to cope with the empirical contradictions that the dominant model confronts while preserving the basic assumption that voter participation can be explained by personal characteristics rather than by political institutions. The point is not that the political context sometimes *offsets* the effects of demographic or social-psychological factors on turnout, but that the political context *determines* whether these factors will have a significant effect on participation at all, and just what those effects will be. The evidence strongly suggests that who votes and who does not has no inherent relationship to either variations in attitudes or socioeconomic status. The reasoning that assumes that an intense politics in the nineteenth century modifies the influence of socioeconomic or attitudinal factors is a tortured effort to sustain the "normal science" model. What the data show instead, according to Kleppner, is "the virtual absence of age and socioeconomic biases in the 19th century"; indeed, he finds that in broad regions of the country, "there is more evidence that electoral turnout was an inverse, rather than a direct, function of economic condition."[71]

The challenge to the "normal science" model generated by crossnational evidence is, if anything, even more compelling. Burnham cites a startling comparison: turnout in Sweden by propertied middle-class voters is no higher than by manual workers (90 percent versus 87 percent in 1960), but in the United States the propertied middle class turns out half again more than the working class (77 percent versus 52 percent in 1972). When education is considered as a determinant of turnout, the Swedish data show no difference between the voting rates of the most and least educated (97 percent versus 95 percent in 1979), but in the United States the most educated vote at twice the rate of the least educated (82 percent versus 44 percent in 1976).[72] Similarly, about 90 percent of Italians with five years or less of formal schooling voted in 1968, while only 38 percent of Americans with comparable educational levels did.[73] Powell's crossnational findings are particularly compelling. Using the same measures employed by Verba, Nie, and Kim,[74] he found a substantial correlation between turnout and socioeconomic status in the United States, but none in ten other countries.[75] Moreover, except for the youngest age group, correlations between age and turnout were quite weak in these countries, as they also appear to have been in the nineteenth-century United States.[76] And most persuasive, the attitudes associated with status or age, regarded by analysts using the dominant model as the intervening variables explaining why demographic status depresses turnout, are *not* correlated with crossnational differences in turnout. Indeed, Americans as a whole have until recently ranked very high on attitudes which are said to facilitate turnout. They are more intensely partisan, feel themselves to be more efficacious, and are more interested in politics. Turnout should therefore be higher here, not lower. Powell sums up his findings:

> Using a combination of aggregate and comparative survey data, the present analysis suggests that in comparative perspective, turnout in the United States is advantaged about 5% by political attitudes, but disadvantaged 13% by the party system and institutional factors, and up to 14% by the registration laws.[77]

In short, the social-psychological model confounds causes and consequences.[78] Features of the electoral system affect different groups differently. Legal and administrative barriers, such as time and place restrictions on registration or voting, impinge less on the well-off and well-educated than they do on the poor and the uneducated. Party strategies to activate and enlist voters are similarly selective in their impact on different groups, and so are the ideological appeals generated by candidates and parties. As Burnham says, "When politics matters . . . people behave as though it matters."[79] The lack of motivation attributed to the apathetic attitudes or educational deficits of nonvoters is not the cause of their marginalization from electoral politics, although it may be one of the outcomes.[80] Similarly, people with lower levels of education voted less in the United States because the party system tended to ignore them, and not because less education is an inherent impediment to voting. Apathy and lack of political skill were a consequence, not a cause, of the party strategies and political culture, which were sustained by legal and procedural barriers to electoral participation. In sum, the political system determined whether participation is predicated on class-related resources and attitudes.

There is an historical irony in the emergence of the social-psychological model as "normal science." The institutional arrangements that combined to narrow the electoral universe were constructed by regional political and economic elites who worked over time to refashion the legal and party basis of mass electoral participation. They were activated by political problems created by an urban immigrant working class, by insurgent western farmers, and by both white dirt farmers and blacks in the South. Step by step, the elites crafted the institutional arrangements which narrowed the electorate, and they did so precisely to demobilize the groups whose politics were becoming threatening and disruptive. Voter registration arrangements were targeted specifically at the cities where the immigrant working class was concentrated. Literacy tests, stricter naturalization procedures, and burdensome voter registration procedures were not so likely to bar the rich as they were the poor, or the well-educated as they were the uneducated.[81] At the same time, the local parties with a motive to enlist these voters were weakened by reform campaigns. Not only do a good many social scientists manage to ignore these developments by treating the racially- and class-biased effects of these arrangements as causes, but they are encouraged to do so by the witless use of multiple correlational analyses. Thus we have studies which attempt to discover whether the inauguration of voter registration arrangements affected turnout *when urbanization, income, and education are controlled.* But urbanization, income, and education cannot reasonably be employed as control variables, since they in fact predict the likelihood that attacks on mobilizing parties along with stringent voter registration procedures will develop in the first place. Voter registration was intended to discourage voting in big cities, and by the poor and less educated. The effects of these institutional changes cannot be sorted out—indeed, they are necessarily obscured—by introducing urbanization, income, or education as controls.[82] This is just another way in which the political underpinnings of voter exclusion are made to disappear in favor of an analysis that searches for an explanation of nonparticipation in the nonparticipants themselves.

We turn now to the history of the development of the contemporary American electorate. We think that history provides compelling evidence of the interaction of legal and procedural obstructions with party mobilization strategies—or the lack of such strategies—in marginalizing a large portion of the American electorate. It also tells us something about the motives of the political actors who played a role in these developments.

CHAPTER THREE

The Mobilization and Demobilization of the Nineteenth-Century Electorate

*B*etween the first decades of the nineteenth century and the first decades of the twentieth, the legal right to vote was successively extended to unpropertied white men, then to black men after the Civil War, and finally to women in 1920. But even before the century-long process of formal enfranchisement was completed, a series of legal and procedural changes were introduced into the electoral system that obstructed the actual ability of many people to vote. At the same time, changes in the party system reduced the motivation and the capacity of the local parties to mobilize voters. For most of the nineteenth century, turnout levels among eligible voters had been high. By the 1920s, however, voting in the South among blacks and most poor whites had been virtually eliminated, and turnout by the immigrant working class had fallen sharply in the North.

The combination of widening formal enfranchisement and narrowing electoral participation is not as paradoxical as it may seem. What explains these contradictory trends was a change in the potential importance of the vote. Under some conditions, the franchise yields people little influence on government; under other conditions, it may yield more. The distinctive methods of organizing voters that emerged in the United States during the nineteenth century produced high levels of participation among the white men who were eligible to vote, but at the same time these methods limited their influence on government. As a result, there was relatively little contention over the right of white working-class men to vote. Toward the end of the century, however, wrenching economic change provoked a series of popular mobilizations that overtaxed the earlier methods of political incorporation that had sustained high electoral participation but limited its influence. Popular demands, especially popular economic demands, began to emerge into electoral politics, and even to dominate some electoral contests. As the possibilities of popular electoral mobilization began to threaten the interests of the ruling groups in the late-nineteenth-century United States, they responded by sponsoring something like a democratic counterrevolution. A series of "reforms" were introduced which weakened the ability of local parties to maintain high participation among lower-strata voters, and which impeded voting by lower-strata people. The effect of these changes was to marginalize potentially contentious groups from the electoral system.

In this chapter, we deal first with what we call the tribalist and clientelist characteristics of nineteenth-century politics that made high levels of mass participation possible even while limiting conflict, especially class conflict. Then we investigate how the increasingly issue-oriented and conflictual politics of the decades after the Civil War strained these arrangements. Finally, we describe the crucial election of 1896, in which a Republican-corporate mobilization defeated the Populists (who had allied with the Democrats), the most important mass electoral movement of the nineteenth century. The election also inaugurated a pattern of sectional one-party dominance, by the Republicans in the North and the Democrats in the South. With the Populists smashed and party competition reduced, the way was cleared for the acceleration of changes in the rules governing voting and in the organization and outreach strategies of the parties. Together, these changes sharply reduced voting among lower-strata voters in the twentieth century. The feudal system of the apartheid South was shored up, the prospects for labor politics outside the South were dimmed, and the ability of popular movements to affect national politics was weakened.

The contraction of the electorate had a telling impact on the evolution of American politics in the twentieth century. Still, without a sober assessment of the terms on which mass participation was sustained in the nineteenth century, it is all too easy to be lulled into a nostalgia that mourns the passing of a democratic era that, in fact, never was.

The "Golden Era" of American Democracy

The spirit and vigor of popular politics in the nineteenth century is the stuff of folklore. Consider Tocqueville's oft-cited impressions in 1831:

> No sooner do you set foot on American soil than you find yourself in a sort of a tumult. . . . A thousand voices are heard at once. . . . One group of citizens assembles for the sole object of announcing that they disapprove of the government's course, while others unite to proclaim that the men in office are the fathers of their country. . . .
>
> It is hard to explain the place filled by political concerns in the life of an American. To take a hand in the government of society and to talk about it is his most important business and, so to say, the only pleasure he knows.[1]

Most political historians echo Tocqueville's characterization: "Political life was rich and vibrant," says Hays, drawing on the Handlins' study of Massachusetts for confirmation.[2] "By 1840," Gienapp exclaims, "the tide of political democracy . . . swept all before it."[3]

And the tide drove up rates of voter participation. Property qualifications that had restricted voting in the eighteenth century were steadily lowered in the early decades of the nineteenth, and the electoral-representative system was gradually expanded so that more officials were required to stand for popular election, including presidential electors, governors, and many of those in local government.[4] With these changes, the already high voter participation among white men rose to unprecedented levels in an era when the United States was the only democratic polity in the world.[5]

Early in the century, turnout levels were still volatile, surging between 1804 and 1818, and then tapering off during the 1820s.[6] That changed with the election of 1828, when turnout began a steady upward swing, reaching 80 percent of the eligible electorate in the presidential election of 1840. Moreover, stable and high levels of participation characterized all levels of the federal system. In the elections between 1824 and 1832, when fifty gubernatorial contests were decided by popular vote, turnout for President exceeded the vote for governor in only sixteen instances.[7] Turnout continued high in the second half of the nineteenth century, ranging from a low of about 69 percent in the presidential election of 1852, just before the electoral realignment that preceded the Civil War, to 82 and 83 percent respectively in the elections of 1860 and 1876. And high levels of voting also continued at lower levels of government. The mean turnout for *all elections* between 1840 and 1860 was 70 percent. Turnout in presidential elections during this period ranged from 69 to 83 percent, and it lagged only modestly behind in nonpresidential elections, averaging 67 percent, which is spectacular by modern standards.[8]

Most historians resort to rhetorical hyperbole in describing the nineteenth-century politics which generated such high levels of participation among the eligible white male electorate. There is an infatu-

Table 3.1. Presidential Turnout Percentages, 1840–1896

	SOUTH	NON-SOUTH	NATIONAL
1840	75	81	80
1844	74	80	79
1848	68	74	73
1852	59	72	69
1856	72	81	79
1860	76	83	82
1864	Civil War	76	76
1868	71	83	81
1872	67	74	72
1876	75	86	83
1880	65	86	81
1884	64	84	79
1888	64	86	81
1892	59	81	76
1896	57	86	79

SOURCE: *Burnham (1981c:100, table 1). Based on total of all citizens legally eligible to vote, aliens excluded.*

ation with the period, evident in the extravagant images of popular democracy with which it is characterized. Scarcely an account fails to remark upon and celebrate the excitement of nineteenth-century democratic politics: the pageantry, the marching bands, the rallies, the hoarsely shouted slogans, the fury and fun—in short, the extraordinary popular enthusiasm that marked election campaigns. "There was no spectacle, no contest, in America that could match an election campaign, and all could identify with and participate in it."[9] But there is good reason to be skeptical of the celebratory depiction of nineteenth-century democratic politics.

TRIBALISM IN THE GOLDEN ERA

To understand the developments which brought the Golden Era to an end, we should identify the modes of political integration that produced high levels of voter participation, and then ask how and why they changed. Indeed, this period suggests parallels to contemporary politics in economically less developed regions abroad where democratic forms coexist with and even seem to nurture decidedly undemocratic realities. One such parallel is suggested by the intensity of ethnocultural issues in nineteenth-century politics, a feature we call "tribalism." Just as the politics of contemporary developing nations are often riven by intense tribal identifications and conflicts, so was popular participation in the nineteenth-century United States strongly marked by ethnic and religious divisions.[10]

The association of religious identification and popular politics was evident from the beginning of the nineteenth century, and religious feelings intensified with the revival movements that swept the North in the 1820s and 1830s. Indeed, Tocqueville's observations in *Democracy in America* in 1831 led him to conclude that "Religion should be considered as the first of their political institutions."[11] Religion gained unique secular force from the proliferation of church-related voluntary associations through which an essentially civil religion was created, and through which religious crusading and partisan fervor were joined. This ethnoreligious infrastructure provided the vehicle, and rapid immigration and associated labor-market competition and conflict provided the stimulus, for the nativist, temperance, and antislavery movements of the midcentury, which in turn strongly marked

the party realignment of the 1850s.[12] High levels of democratic participation, in short, were mobilized through overlapping networks of religious and ethnic associations.

Consistent with these intensely felt ethnoreligious identifications,
popular political enthusiasms had what Gienapp calls the "unseemly"
features of rival ethnic gangs and thugs who fought to control access
to the polls and otherwise participated in the generally inebriated tu-
mult, and whose impact on the exercise of voter choices has received
rather casual attention.[13] This pugnacious aspect of popular politics
also clearly has its parallels in less economically developed societies, as
in the Tillys' descriptions of the battles between gangs from rival vil-
lages in preindustrial Europe.[14]

A number of commentators also maintain that ethnic and religious identities were intertwined with real differences in social position and economic interest, with the consequence that class, ethnic,
and religious identification were mutually reinforcing. Thus Bridges
says that the antebellum partisan appeals of the New York Democratic
Party insisted "that the Democracy was the 'true home of the working
classes'" and tried to drive the point home by employing a rhetoric
that fused the issues of religion, ethnicity, culture, class, and liberty.[15]
Wilentz explains why political appeals of this kind could be made:

> To take a well-studied example: to be an evangelical Protestant in the North
> in the 1830s and 1840s certainly signified adherence to a broad cultural out-
> look, a particular moral viewpoint. It also signified something about a per-
> son's social position or expected social position in an evolving class society;
> even more, that "culture," that moral viewpoint, was in part defined and rein-
> forced by changing class relations, in which inherited religious ideals as-
> sumed new—and in this case quintessentially bourgeois—meanings and
> forms.[16]

Sectional passions should be added to these sources of identification and association that encouraged electoral participation. Bensel
claims that sectional feelings "constitute the most massive and complex fact in American politics and history."[17] That was so in part
because sectional passions were compounded of religious, racial,
and regional identifications. It was also in part so because sectional
identities were shaped by economic interests—indeed, sectional economic interests often strained against and overwhelmed class alle-

giances. After all, on the great political questions of the century concerning currency policy, internal improvements, the tariff, and slavery, capitalists and workers in the Northeast had a common interest, however else their interests may have diverged;[18] in turn, their common interests differed from those of both rich planters and poor farmers in the South.[19] In the wake of the Civil War, sectional identification and conflict intensified. Conflicts of this kind, as they unfold, always create their own reality in the bitter memories of injustices done and losses suffered. The civil war in the United States complicated and sharpened religious, ethnic, and racial identifications with bloody memories of war and fierce sectional patriotism. The war produced scars, says Burnham, "which took at least a century to heal. There was no town in the North without its memorial to the Union dead; no town in the South without its Confederate counterpart."[20]

Nineteenth-century popular politics did not lack class content, but the political force of class interests was complicated and diluted by sectional economic issues that united industrialists and workers in the North and landowners and tenants in the South. Class issues were thus interwoven with ethnocultural and especially sectional issues. Our purpose here is not to disentangle the relative influence of religion, ethnicity, and section, but to make a different point: high levels of mobilization for electoral participation were typically maintained by the overlapping influences of religious, ethnic, and regional identifications. The popular politics organized around these tribal identifications and the conflicts generated by them were intensely felt, and stimulated high participation. But participation on these terms did not lead to challenges to nineteenth-century elites.

CLIENTELISM AND VOTER TURNOUT

The popular politics of preindustrial countries are often marked by clientelist methods of organizing participation, as well as by intense tribal identification. Here too there are striking similarities between the nineteenth-century United States and some contemporary developing nations. As voter participation expanded, so did the reliance by the political parties on government patronage, and on the clientelist linkages to the electorate which government patronage made possible.[21] The complex federated governmental structure with which the United States entered the nineteenth-century exposed the state to penetration by parties which played a central role in coordinating public policy and integrating mass publics.[22] And as in other developing countries, it was clientelist party organizations that emerged to solve the problems of coordination and political integration. Clientelism appears to thrive in situations where formal enfranchisement precedes industrialization and the self-organization of the working class that industrialization makes possible.[23] In the absence of trade unions and working-class parties, voters easily become prey to political operatives who influence them on the basis of preexisting ethnic or territorial loyalties, and enlist their votes in exchange for goods, services, and friendship. In other words, when the franchise is ceded to populations that are unprepared by the experience of industrialization for modern mass politics, those populations are more likely to become the base for clientelist organizations.[24] Also, machine politics is said to take root more readily among people experiencing the social uprootedness associated with economic change, as was true of many people in nineteenth-century American cities.[25]

Clientelism bears directly on nineteenth-century levels of turnout. From the perspective of party entrepreneurs, votes were resources for gaining control of government offices. And control of government offices in turn yielded the patronage on which party leaders depended to organize voters. Reports which celebrate rising turnout and strong partisanship tend to tread lightly on this aspect of nineteenth-century politics. As Formisano says, "accounts of party formation after 1828 contain perfunctory references to the importance of patronage, but hardly a glimpse of the enormous role played by cadre-men appointed to land offices, post offices, customs houses, and the like, in the building of organizations."[26] A clue to the growing significance of patronage is provided by the growth of government employment, which was the most important way that the functionaries of clientelist party organizations were rewarded and supported. The era after 1830 in which party organization flourished was also an era in which the number of government jobs expanded. Between 1830 and 1860, the number of federal employees increased 3.2 times, while the population grew 2.4 times; state employment also expanded rapidly during this period, largely through extensive public works projects;[27] and federal employment continued to expand after the Civil War, doubling between 1860 to 1880, and then multiplying 2.6 times by 1901.[28] Another form of federal patronage grew even more rapidly after the Civil War as Congress virtually blanketed the northern electorate with veterans' pensions distributed through local Republican leagues. As a consequence, Goodwyn says, "From New England to Minnesota, hundreds of small towns, as well as broad swaths of rural America, became virtual rotten boroughs of Republicanism."[29]

If patronage was the fuel of American party politics generally, it was the cities that became the strongholds of patronage politics and (usually Democratic) party "machines," particularly as the nineteenth-century wore on.[30] In fact, it is not farfetched to think that the marked local orientation of American popular politics, especially in the nineteenth-century, owes something to the strength of locally-based machines, both urban and rural. Of course, localism was nurtured by other features of American politics as well: by the simple and unchangeable fact that ordinary people can best organize for politics in the communities where they live and work; by a deep popular animosity toward central government rooted in the suspicion that a remote government inevitably becomes the captive of elites; and by the reality in the United States of a decentralized federal structure in which local government did indeed do many things, although often not the most important things. To all of these conditions that inclined popular politics toward local issues and local government must be added the role of the city machine in delineating alternatives and organizing political participation. And the strength of the city machines, in turn, was made possible by the high degree of decentraliza tion embedded in the structure of the federal system. The authority and resources vested in local and state governments facilitated the growth of decentralized parties with the flexibility to ignore national issues in their campaigns in favor of state and local or even neighborhood issues. Government decentralization also made accessible the patronage resources which permitted local clientelist parties to operate with a large degree of autonomy from the national or even state party organizations.[31] Before 1840, the New York City Democracy had looked to state and federal appointments to support local organization, but by the 1850s, there were seven city departments with substantial payrolls, as well as the resources yielded by multiplying municipal franchises and contracts.[32]

Certainly the political machines mobilized voters in the big cities, where much of the population was already concentrated by the closing decades of the nineteenth century. They brought "party loyalties to a pitch of almost military fervor and discipline," producing peak participation rates of about 80 percent in the presidential elections of 1876, 1888, and 1896.[33] In particular, the machines mobilized immigrant working-class voters, whose enlarging numbers in nineteenth-century cities might otherwise have caused turnout to fall. The machines kept voter participation high by reaching and enlisting these potential voters, often even before they became citizens, inducing them with friendship, favors, small bribes, the promise of some protection from the harassment of city cops, or by threatening them with the loss of any of these things. The cadres of machine operatives who "worked" the wards and precincts were in turn kept diligent and kept loyal with city jobs, real or otherwise, and sometimes with graft. In turn, the votes of the immigrant working-class wards, and often the middle-class wards as well, together with outright fraud, gave the machines control of the municipal and state offices through which they raised the graft and controlled the public jobs that sustained the ward and precinct apparatus.[34] Moreover, just as ethnoreligious political loyalties were often intertwined with class loyalties, so were allegiances to the machine cultivated with class rhetoric (even while machine bosses cultivated their graft-based alliances with key business interests). Thus a spokesman for the New York Democracy could assert in 1868 that the pending election was "pre-eminently one of capital against labor, of money against popular rights, and of political power against the struggling interest of the masses."[35] By these diverse methods, working-class political participation was kept high while working-class political issues were suppressed—a not inconsiderable achievement, especially at a time of intensifying grievances associated with the massive dislocations caused by burgeoning industrialization, rapid urbanization, and devastating depressions.

The usual account of a spirited democratic politics in the nineteenth century tends to skirt the question of how much that apparent spirit was owed to tribal and clientelist modes of political organization. Burnham's commentaries provide a fair example, if only because he is ordinarily so skeptical and penetrating in his analyses of electoral politics. But there is little of that skepticism in his characterization of the nineteenth-century American voters as primarily "independent yeomen who were thoroughly bourgeois and 'modern,'" mostly literate, and immersed in rich written and oral political communications about "political issues of transcendent importance." The conclusion seems to follow that "the United States was unique in that it had a fully operating set of mass-democratic institutions and values before the onset of industrial-capitalist development. In every other industrializing nation of the 1850–1950 period, modernizing elites were effectively insulated from mass pressures."[36] But this characterization hardly matches the realities of nineteenth-century politics. The existence of issue-oriented and informed democratic publics capable of challenging economic elites cannot be inferred merely from the fact of high voter turnouts.[37] To do so ignores the evidence that tribalist and clientelist methods of political activation and incorporation insulated American elites by managing and deflecting mass pressures, at least until the closing decades of the nineteenth century. High levels of popular participation could therefore coexist with tolerable levels of political conflict. After the Civil War, however, a series of wrenching economic transformations strained those methods of incorporating working-class voters and poor farmers, and it was then that popular economic demands emerged into national politics.

The Rise of Issue Politics

In the post-Civil War period, rapid economic growth combined with extreme market instability and the predatory policies of bankers and corporations to spur the rise of popular protests over economic issues. Increasingly, popular demands were directed to the states and even to the national government for action on economic grievances. Foremost among these popular grievances was the deflationary hard-money policy promoted by financiers who held government securities issued during the war. Naturally enough, the financiers preferred that their investments be redeemed in gold rather than in the inflated "greenbacks" with which they had been purchased. The means to this end was the Treasury policy of holding the nation's money supply constant, even while population and production expanded rapidly. The resulting contraction of the currency between the end of the Civil War and the passage of the Gold Standard Act in 1900 drove interest rates up and prices down.[38] It was, as Goodwyn says, a tragedy to the nation's farmers whose debts became steadily more costly, and whose products became steadily cheaper.

The farmers' troubles were worsened by their dependence on the railroads. It was the expanding network of railroads that had lured farmers to the prairies in the first place. Once there, the great distances from urban markets left them with no way to transport their products to market except by railroad, and that made them acutely vulnerable to the exorbitant rates charged. Many farmers simply could not survive the combined pressures of low product prices and high interest and shipping costs. Year after year in the decades after the Civil War, more and more were driven by rising debts into the hands of banks and crop lien merchants, and then, as they lost their land, into tenancy or sharecropping, particularly in the South. In response, an extraordinary series of protest movements emerged. By the early 1870s, farmers in the Midwest, their indignation fired by the not unreasonable idea that the railroads, having benefited from huge government land grants and subsidies, ought properly to have been subject to some government regulation, mobilized in organizations called Granges to do battle over high shipping rates. The Granges did win legislation regulating railroads in a number of states, but over time the power of the railroad interests (and a Supreme Court ruling in 1886 that struck down state laws regulating the railroad rates)[39] ensured that these victories were short-lived. Defeated by the political reach and staying power of the railroad interests, the Grange movement lost momentum.

Railroad rates remained high, as did interest rates, and commodity prices continued to fall, especially after the depression of 1873. In the late 1870s, another farmers' movement emerged, this time among the impoverished cotton farmers of Texas, who formed the first of the "Farmers' Alliances." In the following years, Alliance organizers (called "lecturers") fanned out to build chapters among the debt-ridden farmers of other southern states.[40] These Alliances became the organizational backbone of the Populist movement and of the People's party that the Populists launched.

The Civil War marked a dramatic economic turning point in the Northeast as well, where most of the nation's burgeoning manufacturing enterprises were concentrated.[41] At the beginning of the Civil War, the United States ranked only fourth among industrial nations; by the end of the century, the U.S. had become the world's leading industrial power.[42] The transformation was turbulent and costly, especially for the growing numbers of workers in the new industries. Fierce competition goaded employers to try to lower production costs, mainly by slashing wages. And competition also led to the overproduction that worsened the severe market downturns that punctuated the era.

These changes simultaneously created an industrial proletariat—at first concentrated in the expanding railroads and the growing steel industry—and the conditions for industrial warfare. On the one side, it was the railroad workers and later the steel workers who were in the forefront of the industrial battles which erupted in the late nineteenth century. During the devastating depressions of the era, strikes and riots reached unprecedented levels, spreading like brush fires along the newly created networks of rail routes. On the other side, industrialists, pressed by competition and goaded by the predatory ethos of the age, organized themselves into employer associations and mobilized public and private armies to defeat strikes. Their goal was to smash the possibilities of worker power by both breaking unions and mechanizing production in order to lower wages and gain firm control over the production process.[43] The ensuing conflicts in 1877, 1886, and 1894 were among the bloodiest and costliest in peacetime American history.

These were desperation strikes, prompted by depression and by aggressive employer efforts to cut wages and reorganize production, and the ferocity of the workers' response sent waves of alarm through the ranks of America's upper classes. The strikes of 1877, for example, which were met first by militia and then by three thousand federal troops, left twenty-six dead in Pittsburgh, thirteen dead and forty-three wounded in Reading, Pennsylvania, and nineteen dead and more than one hundred wounded in Chicago.[44] Property damage was estimated at about $5 million.[45] Another wave of strikes in 1886 reached a climax in the Haymarket bombing incident and a wave of lockouts, blacklisting, and yellow-dog contracts. In the 1890s a new and even larger wave of strikes in steel, railroads, and mining again brought out the National Guard and federal troops, culminating in an estimated thirty-four dead in the Pullman strike of 1894, and the massive use of federal marshals to protect railroad property across the country.

These intense economic conflicts led to recurrent efforts by workers and farmers, sometimes separately and sometimes together, to organize independent electoral challenges. It was probably inevitable that contention would take electoral form, given the vigor of political participation in nineteenth-century America, together with government's enlarging role in promoting corporate growth while breaking strikes and thwarting the demands of distressed farmers. Accordingly, as the level of conflict intensified, the links that bound workers and farmers to the major political parties—and to clientelist and tribalist forms of organization—were strained. As early as 1869, the shoemakers in Massachusetts fielded an Independent party which succeeded in electing two dozen state legislators. In 1872, the Labor Reform party was formed by a number of trade union assemblies that were united in the National Labor Union. Also in the 1870s, farmers backed "antimonopoly" candidates in their fight against the railroads and banks. The efforts of the Labor Reform party came to little, but the farmers won important state offices in Illinois and—in coalition with Democrats—in Minnesota, Wisconsin, Kansas, Iowa, and California.[46]

The severe depression that began in 1873 spurred renewed electoral efforts, and in 1876 a farmer-labor coalition emerged under the name of the Greenback-Labor party, which demanded an expansion of the money supply, to be achieved by government resumption of the issuance of the greenbacks that had funded the Civil War. The Greenbacks also called for a shorter work week and government labor bureaus, as well as restrictions on immigration and the use of prison labor. In the midterm election of 1878, in the aftermath of the great railroad strike of 1877, the Greenbacks (running as the National party) captured fourteen congressional seats and over a million votes (although some of this support was for candidates who were also backed by one of the major parties);[47] they elected mayors in a number of industrial and mining towns in New York and Pennsylvania; and they won an astonishing 34 percent of the vote in Maine, 26 percent in Michigan, 24 percent in Mississippi, and 23 percent in Texas.[48] But as the economy recovered, support for the Greenbacks evaporated, and James B. Weaver, their presidential candidate, won only 3.3 percent of the 1880 vote. But other antimonopoly and labor parties took the place of the Greenbacks. In the South, where the one-party "Southern Democracy" was not yet firmly entrenched, a series of insurgent electoral efforts in the 1880s demanded repudiation of state debts, the abolition of crop liens and convict leasing, and tax reform. In Virginia, "Readjusters" joined with Republicans to elect a governor in 1881.[49] Electoral challenges also recurred in the North. In the spring of 1884, the new Anti-Monopoly party declared itself, on essentially the same platform as the Greenbacks, but the economy was stronger, and the party's candidate won few votes. Still, third-party efforts persisted. In 1886, the United Labor party in New York City came close to winning the mayoralty election with Henry George as its candidate.[50]

Then, in the early 1890s, the Farmers' Alliances entered the electoral lists. The Alliances came to third-party politics gradually and reluctantly, for the strategy on which their movement had been built ignored and even scorned "politics." The movement's organizing strategy rested instead on building producer cooperatives in an effort to buoy prices and keep the cost of credit down. But as the cooperatives foundered on business opposition, particularly by banks which denied credit, the movement increasingly turned from the cooperative crusade to an electoral crusade against "centralized capital, allied to irresponsible corporate power."[51] The program adopted by the state Farmers' Alliances meeting in St. Louis in 1889 (and endorsed by the Knights of Labor) echoed and expanded upon most of the demands of preceding third-party movements: the abolition of national banks and the expansion of the currency, government ownership of communication and transportation, equitable taxation, and the adoption of the Alliance "subtreasury" plan through which the federal government itself would underwrite the farmers' cooperatives. "Populism,"

Richard Hofstadter concluded, "was the first modern political movement of practical importance in the United States to insist that the
federal government had some responsibility for the common weal; indeed it was the first such movement to attack seriously the problems
caused by industrialism."[52]

With this program, the Alliances entered a number of state electoral contests in 1890, trying to capture local Democratic organizations in the South, and fielding third-party candidates in the West.
"Conditions in 1890 were ripe for a political push"[53] as drought in the
West added to the perennial problems of the farmers. "Lecturers"
moved across the farm states to build support for Alliance-backed
candidates running on a program for an expanded (and democrati-
cally controlled) currency, and regulation of railroad and granary
rates. When the returns were counted, they had won fifty-two congressional seats, three Senate seats, three governorships, and majorities in seven state legislatures.[54]

After this heady beginning, the Alliances announced in 1892 the
formation of the People's party, convened a national convention, and
prepared to enter the presidential campaign behind the candidacy of
James B. Weaver, the perennial third-party candidate. This time, however, Weaver won 8.5 percent of the vote, supplanting the Democrats
as the opposition party in Nebraska, South Dakota, and Oregon, oust-
ing the Republicans in Texas, Mississippi, and Alabama, and gaining
outright majorities in Colorado, Idaho, Kansas, and Nevada. Weaver's
twenty-two electoral votes were in fact the first to be won by a third
party since 1860. Then, in the watershed campaign of 1896, the People's party coalesced with the Democratic party by supporting William Jennings Bryan, the Democratic presidential nominee. With that
action, the Populists launched a national election campaign in which
economic elites revealed their fear of an enfranchised populace more
plainly than ever before.

The Democratic Counterrevolution
and the Campaign of 1896

In hindsight, the challenge posed by the farmers' movement may
seem to have been hopeless, and for several reasons. For one thing, the
effort by largely Protestant farmers to build a national coalition with

the largely immigrant and Catholic working class ran against the grain of ethnoreligious politics. For another, experience in the United States had already showed how difficult third-party contests were to win, and how elusive the results. From the outset, electoral efforts by the farmers in the South were battered by old-line Democrats who employed frenzied race baiting, as well as force and fraud, to defeat them.[55] Just as serious, in Goodwyn's opinion, was the ingrained loyalty of most southern farmers to "the party of the fathers," a factor which helps account for the reluctance of southern Populists to turn to electoral politics in the first place (and for their eventual alliance with the Democratic Party).[56] Then, as the farmers' cause nevertheless gained momentum, it was often the case that southern Democrats simply overwhelmed the Populists by coopting their issues and their rhetoric. "By the mid-nineties, no stump speech in the South was complete without blasts at the railroads, the trusts, Wall Street, the gold bugs, the saloonkeepers, or some similarly evil 'Interest.'"[57] William Jennings Bryan was just such a master of the rhetoric of the common man, as in the famous peroration of his address to the Democratic nominating convention in 1896:

> You come to us and tell us that the great cities are in favor of the gold standard; we reply that the great cities rest upon our broad and fertile prairies. Burn down your cities and leave our farms, and your cities will spring up again as if by magic; but destroy our farms and the grass will grow in the streets of every city in the country. . . . Having behind us the producing masses of this nation and the world, supported by . . . the laboring interests and toilers everywhere, we will answer their demand for a gold standard by saying to them: You shall not press down upon the brow of labor this crown of thorns, you shall not crucify mankind upon a cross of gold.[58]

Such rhetoric helps to explain why the Populists abandoned their third-party movement and endorsed Bryan, the Democratic candidate. But the price of coalition was high. Very little of the bold Populist critique of industrial capitalism, or of its visionary program of economic cooperation, was evident in the ensuing campaign. Even the currency issue was emasculated: if the Populists had once sweepingly called for wresting control of the monetary system from the nation's bankers, the Democratic-Populist campaign now demanded only the minting of silver currency.

But industrialists and bankers did not have the benefit, if such it is, of the hindsight which seems to make history as it happened inevitable. Their alarm was palpable, not only because the farmers' movement had spread to reach much of the still large proportion of the population in agriculture, but because of the threat that the campaign might become the vehicle through which a coalition would be forged with discontented industrial workers in the Northeast and Midwest. Nor was the possibility of a farmer-labor coalition entirely a fantasy. The campaign took place while the country was mired in the major depression that had begun in 1893, and in the wake of the 1894 strike wave, the largest in the nation's history to that time. The Greenback-Labor party had drawn substantial support from voters in the Northeast in 1878, at a similar conjuncture of depression and class conflict. And beginning in 1886, when the fledgling Texas Alliance had organized a boycott in support of the striking Knights of Labor, the Farmers' Alliance had often worked self-consciously to gain the support of workers. To smooth the way for coalition with the Knights, the National Farmers' Alliance was renamed the Farmers' and Laborers' Union of America in 1889. The meeting in St. Louis in 1892 announcing the formation of the People's party surged with enthusiasm when Ignatius Donnelly took up the rhetorical banner of labor with a ringing denunciation of "corporations, national banks, rings, [and] trusts" not only because they plundered farmers, but because "urban workmen are denied the right of organization for self-protection, imported pauperized labor beats down their wages, a hireling standing army, unrecognized by our laws, is established to shoot them down, and they are rapidly disintegrating to European conditions."[59] The platform adopted by the People's party went on to denounce the Pinkertons, who were, of course, the "hireling standing army."

Of themselves, these pleas for farmer-labor unity would probably not have caused the propertied classes much alarm, particularly since the electoral successes of the Populists had been entirely confined to states in the West and the South. Certainly, the responses by organized labor were not thunderous. The young American Federation of Labor (A. F. of L.) merely endorsed a number of the Populist planks. In 1893, insurgents within the Knights of Labor toppled their increasingly timid leader, Terence Powderly, with the demand that the Knights should support the farmers' third-party challenge,[60] but by this time the Knights were overshadowed by the growing A. F. of L. Still, no one could be sure. Economic depressions had triggered electoral convulsions earlier in the nineteenth century, and the new electoral challenge sought to tap discontents that had surfaced again and again in the preceding decades. Moreover, popular attitudes were becoming more hostile toward business. Galabos sums up his investigations of public opinion during the period:

> [A]n entire generation of Americans had acquired distinctive attitudes toward big business. Each of the occupational groups studied . . . had become increasingly perturbed about the trusts; all had seen the combination movement spread to a wider range of major industries; all had changed their concept of the corporation in some significant way. The most general pattern that emerges is one of mounting hostility. . . . Neutral attitudes gave way as Americans vented their anger against the trusts and syndicates that were remaking the structure of the industrial economy.[61]

Under these unstable and unfamiliar conditions, the Democratic-Populist challenge was alarming, even horrifying—and to wealthy Democrats as well as Republicans.

Accordingly, corporate interests mobilized, and poured unprecedented sums into Republican coffers for the McKinley campaign, while the Bryan campaign was able to raise only $300,000, a small fraction of the funds contributed by Cleveland's supporters in 1892.[62] The huge railroad conglomerates, such as the New York Central and the Pennsylvania Railroad, took the lead, followed by such corporate combinations as Standard Oil, J. P. Morgan, and New York Life. Some $3,500,000 was raised for the operations of the Republican National Committee alone, which then proceeded to organize a campaign whose scale, says McGerr, was "truly original" in American politics.[63] With virtually unlimited resources to draw upon, a campaign strategy unfolded under the leadership of Mark Hanna, himself a wealthy coal magnate, that was to become the model for the twentieth-century big-money political advertising extravaganza. But the themes that were advertised looked backward rather than forward, resonating with nineteenth-century political culture. Across the land, the newly centralized Republican organization raised the alarm about the threat to "sound money" posed by the Democratic-Populist challenge, a monetary doctrine linked by incantation to national honor and prosperity. And the Republican campaign did not hesitate to appropriate the flag and "wave the bloody shirt," reminding the nation of persisting deep sectional fissures with marching companies, "sound money" processions, flag raisings, and a national (but Republican) Flag Day.[64]

The challenge of 1896 was turned aside not only by the sheer weight of the Republican-corporate mobilization, but by weaknesses in the Democratic-Populist fusion as well. In the Metropole, the vast majority of urban workers rebuffed the Populist appeal for a farmer-labor alliance. The Populist coalition with the Democratic party, which had presided over the depression of 1893, the most severe thus far in American history, was surely one reason.[65] Another was the disarray in Democratic ranks in the wake of the depression, as the silverites split with Eastern financial interests, which had helped to account for the rout of the Democrats in the midterm election of 1894. A still further reason for defeat was that urban workers did in fact have grounds to think the Republican economic program was in their economic interests. They would share in the increases in jobs and wages associated with protective tariffs and a sound money policy, while the free silver issue and commodity price inflation that came to define the Democratic-Populist campaign had little meaning to workers in the midst of a depression economy.

Finally, there was the strong and steady hold of tribalism. Whatever the efforts of the Populist leaders to heal the rifts of religion and section, these powerful identifications were deeply rooted in memory and fixed by symbol and association. The farmers remained a movement of Protestants and nativists, now spearheaded by the Bryan of evangelical Protestant oratory, and this must have been alienating to a heavily Catholic urban working class.[66] Similarly, the Republican sectional appeal to memories of the Civil War resonated with the northern workers who had paid the blood price for the war.

All of this helps to explain the Republican victory, won by a substantially larger margin than had decided presidential contests in the preceding decades. McKinley received 7,035,000 votes to Bryan's 6,467,000.[67] More telling, Democratic-Populist support was almost entirely confined to the western and southern periphery of the country. Bryan failed totally in the bid to appeal to urban working-class voters. As Burnham sums it up, the 1892–96 swing to the Republicans was only 2.9 percent in nonmetropolitan areas, but 23.3 percent in metropolitan ones.[68]

The election of 1896 was one of the most decisive in American history, the historic marker denoting the passing of the "populist moment"[69] and the ascendance in national politics of the conservative wing of the Republican party. At a deeper structural level, it was important because it facilitated the introduction of a series of sweeping changes in American electoral institutions which made possible the near total domination of the Republican party by business in the North and of the Democratic party by planter interests in the South. These changes, taken together, constitute what Schattschneider called "the system of 1896."[70] The system's most important and long-lasting feature was the secular decline in voting that it initiated, a decline that with relatively minor variations has persisted throughout the twentieth century.

The Demobilization of the Nineteenth-Century Electorate

The movements of the late nineteenth century culminating in the challenge of 1896 signaled that American popular politics was breaking out of the constrained patterns of participation that were both created and limited by tribalism and clientelism. But even as a more issue-oriented popular politics emerged, voting by poor farmers and workers began to decline. As voter participation steadily contracted, the grievances of poor workers and farmers disappeared from the agenda of national politics. By the 1920s, the low point of electoral turnout, business (and planters) not only dominated both parties, but business rhetoric defined the political alternatives open to Americans.

Between the elections of 1896 and 1920, turnout fell from 79 to 49 percent (table 3.2).[71] The southern declines came first, and were more extreme—from 57 percent in the election of 1896, to 43 percent in 1900, to 29 percent in 1904, to a low point of 19 percent in 1924. Blacks and most poor whites virtually disappeared from the polls. The contraction of the electoral universe outside of the South was less sharp and less rapid—from 86 percent in 1896 to 57 percent in 1924. The decline was concentrated among the immigrant young, large numbers

Table 3.2. Presidential Turnout Percentages, 1896–1924

	SOUTH	NON-SOUTH	NATIONAL
1896	57	86	79
1900	43	83	74
1904	29	77	66
1908	31	76	66
1912	28	68	59
1916	32	69	62
1920	22	55	49
1924	19	57	49

SOURCE: *Burnham (1981c:100, table 1). Based on total of all citizens legally eligible to vote, aliens excluded.*

of whom never appeared at the polls as they came of age.[72] We should note that the northern decline cannot be explained by the low turnout of women, who gained the suffrage in 1920.[73] The downward trend continued in the 1920s even when the lower rates of voting by women are taken into account.[74]

The demobilization of the American electorate in the wake of the election of 1896 was to become a massive influence in the shaping of twentieth-century political development. However, the electoral de-mobilization was gradual, as popular protests continued for a time, forcing issues onto the political agenda that continued to mobilize voters. There was ample provocation. The pace of industrial con-centration that had generated discontent in the North before 1896 did not slow down, and millions of new immigrants poured into the crowded and pestilent cities, and into the maws of the industrial ma-chine.[75] Strikes became more frequent, often leading to local war-fare.[76] Moreover, political radicalism among insurgent workers in-creasingly took form in socialist and anarchosyndicalist associations, such as the Industrial Workers of the World.

Furthermore, because turnout fell gradually in the North, the tri-umph of northern business in the election of 1896 did not entirely suppress electoral challenges. Even third-party efforts reemerged after an interlude of prosperity during the first decade of the twentieth century.[77] In 1912, Eugene Debs's bid for the presidency on the Socialist party ticket captured 6 percent of the vote. Then a resurgence of farmer radicalism in the West, beginning with the North Dakota Nonpartisan League, spread to Minnesota, South Dakota, Wisconsin, and Washington. The Nonpartisan League elected a governor in North Dakota in 1916 and, later, under the banner of the Farmer-Labor party, also elected two senators, two congressmen, and a governor in Minnesota.[78] And in 1917, the Socialists scored impressive victories in a series of municipal and state elections.[79]

Nor during this interim was Republican domination entirely secure. True, Republican majorities in the presidential contests of 1900, 1904, and 1908 were substantially larger than they had been during the closely contested elections of the late nineteenth century; and the Republican party dominated the Congress during this period as well. But the language of one-party hegemony with which historians often describe the outcome of the election of 1896 overstates the firmness and durability of Republican control. As early as 1910, the Democrats made something of a comeback, capturing the House of Representatives and twenty-six governorships, including the state houses in Massachusetts, Connecticut, New York, New Jersey, Ohio, and Indiana.[80]

Accordingly, national electoral politics was not, in fact, insulated from currents of popular discontent, at least not until after World War I. Indeed, contemporaries saw these years as a period of extraordinary reform and innovation, and so do many scholars. The rhetoric of Progressivism employed by national political leaders from Theodore Roosevelt to William Taft to Woodrow Wilson, together with the string of legislative initiatives they sponsored, constitutes persuasive evidence of the seriousness accorded to persisting popular discontents by national elites. However little these reforms may have changed the lot of working people, national politicians nevertheless felt the need to conciliate. Legislation proliferated: tax reform, railroad regulation, antitrust laws, the outlawing of child labor (later ruled unconstitutional), pure-food and meat-inspection, the establishment of the federal reserve system and a new government-sponsored system of agricultural credit, a model workmen's compensation law covering federal employees, and federal aid for highways, vocational education, and agricultural extension services. A constitutional amendment provided for the direct election of senators, and another extended the franchise to women.[81]

The propaganda which accompanied this star-studded array of legislation celebrated the aspirations of the popular struggles of the late nineteenth and early twentieth century, rather than the doctrine of laissez faire. A delegate to the People's party convention of 1908 exclaimed that "Roosevelt's messages read like the preamble to the Populist platform."[82] And four years later when Roosevelt tried to regain the presidency after the Republican party refused to renominate him in favor of the incumbent Taft, he ran under the banner of the new Progressive party and on a platform calling for social insurance to buffer people against the income losses resulting from industrial accidents, unemployment, sickness, and old age, for the abolition of child labor and convict leasing, for the regulation of interstate corporations and corporate securities, for women's suffrage, and for restrictions on labor injunctions. The Democratic platform incorporated the same themes; it denounced trusts, and called for stricter railroad regulation, a national income tax, and the prohibition of corporate contributions to political campaigns. During the Wilson-Roosevelt campaign, Wilson warned that the "great monopoly in this country is the money monopoly . . . of a few men who necessarily, by the very reason of their own limitations, chill and check and destroy genuine economic freedom."[83] Meanwhile, Roosevelt followed suit, proclaiming that "only by [the] power of the government can we curb the greed that sits in the high places . . . [and] exalt the lowly and give heart to the humble and downtrodden."[84]

Of course, none of this was what it seemed to be. Theodore Roosevelt was a big-business president. Hofstadter points out that "the advisers to whom Roosevelt listened were almost exclusively representatives of industrial and finance capital—men like Hanna . . . George W. Perkins of the House of Morgan . . . A. J. Cassatt of the Pennsylvania Railroad, Philander C. Knox, and James Stillman of the Rockefeller interests."[85] And Hofstadter goes on to show that Roosevelt's intention in supporting conciliatory government interventions was to thwart popular demands for stronger intervention.[86] Trust-busting legislation broke few trusts; the new regulatory agencies worked closely with the businesses they regulated; the Federal Reserve system met the demands of the banking industry for a mechanism to regulate finance in an era of extreme instability, not the pleas of hard-pressed family farmers.[87] When Congress passed Section 20 of the Clayton Act in an effort to exempt unions from anti-trust injunctions, the Supreme Court subsequently declared otherwise. And Roosevelt's calls for social insurance, the abolition of child labor, and restrictions on labor injunctions were not to be acted upon for nearly thirty years. The reforms of the Progressive era could be summed up, Kolko thought, as "political capitalism."[88]

While the legislative initiatives of the Progressive era were clearly less than the rhetoric of the period promised, our central point is that the Progressive agenda as a whole constitutes evidence that business domination of electoral politics was still far from secure. Turnout was edging downward, but slowly. Meanwhile, tribalism and clientelism were also weakening, and as they did, popular discontents with industrial capitalism emerged into national politics in the form of movement struggles and electoral challenges. Their impact could be read in the new language of economic reform spoken by contenders for rulership.

Left interpretations of the Progressive era tend to overlook the extent to which it laid the basis for the popular movements and electoral remobilization which occurred during the Great Depression. The rhetorical acknowledgment of grievances helped legitimate them. And the federal legislation of the Progressive period, however biased toward capital, established a framework of precedents which undermined laissez-faire doctrine by exposing it as transparently false. Economy and polity were not the separate spheres they were proclaimed to be, as business demands on government made clear. Taken together, these ideological and structural shifts foreshadowed the interventions of the New Deal.

But Progressivism ended, as voter turnout dropped to half the eligible electorate by World War I, and to far less of the working-class electorate. Once turnout fell, elite domination of electoral politics became more or less complete, with the consequence that government postures and policies became increasingly antagonistic to farmers and workers. To be sure, the wartime need for a production mobilization and the lingering credo of Progressivism led the administration to placate the increasingly mainstream A. F. of L., whose longtime president, Samuel Gompers, had served as first vice president of that flagship of Progressivism, the business-dominated National Civic Federation. But the jingoism associated with the entry of the United States into the war also provided the occasion for a crackdown on working-class radicalism. Insurgent working-class leaders were rounded up and imprisoned, including most of the top leadership of the Industrial Workers of the World, as well as many Socialists who opposed the war, among them Eugene Debs.[89] And when the war ended, the national political climate moved sharply to the right. The strikes that spread in 1919, as workers tried to win higher wages to cope with rapid wartime inflation, were smashed by government firepower. In Seattle, a general strike early in the year was broken by thousands of special deputies and the U.S. Army and Navy. Calvin Coolidge, governor of Massachusetts, achieved national prominence and the Republican nomination for vice president after ordering the National Guard to put down the Boston police strike and then firing the entire striking force. Later that year, 350,000 steel workers struck in an effort to win back the union that had been smashed in 1892. The strike was broken in part by local police and sheriff's deputies and by Justice Department raiders who rounded up striking aliens for deportation, while federal troops protected strikebreakers in Gary, Indiana.[90] Some 120,000 textile workers struck in New England and New Jersey, as well as silk workers in Paterson, New Jersey. By summer, cities such as New York and Chicago were alive with strikes, and most of them were broken by force. Then, on January 2, 1920, Attorney General A. Mitchell Palmer took advantage of labor turmoil (and alarm over the Bolshevik revolution) to announce that there was a radical plot to seize power in the United States, and then rounded up four thousand alleged revolutionaries, mainly foreign-born workers.[91]

In the election of 1920, the Republican platform roundly denounced strikes and lockouts; its only concession to farmers suffering once more from plummeting agricultural prices was to call for the "scientific study of agricultural prices and farm production costs"; and it condemned the League of Nations.[92] Among those still voting, the Republicans won overwhelmingly and Harding took office in the midst of another depression. At a time when European governments were inaugurating unemployment insurance, Harding turned to the high-tariff policies of the nineteenth century for a solution that clearly protected industry more than it protected workers.[93] Then, as farm prices plummeted still further, he announced that "It cannot be too strongly urged that the farmer must be ready to help himself."[94] And in 1923, Congress passed the Mellon Plan, sponsored by Secretary of the Treasury Andrew Mellon, which cut taxes in the top brackets by half, from 50 percent to 25 percent, while reducing the lowest bracket from 4 percent to 3 percent.[95]

The 1924 election produced another business and Republican government. The Democrats were in disarray, torn between the southern and western wing, whose candidate William Gibbs McAdoo tacitly accepted the support of the growing Ku Klux Klan, and the big-city politicians led by Al Smith. The deadlocked convention went through 103 raucous ballots before settling on John W. Davis, a conservative Wall Street lawyer. Meanwhile, the Republicans nominated Calvin Coolidge over Robert La Follette by 1,065 votes to 34. The election itself was a landslide, and another business president ascended to power. Coolidge slashed the federal budget, proclaimed laissez-faire as the guiding doctrine of his regime (the tariff excepted), complacently staffed the federal regulatory agencies that had been created in response to the popular struggles of earlier decades with representatives of industry, and vetoed a proposal for the development of public power at Muscle Shoals, as well as a series of farm bills intended to stabilize crop prices.[96] The corporate forces that had mobilized in the context of 1896 were now in full command.

The domination of both parties by economic elites would have been less total were it not for the sharp decline in voting. As turnout fell, national politics moved sharply to the right, each development both cause and consequence of the other. We turn now to the question of what it was about "the system of 1896" that explains why that drop occurred. After nearly a century of vigorous participation, how were large sectors of the American electorate demobilized?

CHAPTER FOUR

How Demobilization
Was Accomplished

A good deal of what has been written in explanation of declining
turnout at the close of the nineteenth century fastens on the
consequences of the election of 1896—its impact on party competition and especially the impact of the crushing electoral defeat of the
Populists. We think the preoccupation with the election is misleading
because it presumes that this particular defeat was more telling and
enduring than earlier electoral defeats, including the massive reversals
that the Republicans suffered only a few years earlier in the elections
of 1890 and 1892.[1] It also fails to explain why the subsequent restoration of party competition—first in the North during the 1930s and
then in the South in the 1960s—was not accompanied by a return to
nineteenth-century levels of turnout. An adequate explanation must
look beyond the election of 1896 to the reconstruction of electoral institutions that unfolded at the end of the nineteenth century and the
beginning of the twentieth.

The impact of the election of 1896 was lasting because it occurred
in the context of a series of legal and procedural "reforms" that both
reduced the ability of the parties to organize voters and disenfranchised many voters. The elite mobilizations which secured these re-

forms were not simply a response to the contest of 1896, although the outcome of that contest may have smoothed the way. Rather, the reconstruction of the legal and procedural underpinnings of party organization and voter participation began before 1896 and continued afterward. And this development can be understood as a widespread response by American elites to the rising level of conflict and electoral challenge during the closing decades of the nineteenth century. Only by attending to the interaction between the changing patterns of party competition and the rules governing party organization and voter participation can the decline in voter turnout be satisfactorily explained.

The Decline of Party Competition

Party competition virtually collapsed in much of the country, with the result that the parties lost their incentive to enlist voters and people their incentive to vote. Schattschneider underlines this feature of the system of 1896 in the single most influential explanation of the ensuing transformation in electoral politics. Before 1896, the major parties were more or less in equilibrium. To be sure, the sectional alignment that crystallized in 1896 was prefigured in the third-party system created by the Civil War, in the sense that Republican strength was already concentrated in the North, and Democratic strength in the South and Border states. But neither region was exclusively dominated by one party, and national elections were contested on roughly equal terms.[2]

The outcome of 1896 left the Democratic party greatly weakened in the North and the Republican party virtually destroyed in the South. Burnham shows that in the northeastern and north-central states, Republican presidential pluralities increased from a mean of 3.6 percent in the period 1876 to 1892, to a mean of 21 percent in the period from 1896 to 1928. Moreover,

> There is an enormous increase in noncompetitive Republican bulwarks at the grass roots level. The pattern is not monolithic as in the South. But among the most industrially and socially developed states in the Union, we find one-party Republican hegemony throughout lower New England, Pennsylvania, Illinois, Michigan, Wisconsin, and California. [Later] these states [were]

joined by Ohio and New Jersey. Of the fourteen states of the Metropole, three were one-party Republican bastions in the 1874–1892 period, nine in the 1894 period, eleven in the 1911–1930 period, and four in the 1932–50 period.[3]

Meanwhile, in the South, where party competition had always been weaker, Democratic party pluralities in presidential contests increased from 28.9 percent in the period before 1896 to 42.3 percent in the later period.[4] "The resulting party lineup was one of the most sharply sectional political divisions in American political history."[5]

A related change was the increasingly oligarchical character of both parties. Coming after several decades of turbulent agrarian and industrial conflict, the events of 1896 mobilized northern manufacturing interests to participate in electoral politics through the Republican Party on a larger scale than ever before. In the South, the decade-long organizing efforts of the Farmers' Alliances provoked commercial, landowning, and financial elites to line up behind the region's traditional Democratic party leaders. Once the Populist organizing campaign had been wrecked, these groups gained undisputed control of southern state governments.[6] Meanwhile, "There seems little doubt that, at some point in the second decade of the system of 1896, a very large class skew in [voter] participation opened up and that it tended to grow across the lifetime of the system."[7]

These changes were mutually reinforcing. The elimination of party competition facilitated internal oligarchy, and sustained it over the longer run. Once electoral contests were reduced to largely internal party affairs in much of the country, at least in national elections, the influence of voters on the calculations of party leaders diminished, and the influence of economic elites commensurately increased. "The results of the big Republican monopoly in the North and the little Democratic monopoly in the South were much the same," says Schattschneider.[8] As the absence of party competition made voters less important to party leaders, "both sections became more conservative because *one-party politics tends to strongly vest political power in the hands of people who already have economic power.*"[9] Hence, the sectional realignment of 1896 and the accompanying decline of electoral competition buttressed the rising power of corporate elites in the Republican party, and of regional southern elites in the Democratic party.

Schattschneider and Burnham also think that as the parties came more firmly under the control of economic oligarchs in the North and South, issue appeals disappeared from campaigns. We suspect that this is only partly right. While the parties of the system of 1896 did not articulate the issues which divided a rapidly growing industrial society, neither had the tribalist and clientelist parties earlier in the nineteenth century.[10] As it unfolded, the system of 1896 inhibited the development of a class- and issue-oriented politics that was perhaps becoming possible as the clientelist party system weakened. This was its main significance (a point to which we return in chapter 5).

Uncontested elections and internal oligarchy help to account for the failure of the parties to mobilize voters.[11] The resulting voter disinterest or alienation, in turn, is one explanation of the steady slide in turnout levels after 1896. This is consistent with the widely held view that voter turnout generally falls, and party-voter linkages generally weaken, when competition declines. Thus Burnham describes the alignment established by the election of 1896 as

> a structure of electoral politics marked by a continuous narrowing of organizable general election alternatives. It is, or should be, axiomatic that close relationships exist between the cohesiveness and competitiveness of parties as structures of collective action and the willingness or even the ability of the public to participate in general elections.[12]

That declining party competition produced declining turnout makes sense. Still, this explanation is hardly complete.[13] The election of 1896 is frequently described as a landslide which both crushed the Populists and demolished the Democratic party in the North. But why did a defeat in one election, even though it was a shattering one, have such pervasive and lasting effects? Why was the Republican party able to maintain virtual domination of the North for three decades after 1896, and why was the Democratic party able to maintain even more complete domination of the South until the 1960s? In short, how was the alignment of 1896 institutionalized?

The System of 1896:
The Legal and Institutional Bases

At least part of the answer lies in a series of legal and institutional changes that began in the closing decades of the nineteenth century and continued into the twentieth century. One set of changes weakened the ability of the local party organizations, especially in the big cities, to enlist working- and lower-class voters. A second set disfranchised many potentially contentious working- and lower-class voters in the cities, as well as southern blacks and many poor whites in the South. Disfranchisement was accomplished either by legislating new qualifications for the suffrage or by erecting procedural obstructions, mainly in the form of voter registration requirements such as literacy tests. These several legal reforms were cumulative in their effects. Once the local parties were stripped of organizational resources, they were less able to help their constituents hurdle or circumvent the new legal and procedural obstacles to the suffrage.[14] In the absence of party mobilization, procedural barriers to lower- and working-class turnout were more effective. As a result, the groups who had been constituencies for the electoral challenges of the late nineteenth century were gradually purged from the active electorate.

THE ASSAULT ON THE PARTIES

There are different explanations for the decades-long wave of reforms that weakened the political parties, especially by diminishing their ability to activate and organize lower-status voters. The reformers themselves raised the twin banners of eliminating fraud and inefficiency in city government. These charges had a real basis. The clientelist parties were riddled with corruption and often run by ethnic bosses with little interest in the ideal of efficiency, understood as government run on business principles in business interests.

However, the deeper reason for the rise of antiparty and antisuffrage agitation among businessmen and upper-class professionals had to do with the large economic and political changes taking place in post–Civil War America. The rise of business-backed reform can be understood as a defensive response on the one hand to the political disturbances of the late nineteenth century, and on the other as an aggressive effort to gain undisputed control of governmental functions. Business and professional leaders were unnerved by the hordes of immigrants concentrating in burgeoning city slums, confounded by the strength of the new city political bosses made audacious by their grip on immigrant and working-class voters, shaken by the waves of strikes and riots that began in the 1870s, and then finally jolted by the series of insurgent electoral challenges that culminated in 1896. Nor were they entirely reassured by the victory of 1896, given the scale and persistence of the disturbances associated with the enlarging working class.

At the same time, businessmen were prompted by economic expansion to try to assert firmer control of government, especially of those state and local agencies that managed policies important to economic development. In the mid-nineteenth century, government had been only intermittently involved in economic affairs, mainly by dispensing particularistic benefits, such as land grants and favorable tariff rates. But in the decades of rapid and unregulated industrial growth after the Civil War, economic elites began to demand much more. These demands anticipated the large role that government on all levels would eventually come to play in a developed capitalist economy—by bringing order to markets, reducing barriers to entry, assuming many of the costs of production, and by alleviating some of the side effects of untrammeled capitalist growth. This was a crucial moment in American development, for the increased dependence of business on the state suggested at least the possibility that new accomodations would have to be reached with the parties and their lower-strata constituencies. Instead, however, as the need for enlarged government intervention began to emerge, the parties, especially local clientelist parties, increasingly came to be seen as a nuisance and an obstruction. American businessmen wanted a widening array of governmental supports without the necessity of dealing with party intermediaries or their voter constituencies. The code words in this effort were efficiency and expertise in government.[15]

Accordingly, during the closing decades of the nineteenth century, the local parties came under progressively more intense assault from a series of business-backed reform movements.[16] The principal targets of the antiparty reformers were the local machines, and the reformers moved on several fronts to weaken them. They formed crusading watchdog organizations to expose corruption and to campaign for efficient government;[17] they fielded reform slates to challenge the machines in local elections; and they mobilized to influence state governments to intervene in city politics. These efforts slowly bore fruit as city and state governments were reorganized. Beginning in the 1870s, public jobs were gradually removed from party control through civil service reform.[18] Key city functions were reorganized and set up as independent agencies shielded from party influence on the grounds that municipal affairs should properly be run on a nonpartisan basis. And many smaller municipalities whose machine leaders carried less weight in state government were simply put under the control of "expert" city managers or commission forms of government on the grounds that city affairs were properly not political at all.[19] All of this, of course, gradually stripped the urban-based political parties of their patronage resources.[20]

During roughly the same period, a series of electoral reforms—including nonpartisan and at-large elections, the introduction of officially printed ballots (called Australian ballots) during the 1880s and 1890s and, somewhat later, direct primaries—made it more difficult for machines to enlist and control voters. For example, before the introduction of officially printed ballots, each party printed and distributed its own ballot, listing only the names of its candidates, and these were deposited in the ballot box by voters. Party workers could "persuade, cajole, intimidate, and bribe voters to take their ballots as the voters walked to the polling place."[21] Official ballots dealt the clientelist parties a serious blow since, as Banfield and Wilson say, "the existence of the machine depends upon its ability to control votes."[22] And with less ability to control votes, the machine's grip on city and sometimes state governments loosened.[23]

Business-backed reforms gradually weakened the clientelist parties, and diminished their ability to mobilize voters. The alignments in these reform-vs.-machine battles were complicated, however. The machines were also closely allied with major business interests, as Lincoln Steffens made vividly clear in *The Shame of the Cities*. The main basis of that alliance was everywhere similar. Machine politicans used their control of public office to dole out franchises, contracts, and the use of the public treasury to businessmen in return for graft. Moreover, clientelist party organizations helped to deter the political mobilization of working people in opposition to business interests. In other words, the machine provided a method of incorporating working people into politics while keeping their political issues off the electoral agenda, a conclusion reached by Gosnell more than half a century ago.[24] This may well explain why it was in those rural states where clientelism never took root as strongly that a broad popular movement with a bold political agenda emerged in the late nineteenth century.

Nevertheless, business interests were from the start divided in their responses to the machines. One reason was simply that many businessmen resented the high price machine politicians extracted in taxes and graft, often for indifferent services, or unreliable municipal services and favors. Bridges tells of efforts of New York City businessmen to organize a reform movement as early as the 1850s. The reformers were spurred by the failure of the city council to deliver contracts to businessmen from whom bribes had already been accepted, as well as by rising taxes and the increasingly precarious fiscal circumstances of the city.[25] As the economy and the cities expanded together after the Civil War, the ability of the machines to make some businessmen rich through contracts and franchises expanded. But so did the ire of other major elements in the business community, both because of rising municipal costs, and because of the failure of the local parties to deliver efficient and reliable public services and infrastructures. The recurrent reform campaigns in cities across the country during the second half of the nineteenth century were fueled largely by these discontents.

Business interests were also divided in their attitude toward the machines as a reflection of their sharp differences on national economic policy, and particularly the issue of protective tariffs, which pitted low-tariff commercial and financial interests against high-tariff industrial interests. Since the national Democratic party opposed tariffs[26] and since the local clientelist parties in the cities of the North were mainly Democratic and were crucial to the fortunes of the national party in the closely contested elections of the 1870s and 1880s, pro-tariff industrial interests had reason to want the machines weakened.[27]

The election of 1896, however, resolved the tariff question in favor of high-tariff industrial interests. At the same time, the Republican sweep dissipated the threat of electoral insurgency from below, and thus made the role of the machine in integrating and controlling the working class less valuable. These developments smoothed the way for the introduction of a new series of legal reforms that struck further blows at the capacities of the party organizations to activate and organize voters.

One change was the introduction of the direct primary in the years between 1903 and 1915. Both V. O. Key and Burnham argue persuasively that the direct primary worked to reinforce one-party domination where it was adopted.[28] And what Burnham calls the "democratic-participatory symbolisms" evoked by the direct primary almost surely made it more difficult for third-party challenges to the dominant parties to emerge.[29]

More frontal assaults on the local clientelist parties also accelerated, usually mounted from the state capitols where the urban-based clientelist parties could be overwhelmed by business-reformers who staged spectacular investigations of machine corruption. The state legislature redrew the municipal boundaries of New York City in 1898, for example, incorporating the outer boroughs in an effort to swamp the Manhattan-based Tammany organization. Meanwhile,

> the first fifteen years of the twentieth century . . . more precisely, the brief period from 1904 to 1908 saw a remarkable compressed political transformation. During these years the regulatory revolution peaked; new and powerful agencies of government came into being everywhere. At the same time voter turnout declined, ticket-splitting increased, and organized social, economic and reform-minded groups began to exercise power more systematically than ever before.[30]

Very rapidly, investigations of machine–business corruption were initiated in one state after another, involving the life insurance industry in New York, public utility corporations in San Francisco, the railroads in half a dozen states in the Midwest and South, streetcars and utilities in Denver, the liquor industry in Iowa. The result was a battery of new state laws—McCormick counted 130 laws in selected categories between 1903 and 1908—regulating lobbying, prohibiting corporate contributions to campaigns, regulating or limiting free railroad passes for public officials, and establishing commissions to regulate railroads.[31]

"Electoral mobilization," in Kleppner's recapitulation, "has always depended on the active intervention of mobilizing agents—political parties."[32] Whatever the limits of voter participation built on the clientelist and tribalist appeals of the nineteenth century, the investment in these appeals by the parties did signal that party leaders needed working-class voters and had the organizational capacity to activate them. But after the turn of the century, the local parties, weakened by relentless reform assaults, were less able to reach voters, by any method at all. The great spectacles and celebrations, the marching bands and parades that had punctuated earlier campaigns faded away. Even ethnoreligious election appeals lost the force and fire of an earlier era, and Republican campaigns in particular became almost ecumenical.

As party connections to the working-class electorate atrophied, a gradual demobilization of voters occurred. The slide in turnout was one sign. Another, more specifically revealing of the attenuating connection between party and electorate, was the erosion of party-line voting, with the result that a degree of fragmentation began to appear in electoral results that was unknown earlier in the nineteenth century. Republican hegemony in the North in national and especially presidential contests was modified by the simultaneous erosion of the partisanship that had characterized nineteenth-century voting patterns. State and local election results increasingly diverged from national results, so that Democratic victories on the state and local level were not unusual. Burnham characterizes this development as the beginning of the "fragmented" politics of the modern era, by which he means the dissolution of strict partisanship and the emergence of diverse coalitions at different levels of government.[33] Shefter makes a similar point when he says that the notion of a "one party North" is exaggerated, and points to the vigorous party competition that persisted in New York state politics throughout the period.[34]

LEGAL AND PROCEDURAL DISFRANCHISEMENT

The closing decades of the nineteenth century also witnessed a wave of legal reforms that had the effect of disfranchising what McCormick calls "discordant social elements."

> Southern blacks and poor whites, by participating in the Populist movement, and new immigrants, by supporting the most corrupt city machines and

flirting with socialism, convinced elites everywhere that unlimited suffrage fueled disorder. Under the banner of "reform," they enacted registration requirements, ballot laws, and other measures to restrict suffrage.[35]

Developments in the South provide the clearest illustration of the impact of legal and procedural changes on voter turnout. Disfranchisement was part of the broader effort by the southern planter class to erect a system of political, economic, and social coercion over blacks which would permit the reestablishment of a quasi-feudal labor system. Experience showed that black enfranchisement interfered with this objective. As late as the turn of the century, blacks were still able to elect representatives to state and local office over much of the South, impeding the uses of the apparatus of state and local government to reestablish the caste labor system. Moreover, black voters could strike alliances with dissident electoral movements, as they had with northern-backed Republicans in the South after the Civil War. Later, as the radical farmers' movement grew and opened new opportunities for insurgent black-white alliances, the pressure for disfranchisement grew, and was extended to poor whites as well. Indeed, the model for a new kind of polity which left formal voting rights intact but stripped poorer and less educated people of the ability to exercise those rights was pioneered in the South.

From the period of Reconstruction, black voting rights had been countered by reigning Democratic parties and their Bourbon allies with an extraordinary repertoire of inventive techniques ranging from trickery and fraud to outright violence.[36] And fraud, trickery, and violence, which spread after federal troops were withdrawn in 1877, went far toward reducing black voter turnout. But apparently not far enough, since even moderate levels of black participation helped keep southern Republican parties alive, and provided significant potential support for Populism in the 1890s.[37] Furthermore, fraud, trickery, and force were inherently unstable solutions, for their effective deployment depended on vigilant local organization, and they also made the Southern Democracy vulnerable to national outcry and federal intervention, a danger which persisted long after Reconstruction.[38] According to Bensel, "the prospect of federal enforcement of suffrage rights provoked anger, frustration and fear," for federal intervention was rightly seen to put marginal districts in jeopardy.[39] Legal methods of disfranchisement "simultaneously released the Bourbons from the twin threats of federal intervention and agrarian class-based radicalism."[40]

The southern solution to the problems posed by the black franchise was to attach conditions to the right to vote that did not mention blacks, but which blacks could not fulfill, thus avoiding a direct violation of the Fifteenth Amendment. These disfranchising devices were not created all at once. Rather, the campaign occurred in waves. As federal troops withdrew and the interest of northern reformers in the freedmen waned, the southern states gradually developed the arrangements which would eventually strip some three-quarters of the population, black and white, of the right to vote:

> Each state became in effect a laboratory for testing one device or another. Indeed, the cross-fertilization and coordination between the movements to restrict the suffrage in the Southern states amounted to a public conspiracy.[41]

Some of the methods were already on the books. Georgia retained an optional poll tax from the time when the payment of taxes was a common condition for the exercise of the suffrage. In 1877 the state simply moved to make its poll tax mandatory and far more onerous,[42] and turnout dropped precipitously.[43] Shortly afterward, in 1882, South Carolina adopted an "eight-box" law, followed by Florida in 1889, a device which required the voter to deposit separate ballots in each of the boxes marked for different candidates, making it virtually impossible for the illiterate to navigate the balloting process:

> In South Carolina, the requirement that, with eight or more ballot boxes before him, the voter must select the proper one for each ballot, in order to insure its being counted, furnished an effective means of neutralizing the ignorant black vote; for though the negroes, unable to read the lettering on the boxes, might acquire, by proper coaching, the power to discriminate among them by their relative positions, a moment's work by whites in transposing the boxes would render useless an hour's laborious instruction.[44]

The introduction of officially printed ballots, organized by office rather than by party, was similarly confusing to the uneducated. These arrangements anticipated the straightforward literacy tests which were to come later. Meanwhile, the South developed voter registration procedures that were distinctive for the discretion which they granted local election officers in deciding whether potential voters were in fact qualified. These procedures were particularly useful in purging the electorate of blacks and poor whites in anticipation of constitutional conventions where more sweeping disfranchising laws could then be enacted.[45]

As Populist dissidence mounted in the late 1880s, the southern disfranchisement movement accelerated. Mississippi was another pioneer, introducing both a $2.00 poll tax and a literacy test in its constitutional convention of 1890, arrangements which drove voter participation down to 17 percent by 1900.[46] Florida and Tennessee followed quickly after, and then, in 1894, Arkansas fell in line. Kousser offers persuasive evidence of the impact of these disfranchising measures in simultaneously depressing turnout and reducing support for oppositional Republican or Populist parties in the states that adopted them during the early 1890s, when southern electoral challenges peaked.[47]

The momentum of the disfranchising campaign accelerated again after 1896, as the earlier measures proved their effectiveness, and as the resistance offered by southern Populists and their poor-white constituencies dissipated. The fact that national Republican leaders seemed to lose interest in protecting the electoral base of southern Republicanism once the party's national dominance was assured by the 1896 sweep of the North probably encouraged the disfranchisers. The rising wave of race-baiting after Bryan's defeat also helped pave the way by appealing to the racism of poor whites in an effort to win their support in completing the legal system of disfranchisement.

Accordingly, after 1896, the remaining southern states followed the path laid out by Mississippi, introducing poll tax laws where none yet existed, or making existing poll tax measures more restrictive by raising the amount of the tax or by making it retroactive. In Texas, a poll tax had first been proposed in 1875, on the ostensible grounds that it would eliminate "irresponsible voters." But Texas was the birthplace and organizing center of the Farmers' Alliance, and it was not until 1902, when the Populists had disappeared, that a constitutional amendment establishing the poll tax was approved, this time frankly presented as a white-supremacy measure.[48] By 1904, turnout in Texas had plunged to 30 percent from its peak level of 80 percent twenty years earlier.

And after the debacle of 1896, the southern states also acted rapidly to add literacy test barriers to poll tax barriers. To overcome the opposition of the poor and illiterate whites who would also be disfranchised by these measures, complicated loopholes were introduced that could in principle refranchise some of those who were being disfranchised. Thus, "good character" clauses were added that permitted voter registrars to make exceptions, or clauses permitted registrars to accept "understanding" of some portion of the state constitution as a substitute for literacy, or grandfather and "fighting grandfather" clauses permitted exceptions to be made for those whose grandfathers had voted, or whose grandfathers had fought for the Confederacy. But these gestures to overcome the opposition of poor whites were usually allowed to lapse. In any case, the loopholes did not work and were probably not intended to work. Most poor whites were unwilling to risk the humiliation of failing the new voter tests.[49]

No one disputes that the southern system "worked." In the 1880s and 90s, turnout in the South had regularly exceeded 60 percent, and sometimes reached 85 percent.[50] Phillips provides some dramatic examples of the change. In Arkansas, turnout dropped from over two-thirds to just over one-third between 1884 and 1904; in Mississippi, from almost 80 percent in 1876 to less than 17 percent in 1900; and in South Carolina participation plummeted from 83.7 percent in 1880 to

Table 4.1. Relationship of Poll Tax and Literacy Test Laws to Presidential Turnout in Southern States, 1892–1916

	ABSENCE OF LITERARY TEST	PRESENCE OF LITERARY TEST
Absence of poll tax	72	57
Presence of poll tax	40	24

SOURCE: *Rusk (1974:1043). Cell entries are presidential turnout means computed over all years, 1892–1916, for states having the legal combination listed.*

Table 4.2. Southern Presidential Turnout Percentages
by Race: 1876–1892; 1900–1916; 1920–1924

South	1876–1892		1900–1916		1920–1924	
	White	*Black*	*White*	*Black*	*White*	*Black*
Black-belt counties	75	44	47	5	27	0
White counties	62	79	53	0	35	0
Total	69	60	50	2	32	0

SOURCE: *Kleppner (1982:53 and 65, tables 3.6 and 4.4). Black-belt counties defined as 30 percent black.*

18 percent in 1900.[51] As the system of legal barriers was put in place, the black vote dwindled and then disappeared, and white turnout shrank as well. In Kousser's words, "the security of the black belt and the Democratic party had been purchased at the cost of abandoning popular government."[52]

Scholarly debate over the causes of turnout decline in the South turns on a rather narrow dispute having to do with the *relative weight* of force and fraud on the one hand, and legal barriers on the other hand. On the larger points, there is in fact no dispute: millions of blacks and poor whites were disfranchised, and legal barriers mattered in that process. The boldness of the disfranchising movement in the South makes the motives of the disfranchisers and their techniques clear. The South also provides strong clues, we think, to developments in the North: "The South is properly viewed as an extreme rather than a wholly deviant example of processes more generally and diffusely at work."[53]

Indeed, southern elites learned many of their arguments for disfranchisement from reformers in the North, just as reformers in the North learned some of their methods from the South. The decades after the Civil War when techniques for disfranchising blacks and poor whites were being perfected in the states of the Confederacy were also the decades when something very much like a democratic counterrevolution swept across the North, leaving in its wake a new system of rules governing electoral participation.

Limiting the suffrage was a solution that came easily to the minds of northern reformers. Restricting the vote to the better sorts of people would work toward restoring firm control of government and politics to business and professional leaders. Otherwise, the *Nation* warned in 1877, immigration would lead to "the severance of political power from intelligence and property."[54] Nor at the time could this sort of solution have seemed so farfetched. It was after all still early in the "age of democracy." As late as 1828, fourteen states still imposed property or tax-paying restrictions on white male suffrage; Connecticut, Louisiana, and New Jersey retained these restrictions into the 1840s, Virginia until 1851, and South Carolina through the Civil War. Dorr's Rebellion against suffrage restrictions in Rhode Island in 1841 had in fact ended in a draw that established different property tests for native-born and naturalized citizens.[55] And the democratic counter-revolution gained momentum in the United States at a time when most European workers had not yet won the right to vote, so that precedents elsewhere offered no defense of the franchise.

The straightforward attack on the right to vote for the unpropertied remained largely rhetorical, however, perhaps because it was so unlikely to receive the support of politicians who, pending the success of the disfranchisers, would have to risk the ire of the unpropertied at the polls. In 1875, Governor Tilden of New York appointed a bipartisan commission to reform city governments, which recommended restricting the franchise in municipal elections to taxpayers and rent-payers, with property and rental payment floors graduated by city size. In New York City, it was proposed to restrict the franchise to those with more than $500 in property, or those with annual rental payments over $250. The Tilden Commission recommendations were received enthusiastically by New York City businessmen, including the Chamber of Commerce, the Stock Exchange, the Produce Exchange, and the Cotton Exchange, all of whose representatives rallied to its support, along with a roster of prominent and wealthy New Yorkers. But the strategy was too obvious, and too drastic in the effects it promised to have, particularly on Tammany Hall, which led the opposition and worked to defeat legislators who supported the plan. The Tilden Commission plan ultimately failed.[56]

Other and more circumspect routes to the same end were explored. Seven nonsouthern states increased the length of their resi-

dency requirements,[57] and eleven states repealed older laws or constitutional provisions that had permitted immigrants to vote if they
declared their intention to become citizens.[58] Educational requirements were another and broader solution, and one which matched the
reformers' repeated rhetorical calls for a more intelligent electorate.[59]
Moreover, there was something like a modest precedent in the literacy
requirements which existed on the books in Massachusetts and Connecticut (although these had not been enforced). Between 1892 and
1910, seven states in the South imposed literacy requirements, and between 1890 and 1928, eleven states in the North and West followed suit.
Literacy tests, says Kleppner, were aimed at the lower class, and especially (in the North) at naturalized voters.[60] In 1953, Riker summed up
the case:

> The real political purpose, so artfully concealed, is to deprive of citizen rights
> certain minorities believed to have a low literacy rate. Eighteen states have
> adopted the test, seven to disfranchise Negroes, five to disfranchise Indians
> and Mexicans and Orientals, and six to disfranchise European immigrants.[61]

Riker goes on to give the example of New York, where the administration of literacy tests during the 1920s disfranchised almost 20 percent
of the people who took them.[62]

But residency requirements or literacy tests were of themselves not
sufficient to achieve the ambitious goal of restricting electoral participation, especially in circumstances where local party organizations
were intent on recruiting voters, literate or not. Nor indeed were any
new restrictions likely to be very effective without a procedure to implement them. An administrative mechanism was needed that would
sort out those who were eligible from those who were not. The obvious mechanism was a voter registration system. These systems in fact
served a double purpose. On the one hand, they implemented the new
restrictions; on the other hand, they also provided a potentially flexible and selective administrative mechanism that would of itself make
it more difficult for some to vote and easier for others.

Over time, efforts to restrict the suffrage concentrated more and
more on the procedures for certifying eligible voters, or voter registration. In fact, Massachusetts had required registration as early as 1800,
and Connecticut and Maine also adopted early registration systems.[63]

And there had been episodic efforts to impose registration requirements in other states, although these efforts frequently failed, or the
systems were weak or indifferently applied, at least until the closing
decades of the nineteenth century. Between 1876 and 1912, however, almost half the northern states introduced amendments to their constitutions providing the authority for voter registration requirements.
Others already had such authority, or simply legislated it without constitutional provision.[64] By 1929, when Joseph Harris compiled his review of voter registration in the United States, all but three states (Arkansas, Texas, and Indiana) had instituted registration procedures,
and these states would soon fall in line.[65]

A system for registering voters seems at first glance a reasonable
development. It was, after all, simply a means of compiling a list of
those who were eligible to vote, a procedure that became more necessary as the population grew, and as the vote fraud perpetrated by the
clientelist political parties became more common. In practice, however, the way the lists were compiled had a great deal to do with who
was likely to be on them, and who was likely to be omitted. The procedures for certifying voters had, in other words, political significance,
a fact recognized from the earliest days of mass suffrage. For that reason, voter registration procedures have always been the object of conflict. An attempt to introduce an amendment to the New York constitution in 1821 providing for a registry of eligible voters provoked the
charge that men would be compelled to make an extra journey, perhaps of some great distance, with the result that "a few shall rule the
many, who have a desire that aristocracy shall triumph but honest republicans will never take such pains."[66] The amendment failed, by a
vote of 60 to 43.[67] Similarly, when Pennsylvania enacted its first registration law in 1836, requiring the assessors in the county of Philadelphia to make up a list of qualified voters, and providing that no one
would be permitted to vote who was not on the list, there were protests
in the constitutional convention the following year. The law, it was
charged, was designed to reduce the Philadelphia vote, and to cut
down the vote of the poor:

> When the assessors went around, the laboring men were necessarily and of
> course absent from their homes, engaged in providing subsistence for them-

selves and their families; and not finding the men at home, did not go again. When the election came on these men ... were spurned from the ballot boxes. They were told their names were not on the registry, and that, therefore, they had no right to vote. ... But how was it with the rich man? The gold and silver door plate with name was enough, and there was no danger that the assessor would overlook that.[68]

These early objections only hint at the variable political consequences of different registration procedures. In fact, compared to the personal voter registration arrangements developed later, these early "nonpersonal" registration systems were relatively benign, for they placed the burden of compiling lists of eligible voters on town or county officials.[69] However, as political insurgency spread in the late nineteenth century and the movement to reform the franchise gathered momentum, voter registration arrangements became not only more widespread, but also increasingly restrictive. The trend was toward ever more onerous procedural requirements: from nonpersonal registration lists compiled by local officials to personal registration lists that required citizens to appear before those officials at given times and places; from permanent registration to periodic and even annual registration; to earlier closing dates for registration, so that campaigns no longer served to stimulate voters to register;[70] and toward more centralized administration of voter registration, which not only removed registration to less accessible and less familiar sites but also was more likely to remove it from the control of local politicians with an interest in maintaining existing patterns of voter participation.[71]

Logically enough, the big cities were marked from the beginning as the target of these increasingly restrictive registration requirements. Partisan motives, class interests, and animus against the machines combined to explain the urban focus. Democratic party strength (outside of the South) was based on the immigrant working class and the political bosses, and they were based in the cities. McGerr quotes Theodore Dwight Woolsey, a liberal reformer and past president of Yale, in 1878: "The cities are to be dreaded ... They take the lead in all commotions, they have less wisdom and stability, but more energy and political fanaticism." And the historian Francis Parkman agreed: "It is in the cities that the diseases of the body politic are gathered to a head, and it is here that the need of attacking them is most urgent. Here the dangerous classes are most numerous and strong, and the effects of flinging the suffrage to the mob are most disastrous."[72]

Thus Pennsylvania's early nonpersonal system of registration applied at first only to Philadelphia, and each time the registration system was made more restrictive, it was Philadelphia that was singled out for the new procedures.[73] In 1906, the state legislature amended the registration procedure again, to require annual personal registration in Philadelphia, Pittsburgh, and Scranton.[74] When New Jersey Republicans succeeded in legislating a permanent system of personal registration in 1870, their earlier legislative victory having been repealed by the Democrats, they applied the system to the seven cities in the state with populations of more than 20,000.[75] Subsequently, after a series of revisions, the registration system was changed so that voters in cities over 15,000 had to register in person each year.

The fears inspired in elites by the climactic national electoral challenge of 1896 naturally gave greater impetus to efforts to strengthen registration requirements, while the landslide Republican victory in much of the North, by weakening Democratic opposition to the requirements, smoothed the way for acting on those fears. Harris summarizes the consequences:

> In the period from 1896 to 1924, when the turnout declined almost steadily, state after state enacted registration laws which typically required registration annually and in person of all voters in the nation's large cities; the registration procedures of this era have been described . . . as "expensive, cumbersome, and inconvenient to the voter."[76]

Kleppner makes the same point:

> Beginning in the 1890s, stronger types of voter-registration systems replaced the weak ones that had been used earlier in some states. The key feature of this change was the imposition of a personal-registration requirement, a provision that shifted the burden of establishing eligibility from the state to the individual. By 1920, 31 nonsouthern states had put some form of personal registration requirement into effect.[77]

Thus, for example, Massachusetts had been more or less content with its registration system of 1800, which remained unchanged until in 1896 the citizens of Boston were made subject to a personal periodic registration requirement, at a central location.[78] And in New York, where the first registration law passed in 1859 had authorized precinct officers to prepare lists, the 1894 constitution required personal annual registration in cities over 5,000. In 1898, a state agency was created to detect election fraud, and for the first few years it focused almost exclusively on registration fraud in New York City.[79] Delaware moved from permanent registration to biennial registration in 1899, and in 1896 Maryland required annual registration in the city of Baltimore, where the police also purged the lists each year by means of a house-to-house canvass.[80] Annual purges of this type, which were also instituted elsewhere—in Boston and Milwaukee, for example[81]—are especially revealing of the purposes of the new voter registration arrangements. Where once the door-to-door canvass had been used to add electors to the list, now it was used exclusively to eliminate them.[82]

Finally, the very intricacy inherent in variable registration systems operated by state, county, and municipal officials was important, for the execution of these complex arrangements inevitably gave officialdom the latitude for uneven and selective enforcement of the new procedures. Literacy tests, for example, could be administered differently in different places, and differently for different people. The new voter registration apparatus also permitted the introduction of a series of informal barriers, having to do with the days and hours that voter registration was available, where the offices were located, how people were informed of where and when, and the manner in which they were treated by the officials who administered the procedures. Inevitably, over the long run, these informal barriers tended to exclude those who were less educated and less self-confident, and were often administered so as to secure that effect.[83]

The new procedures gradually took their toll, and voter turnout dropped, specifically as a result of voter registration. Kleppner, who thinks the decline in electoral competitiveness is the principal explanation of falling turnout, nevertheless concludes that voter registration requirements accounted for between 30 and 40 percent of the turnout decline where they were in force.[84] Burnham comes to a similar conclusion, conceiving of these obstacles as one of the ways in which the rules of the game were intentionally changed to limit access to the ballot at the end of the nineteenth century. And he credits the new requirements with responsibility for part of the decline in turn-out that occurred, although he thinks the effect less important than party-behavior depressants of turnout. In a statistical comparison (similar to Kleppner's) of counties with personal registration with nonregistration counties between 1890 and 1910, Burnham finds that the turnout decline in the registration counties is "only" 14.5 percent greater.[85] Overall, however, Burnham concludes that about a third of the decline in voter turnout that occurred in the early decades of the twentieth century was attributable to rule changes, and particularly to voter registration.[86]

Our argument, however, suggests caution in attempting to disaggregate the effects of the several main features of the system of 1896. Changes in the party system, including a decline in party competition, and weakened and reorganized parties worked together with changes in the rules, each reinforcing and compounding the effects of the other, with the consequence that voter participation by the less-well-off steadily fell in the first decades of the twentieth century.

CHAPTER FIVE

The New Deal Party System: Partial Remobilization

*B*y the 1920s, low levels of electoral participation had become a central fact of American political life. During the decades since, successive cohorts of tens of millions of nonvoters have constituted the most unstable element in American politics. At different times, fractions of these marginalized populations were drawn into the electorate, or allowed to drop out of it, and these successive expansions and contractions of the voting universe have played a critical (if often unacknowledged) role in the dynamics of electoral change.

The metapolitics of participation had three distinct phases. The first is associated with the New Deal, though it began in 1928 with a partial remobilization of northern working-class voters stimulated by the intense ethnocultural conflict evoked by Al Smith's candidacy against Herbert Hoover. The participation of these working-class voters in the Democratic party expanded further during the New Deal, and was sustained by the extraordinary programmatic and structural innovations of the decade which, among other things, created a party apparatus to enlist working-class voters. The constrictions on electoral participation established by the system of 1896 persisted through all of these developments, however, shaping the Democratic party that emerged from the New Deal realignment. As a result, voter turnout among working-class voters did not rise as much as it might have, signaling that the previous patterns of legal restrictions and skewed party-electoral linkages had been modified but not overturned. Perhaps even more important, the southern wing of the system survived the upheavals of the New Deal period intact, with the consequence that blacks and poor whites remained effectively disfranchised there. Meanwhile, the role of the South in national affairs enlarged because it was key to the majority status of the reigning Democratic party. Consequently, the South could exert a powerful conservative weight that tempered the influence—and over time the Democratic allegiance—of the northern working class.

The second phase saw the breakdown of one-party politics in the South, and the resulting partial breakup of the New Deal electoral coalition. This phase too can be understood as a series of challenges to the terms of electoral participation associated with the system of 1896. The civil rights movement raised one set of challenges and ultimately created the political conditions that forced reluctant national Democratic leaders to intervene in the southern system to enforce the partial refranchisement of southern blacks, although at great cost in white southern support. Political modernization in the South also resulted in the refranchising of less-well-off southern whites, many of whom entered the electoral system under the banners of the Christian Right's remarkable late-twentieth-century revival of tribalist politics. These events completed the collapse of the one-party South, and led to a revival of the Republican party.

The third phase in the politics of participation unfolded in the North, where support for the New Deal was also weakening. Most explanations emphasize working-class defections prompted by the conflicts which emerged in the 1960s, particularly over race and the issues associated with the New Politics. We think, however, that there was a deeper and more longlasting problem. The apparatus created by the New Deal leadership during the 1930s to reach and hold its new working-class constituency consisted largely of revived clientelist local parties, and a network of new party-linked labor unions. After World War II, as the composition of the working class gradually shifted from industrial workers to include large numbers of minorities and women in the emerging service sector, this apparatus for mobilizing voters became progressively less effective, paralyzed partly by organizational stasis and partly by antagonisms between its old working-class constituents and the new working class.[1] The Kennedy and Johnson administrations tried to reach past malfunctioning local parties and city bureaucracies by intervening in the cities with new "Great Society" programs. But the voting apparatus itself remained firmly under the control of state and specifically local parties. One result was that the partial remobilization of the working class which had made the construction of the New Deal coalition possible was gradually reversed. Voter turnout again began to decline, and once again it declined most among the less-well-off. We begin in this chapter with a discussion of the New Deal remobilization, and the conditions which limited it. Then, in chapter 6, we turn to the developments which led to the breakdown of the party system established under the New Deal.

Realignment, Incomplete Remobilization, and the Role of Social Movements

The origins of the New Deal realignment are often located in the presidential contest of 1928, when the Democrats nominated Al Smith —New York machine boss, Catholic, and wet.[2] Intense feelings about religion, immigrants, and Prohibition dominated the election, and large sections of the South actually defected to Hoover rather than vote for "a subject of the Pope."[3] Meanwhile, Catholics and immigrants rallied to Smith, who became the first Democratic presidential contender since Cleveland to carry the ten largest cities.[4] It was, in short, a contest, and it was about matters of cultural identity that stir passions. And for the first time since 1896, turnout rose significantly; it jumped from 19 percent to 23 percent between 1924 and 1928 in the South, and from 57 percent to 66 percent in the North (table 5.1). It is testimony to the persistence and force of the ethnocultural attachments which figured so largely in nineteenth-century politics that the contest of 1928 actually produced a larger jump in turnout than the realigning elections of 1932 and 1936.[5] But a contest between Protestants and Catholics did not, of course, break the pattern of Republican and business control of the national political dialogue that had unfolded with the system of 1896. John J. Raskob, a General Motors executive,

Table 5.1. Presidential Turnout Percentages, 1924–1940

	SOUTH	NON-SOUTH	NATIONAL
1924	19	57	49
1928	23	66	57
1932	24	66	57
1936	25	71	61
1940	26	73	62

SOURCE: *Burnham (1981c:100, table 1). Based on total of all citizens legally eligible to vote, aliens excluded.*

became chair of the Democratic National Committee; business slogans dominated the rhetoric of both parties; and Smith was routed, winning only 87 electoral votes, while Hoover ascended to the presidency with the largest Republican congressional majority since 1920.[6]

When the crash of 1929 hit, entire industries were stricken, whole towns devastated.[7] But people did not turn to electoral politics for solutions; in 1930 and 1932, there was no additional turnout rise *at all* in either the North or South. In the depressions of the 1870s and 1890s, by contrast, economic catastrophe had drawn people to the polls. Turnout had jumped in the midterm elections of 1874 and 1894, each of which came on the heels of a major depression.[8] The dislocation and distress occasioned by the depression of 1929 was probably more severe, if only because so much of the country was by that time urbanized and industrialized and totally exposed to market fluctuations. Still, the system of 1896 had gradually restricted the participation of the less-well-off, and popular economic grievances had disappeared from party agendas by the 1920s. Those who voted spurned the incumbent regime, to be sure, and Roosevelt carried all but a few states in the Northeast. But this expressed a reaction by voters of all strata against a president and a party that had presided over the economic calamity:

> In 1930 and 1932 the available political alternatives failed to stimulate political consciousness among the deprived or to increase greatly their interest in electoral politics. Neither major party effectively gave meaning to and mobilized economic discontent. What occurred in these elections was a decisive rejec-

tion of the party of "hard times" and of its most visible officeholder, Herbert Hoover. The anti-Republican swings that shaped those outcomes extended to virtually all categories of voters, but they did not restructure the fault line of partisan combat.[9]

The usual view is that the upturn in voting that eventually occurred among the less-well-off was a response to the Depression and the New Deal.[10] Of course, in some sense that has to be true; something about the 1930s galvanized higher voter participation. But the rise did not begin until the midterm election of 1934—five years after the collapse—and turnout rose again in both 1936 and 1940. What the timing of rising turnout makes clear is that it was not a simple response to economic distress. Moreover, while the New Deal initiatives helped to motivate new voters to try to contend with the registration process, these initiatives themselves have to be explained.

The role of popular movements is missing from most accounts of rising turnout in the 1930s (and, indeed, missing from most accounts of the New Deal more generally). To be sure, New Deal reforms helped increase turnout in the North in ways that we will describe. But the reforms themselves were forged by the interaction between political movements and electoral politics.[11] The Roosevelt administration reached out to people in the middle and the bottom of American society because its hand was forced by popular mobilizations and the uncertain electoral repercussions which they produced. Even the 1932 campaign appeals, which restored to national politics a rhetoric celebrating the common man and denouncing the economic royalists that had been absent since the Progressive era, and the fact that Roosevelt came to office prepared to inaugurate some relief measures and to buoy commodity prices by imposing controls on agricultural production, were influenced by early waves of popular protest. That said, however, the new administration's initial plans were mainly oriented to reviving business by bringing order to the financial markets, and by adopting a plan for industrial price and production controls proposed by the U.S. Chamber of Commerce. The protest movements caused sufficient disruption and electoral dissension to change that. The movements transformed vague campaign promises into contentious issues with which the Roosevelt administration had to cope, or risk both escalating disruptions in the streets and factories, and disaffection among elements of its still insecure electoral constituency. Popular protest compelled the administration to inaugurate massive relief programs, to support legislation giving workers the right to collective bargaining, and to initiate sweeping social security legislation. The New Deal programs, in short, were importantly a response to an electorate galvanized by movements.

The movements in turn were also energized by the comparative responsiveness of the new administration: they were not simply a reaction to economic calamity. Protest emerged and spread because of the new political possibilities suggested by the partial erosion of the system of 1896 and the instabilities associated with electoral realignment. Those possibilities were not just vaguely sensed. They were evident from the changed rhetoric of political leaders, and from the early initiatives they took to appease popular unrest. The campaign promises, Roosevelt's overwhelming victory, and the dramatic legislative initiatives during the first hundred days encouraged people to think that public issues had some bearing on their private troubles.

The sense of popular power and programmatic possibility that was communicated by politicians who were trying to ride out the currents of electoral instability helps to explain the emergence of what were surely the largest protests of the unemployed in American history. People marched and demonstrated for "bread or wages" and battled the police to stop evictions in many of the major cities of the country.[12] The emergency relief measures of 1933, initiated within weeks of Roosevelt's inauguration, were a response to these protests and to the alarm they generated among politicians generally, not least among panicked local government officials whose efforts to provide unemployment relief were leading to local fiscal disaster. A Social Science Research Council Bulletin put it this way:

> By the time the new federal administration came into power in 1933, the pressure for more money had become so nearly unanimous that it was politically desirable for congressmen and senators to favor large appropriations for relief; candidates were elected often on a platform which predicated adequate relief appropriations by Congress.[13]

The changed climate also encouraged other hard-pressed groups —workers, the aged, farmers, and farm tenants. Rural mobs resisted farm foreclosures; the aged campaigned for government pensions to the battle hymn of "Onward Townsend Soldiers"; mass encampments of displaced tenant farmers demanded government aid; and, as the economy finally began showing feeble signs of recovery in 1934, industrial workers erupted in strikes and sitdowns to win collective bargaining rights. These popular actions were incited by the hopes that the New Deal stimulated.

In turn, mass action transformed hope into demands and galvanized voters around those demands, helping to shape the New Deal programs and rhetorical appeals. By raising issues and polarizing alternatives, the dynamic between movements and the New Deal almost surely helped sustain and enlarge voter turnout, particularly in the elections of 1934 and 1936. However, the larger impact of movements on turnout was indirect. The combination of electoral instability and protest thus forced the New Deal administration to intervene in the structure of the federal system, in the economy, and in the lives of ordinary people in ways that Roosevelt and his brain trust had almost surely never contemplated, and this too affected turnout. In the American federal system, the impact of national policies on the everyday life of most people had always been obscure. This was no longer so. Now new federal programs overrode state and local governments to reach out directly to the citizenry; or federal program dollars (and New Deal popularity) were used to press sometimes reluctant state and local governments into collaboration. Kleppner describes the resulting change in the relationship of masses of people to the national government:

> Never before had so many citizens experienced the effects of federal actions so directly or been able to see their consequences so concretely. Federal relief agencies—the Civil Works Administration, the Federal Emergency Relief Administration, and the Works Progress Administration—provided jobs for over seven million adults, as did the National Youth Administration for over seven million young Americans. The Home Owners' Loan Corporation helped refinance one out of every five mortgages on private urban dwellings in the country. The Social Security Act created a system of old-age insurance and established a federal-state system of unemployment insurance. The Tennessee Valley Authority and the Rural Electrification Administration brought electric power to millions of rural homes and farms.[14]

The vast new federal or federally funded programs provided the New Deal with an infrastructure linking program beneficiaries to the Roosevelt wing of the Democratic party and providing the organizational vehicles to mobilize voters from the bottom. Thus the various relief programs provided part of the foundation on which the Democratic party's apparatus to recruit voters was rebuilt:

> Econometric analysis of state-by-state relief expenditures shows that political considerations (like closeness of the vote) far overshadowed poverty in explaining the distribution of billions of dollars of relief money. Historians examining the situation by states and cities concur that politicized relief, especially as channeled through Democratic organizations, played a major role in rebuilding the Democratic coalition. At one time or another during the decade, somewhere between 40 and 45 percent of all American families received federal relief. Gallup polls show that families receiving politicized relief (WPA, CCC, NYA, and related programs) voted much more heavily Democratic than did poor people not on relief. In August 1936, for example, reliefers were 82 percent for Roosevelt; the lowest one-third income group was 70 percent; and the highest third, only 41 percent.[15]

Some of the main intermediaries in establishing these links between working-class voters and the Democratic party were the old political machines, which in many places had become debilitated by municipal fiscal crises (as well as by the effects of decades-long reform campaigns). With federal program monies, however, they could be reinvigorated. Roosevelt collaborated with the local clientelist parties,[16] and they in turn supported the New Deal: "Far from rendering the machine[s] obsolete, Roosevelt reinvigorated [them] for at least another decade."[17] The most famous instance was the New Deal relationship with the Chicago machine—initiated in return for Mayor Anton Cermak's support at the 1932 convention—where federal funds made possible the centralization of the fractious ward-based Chicago bosses.[18] The distribution of federal benefits could also be wielded to punish enemies. Roosevelt used federal relief and public works funds in New York City to help destroy Tammany Hall and the base of Al Smith, his archrival. Tammany was already reeling from a series of investigations of corruption initiated by Roosevelt while he was governor. Then, in 1933, Roosevelt's allies collaborated in fielding a New Deal-backed competitor to the Tammany candidate who divided the

Democratic vote in the mayoralty contest and threw the election to Fiorello La Guardia, the reform-Republican candidate. La Guardia's subsequent firm hold on the mayoralty was at least partly due to the liberal allocations of federal monies to New York City. Taken together, these actions were probably fatal—or as near fatal as any particular set of measures ever had been—to the hardy "New York Democracy."

The unions came to constitute a parallel infrastructure to mobilize voters. After Roosevelt reluctantly ceded industrial workers government protection for the right to organize, the national Democratic party developed strong organizational ties to the new CIO unions. In many places, the unions functioned as local parties, turning out their own members for the Democratic slate, and organizing campaigns in their localities. As early as 1936, the CIO threw itself into the effort to reelect Roosevelt by staging rallies, paying for radio time and leaflets, and spending nearly a million dollars in the industrial states of New York, Pennsylvania, Illinois, and Ohio. In addition, the constituent unions of the CIO contributed $770,000 to Roosevelt's campaign fund, most of it from the mineworkers' treasury, a sum which dwarfed the A. F. of L.'s earlier political contributions, which had totalled a mere $95,000 over the entire previous thirty years.[19] In subsequent elections, the CIO commitment to the Democratic Party became firmer. In 1940, union delegates figured prominently in the national Democratic convention, and Roosevelt ran strongest in the industrial counties where the CIO was concentrated.[20] And in 1944, every constituent CIO union endorsed Roosevelt, the CIO campaign contribution was raised to $1,328,000, and an apparatus involving tens of thousands of workers was created under the newly launched Political Action Committee.

If the timing of the rise in turnout supports our view that new voters were drawn to the polls by the interaction of popular protest and the New Deal programmatic and mobilizing initiatives that protest had forced, the changing social composition of the active electorate provides additional support. Turnout increased most among the lowest economic categories—those hard hit by unemployment and the recipients of relief assistance. It rose more among immigrants and those of immigrant parentage. "Overall," Kleppner concludes, "the increased turnout resulted from new mobilization among immigrant-stock voters, the young, those toward the bottom of the economic ladder, the unemployed, reliefers, and citizens" who had not voted in the 1920s.[21] And as turnout rose, the electorate polarized along class lines. These two developments were related in the sense that both were ultimately responses to the politics of protest, and to the initiatives which protest had forced. In 1932, Roosevelt outpolled Hoover among every category of voters, including the highest income category. By 1936, however, "businessmen switched to Landon while workers went the other way":[22] Roosevelt ran 29.1 percentage points behind the Republican candidate among high-income voters, and his lead among voters on relief rose to 68.8 percent.[23] In early 1940, the *Public Opinion Quarterly* summarized Gallup poll data showing that 64 percent of upper-income respondents preferred the Republicans, while 69 percent of lower-income respondents preferred the Democrats.[24] Similarly, table 5.2 shows sharp class differences in response to the question from the same poll, "In politics, do you consider yourself a Democrat, Independent, Socialist or Republican?"

Not surprisingly, as electoral polarization along class lines increased and voting levels rose, the turnout gap between the well-off and the poor narrowed.[25] These developments indicated that several important changes had occurred in the electoral arrangements associated with the system of 1896, and especially in the pattern of partisan competition and party-constituency linkages. Economic collapse

Table 5.2. Party Identification Percentages, 1940

	REPUB-LICAN	DEMO-CRAT	INDEPEN-DENT	OTHER
Total sample	38	42	19	1
Professional	44	29	25	2
Business	48	29	22	1
White-collar workers	36	40	22	2
Skilled workers	36	44	19	1
Semiskilled workers	33	47	18	2
Unskilled workers	27	55	16	2

SOURCE: *Sundquist (1973:202). Based on a Gallup poll question asked in early 1940.*

toppled the Republican party from its position of dominance in much of the country. The ensuing electoral instability, combined with popular protest, oriented the Democratic Party toward the urban working class, and even prompted at least a partial reconstruction of organizational linkages to the working class.

But the party mobilizing apparatus of big-city political organizations and unions was limited in its reach and, as we will soon note, riddled by contradictory political pressures. Meanwhile other elements of the system of 1896 persisted, and inhibited the extent of party recomposition. In particular, voter registration barriers partly choked off the surge in turnout among those who suffered most from the economic collapse and benefited most from the New Deal concessions. It has become commonplace to speak of soaring turnout during the mid-1930s. But considered in the light of the extraordinary economic and political events of the period, the increase in turnout was not what it might have been. Nationally, voting rose from 57 percent in 1932 to 61 percent in 1936, and to a peak of 62 percent in 1940.[26] Given the momentous political events of these years—the cataclysmic depression, the spread of mass protest movements, the extraordinary New Deal policy initiatives, and the exceptional efforts to enlist voters—why didn't many more people flock to the polls?

We think the surge that might otherwise have occurred was restrained by the elements of the system of 1896 that did not change. In particular, the restrictions on the franchise associated with literacy tests, residence requirements, and voter registration procedures persisted. Indeed, voter registration requirements had spread in the course of the preceding decades, as more and more counties were covered by state registration laws.[27] Literacy tests and residency requirements barred some people outright from voting, no matter the political stimuli of the era. The administrative barriers of the voter registration process were more flexible, for the better educated or more confident or highly motivated might overcome them. And many people did overcome them. Nevertheless, there is persuasive evidence that personal voter registration requirements continued to inhibit access to the ballot for many others, if only by discouraging them, and thus dampened the electoral mobilization of the 1930s. According to Kleppner's analysis, the difference in turnout between counties with and without personal voter registration requirements in the urban and industrial Metropole was about 8 percentage points.[28] Thus the intense politics of the decade did raise turnout, but less than might have been the case had the restrictive electoral machinery of 1896 not been in place. The electoral universe remained skewed, and that is surely a main reason that the class reorientation of the Democratic party was as partial and short-lived as it was.

Another reason is also traceable to persisting features of the system of 1896. The electoral mobilization that spread across the country in the 1930s never reached the one-party South. Turnout had risen from 18 percent in 1924 to 23 percent in 1928 in response to the ethnocultural challenge of the Smith campaign. But there was no upsurge in the 1930s: turnout rose by a mere 3 percentage points over the decade, reaching 26 percent by 1940. Neither the protest movements nor the New Deal electoral organizing efforts of the 1930s penetrated the southern political oligarchy, and arrangements which disenfranchised blacks and most poor whites stayed in place.

Franklin Delano Roosevelt constructed a peculiar electoral coalition between the northern urban industrial working class and well-off southern white elites. True, the outlines of that coalition were long-standing. The Democratic party had harbored the big-city machines and southern oligarchs in uneasy coexistence since the nineteenth century, and the party had sometimes been rent by conflict between these constituencies, especially in the 1920s. But two things were different in the 1930s. A national Democratic party dependent on southern support now held national power. And the urban working class had become both more assertive and a more important element of the coalition than it ever had been before. Accordingly, the party tried to craft programs that would knit together the diverse constituencies which made up its new voter majority while suppressing conflict between them. The relief and public works programs that we usually think of as oriented to the urban working class were also a lifeline to the devastated South:

> During the Depression the "colonial" economy of the South was ravaged far beyond the comprehension of most contemporary northern residents. The prostrate condition of the periphery led its congressmen to support progressive taxation (which raised comparatively more revenue from core industrial

regions) and vast relief programs (which, while they favored the North, still redistributed income to the South because they were financed through progressive tax schedules). On these policies, both the plantation elite and northern labor could agree.[29]

And just as the lifeline to the urban working class bolstered big-city machines, the lifeline to the impoverished South bolstered the state and local parties. At the same time, to mute conflict between the northern and southern wings, the administration of many of the New Deal programs was decentralized. This is what Bensel calls "cooperative federalism." Federal authority in some of the new programs was limited largely to fiscal support of state and local initiatives; other programs were located in independent agencies, spun off from federal oversight to enable them to bend to local interests; or vast legislative powers were delegated to existing executive agencies so as to avoid intractable conflict on the floor of the Congress. New Deal public works or relief or labor programs could thus be tailored to the requirements of the southern system. This means that the programs did not interfere with "the cheap and captive labor pool that segregationist institutions provided for rural plantation owners and low-skill manufacturing industries. . . . For this reason, agriculture and most seasonal activities such as canning and cotton ginning were exempted from minimum wage and union legislation."[30] The New Deal, in short, did not challenge segregation, the plantation system that kept sharecroppers in bondage to the planters through constant debt, or the low wage rates on which southern manufacturing depended. Roosevelt even refused to sign an antilynching law. In these ways, the New Deal helped to entrench the Southern Democracy associated with the system of 1896, a system that rested on the legal disfranchisement of the vast majority of blacks and poor whites.

These arrangements also set narrow limits on the political development of the national New Deal coalition. The persisting one-party system in the South meant that its congressional representatives had the seniority to dominate the committee system in the Congress, with the result that a bipartisan congressional coalition of southern Democrats and Republicans continued to hold national Democratic policies hostage for at least the next four decades. And over the longer run, it also meant that the market strength and organizational capacities of northern workers would be undermined by the low-wage labor system in the South which the "cooperative federalism" of the New Deal left untouched.

The limits on the possibilities of electoral politics inherited from the system of 1896 worked together. Because participation by the working class and the poor in the North continued to be constrained, Democratic control of the urban North was contingent and uncertain, and the party could not aspire to national power without the support of the South. This made the party doubly dependent on the South. It depended on southern support in the Congress for its legislative agenda, and it depended on southern votes in presidential contests.

In the absence of these severely limiting conditions, it seems reasonable to surmise that the Democratic party that emerged from the New Deal might have developed to resemble a European social democratic party. Of course, other things were also supposedly different in the United States, including the vigor of a popular culture of individualism, and the single-minded greed of American business. Still, popular political attitudes change as party formations change, and business is sometimes defeated. If party leaders had been confronted by a full complement of working-class voters in the cities, and a full complement of impoverished black and white laborers and tenants in the South, who can be sure that a labor-based political party would not have emerged?

CHAPTER SIX

The Decline of the
New Deal Party System

*T*he New Deal coalition could not last. Its peculiar construction made it susceptible to deep tensions. Elements of a modern labor party had been added to the Democratic party that emerged from the system of 1896, but that nascent labor party was stifled by the power of the one-party South in the Democratic coalition. Strain and ultimately dissolution were probably inevitable.

Dealignment and Remobilization in the South

The resurgence of conflict over race and section began early, and was ultimately rooted in the modernization of the southern economy. On the one side, New Deal policies favored the industrial development of the South, a bias that was first observable in the decisions of the World War II War Production Board.[1] The bias persisted in the postwar period because the seniority of southern representatives enabled them to influence the location of military installations and the allocation of defense contracts for the next forty years. At the same time, federal accommodations to the South in labor and social welfare legislation ensured that wage rates remained low, and attractive to northern investors.[2] Taken together, these developments fueled the economic growth that greatly enlarged the southern middle class, and helped spur a Republican revival.

On the other side, southern agriculture became more capital-intensive during and after the war, again partly as a result of federal agricultural policies which were dominated by southern congressmen. Millions of black and white tenants, day laborers and sharecroppers, as well as small farmers, were steadily forced off the land. The displaced whites largely remained in the South, but about half of the blacks forced off the land migrated to the big cities of the North, where they became voters and constituents of the urban and northern wing of the Democratic party.

In other words, key constituent blocs of the New Deal electoral coalition were being set in motion, economically, geographically, and inevitably politically as well. Northern blacks had become Democrats in 1934, largely in response to the help extended to them by New Deal welfare programs, as well as the symbolic assurances associated with Eleanor Roosevelt's cultivation of black leaders. But their numbers were not large, and they only mattered in close elections. The migration northward meant that steadily growing numbers of blacks concentrated in the big cities, where those who voted could sometimes determine how the big industrial states swung in presidential contests. Harry Truman's attempt to conciliate blacks by appointing the U.S. Commission on Civil Rights just prior to the 1948 campaign was an early sign that northern black votes were beginning to matter to national Democratic politicians, and especially to Presidential contenders.[3] And when four state delegations from the Deep South walked out of the Democratic convention that year to form the States' Rights party, because some of the recommendations of the Civil Rights Commission were incorporated in the Democratic platform, it was an early sign of the pending hemorrhage in the New Deal's southern support. Truman survived, but with only 53 percent of the southern white vote compared to FDR's 85 percent in 1936.[4]

Just as Roosevelt's rhetorical appeals to hard-hit working-class voters had raised hopes and stimulated protest, the gestures of national Democratic politicians toward the enlarged number of northern blacks in denouncing the southern system helped to raise hopes and stimulate protests. Increasingly liberal national rhetoric on the race issue, especially on voting rights in the South, ignited the civil rights movement in the mid-1950s. The result was more than a decade of wracking conflict that began in the South and spread to the North. National rhetoric about civil rights for blacks, and the 1954 Supreme Court ruling against segregated schools, goaded southern politicians and white segregationist organizations into a "movement of massive resistance" challenging the authority of the federal government to intervene in the southern system.[5] But these events also incited southern blacks to demand federal intervention, beginning with the Montgomery bus boycott in 1955 and continuing with more boycotts, lunch counter sit-ins, freedom rides, marches, and voter registration campaigns, all of which defied caste rules and provoked massive confrontations with southern mobs and police. Throughout the 1950s, the Democratic party vacillated over civil rights, trying to hold both its traditional southern white constituencies and the growing number of black voters in the North. Events would soon force a choice.

As the conflict escalated, southern electoral tactics to keep the national Democratic party from acceding to demands for civil rights legislation intensified. The Dixiecrat revolt in 1948 had deprived the Democratic ticket of the votes of Alabama, Louisiana, Mississippi, and South Carolina. Thereafter, southern political leaders turned to a strategy of "presidential Republicanism," encouraging their constituents to vote both for Republican presidential contenders and for Democratic congressional and state candidates. In 1952 and 1956, the resulting southern defections cost the Democratic presidential ticket four states in the Outer South—Florida, Virginia, Tennessee, and Texas—as well as Louisiana in 1956. Furthermore, the increasingly unsuccessful national Democratic presidential strategy of trying to placate the white South by dragging its heels on effective civil rights legislation began to provoke defections among the enlarging number of blacks who were gaining the franchise as they migrated to the northern cities. Stevenson won 80 percent of the national black vote in 1952, but only 60 percent in 1956, and his "states-rights" position on civil rights was surely a main reason. Kennedy fared somewhat better after having campaigned specifically for black votes, winning 68 percent of their ballots, but he lost Florida, Tennessee, and Virginia as well as Alabama and Mississippi, whose electors were unpledged.

By the early 1960s, the scales began to tip against the white South and in favor of civil rights. The allegiance of many of those white southerners who were in the active electorate seemed to be lost, and incipient black defections portended trouble in the northern strongholds of the Democratic party. In the wake of the demonstrations in Birmimgham, the March on Washington, and a summer in which the U.S. Department of Justice recorded 1,412 separate demonstrations, Kennedy finally agreed to sponsor civil rights legislation, and Johnson carried through on that pledge after Kennedy's assassination. The first civil rights bill in almost a century with effective enforcement provisions was signed into law on July 2, 1964. Lyndon B. Johnson went on to win a landslide victory, no doubt benefiting as the successor to a slain president, as well as from the weakness of the Goldwater candidacy. Aside from Goldwater's home state of Arizona, Johnson carried every state except four in the Deep South. The landslide notwithstanding, the results were ominous for the New Deal coalition. As Evans and Novak pointed out shortly afterward, "Behind the statistics was a revolution in American politics. The first Southern President since the Civil War captured 90 percent of the Negro vote and lost the Deep South by large margins."[6]

If the election of 1964 again showed the extent of white southern defections, it also revealed something quite new: the southern black vote was emerging as a major factor in the region's politics. As criticism of the southern system by national political leaders had mounted during the previous two decades, and as black protest emerged, the proportions of blacks who were registered to vote in the South had also begun to increase, from 4.5 percent in 1940, to 12.5 percent in 1947, to 20.7 percent in 1952, to 29.1 percent in 1960 and 35.5 percent in 1965,[7] just before the passage of the Voting Rights Act. Rising turnout, furthermore, was correlated with "a new surge of political awareness among southern blacks. In less than a decade, the proportion of apoliticals had fallen from 28 percent to about 3 percent."[8] Blacks were becoming voters, and staunch partisans of the national Democratic party that was championing the civil rights cause. (Conflict also stimulated increases in southern white turnout, from an average of 54.9 percent in the 1952–60 period, to 59.6 percent in the 1964–80 period, and there was a slight tendency for a larger rise among lower-strata whites.[9] However, the events that led to increased white turnout were also leading many of these voters to defect from the Democratic party, at least in presidential contests.)

Had it not been for black support, the Democratic party would have lost four additional southern states in 1964 (Arkansas, Florida, Tennessee, and Virginia). These developments almost surely influenced Johnson's subsequent support for the Voting Rights Act of 1965. Nearly a century before, the Republican party had similarly recognized that the black vote was crucial to the party's fortunes in the South. The Force Bill of 1890, which would have permitted federal supervision of southern elections under certain conditions, was an early version of the Voting Rights Act, and it had the support of President Benjamin Harrison:

> [T]he primary purpose of the legislation was to secure Republican control of the national government by recapturing marginal areas in the south. The president viewed federal protection of the black vote as the only way to promote a Republican revival in the region and believed that such a revival would create a permanent majority for the protective tariff.[10]

As it happened, the Force Bill failed because too many Republicans were unwilling to risk disrupting the South, which had by then become a stable environment for northern commerce and investment. By 1965, the national Democratic party was in a position similar to the Republican party a century before with regard to the South, and the black movement had helped bring it there. If it was to hope to hold southern states in presidential elections, it needed the votes of blacks to replace some of the white Democrats, whose numbers were being depleted both by defections over the race question and by the growing Republican identification among the enlarging middle class. In this sense, the Voting Rights Act widened and institutionalized electoral changes that had already been set in motion by economic modernization and the civil rights movement.

The eventual result of this series of developments was to erode the one-party South that had survived from the system of 1896 to undergird the New Deal coalition. As party competition grew in the South, national Democratic leaders had no choice but to support legislation overturning the more blatant methods of disfranchisement that had prevailed since the late nineteenth century. Southern registration levels leaped upward after federal intervention in southern electoral systems was first authorized under the Voting Rights Act.

Subsequent elections confirmed these changes. Carter, the first president from the Deep South since before the Civil War, failed to win a majority of white southern votes in 1976, and he won only one-third of white southerners in his 1980 reelection bid.[11] Mondale did worse, winning only 25 percent of the southern white vote in 1984. Between 1980 and 1984, fully half of the Republican party's gains among whites came from the South, as did half the party's gains in the House of Representatives (it captured four Democratic seats in Texas, three in North Carolina, and one in Georgia, while losing a seat in Arkansas).[12] In the 1930s, 117 of 120 southern seats in the House were held by Democrats; only 85 of 124 were in 1986.

Meanwhile, the Democratic party's ability to compete in the South depended increasingly on the black vote. In 1986, when the Democrats won five new Senate seats in the South (and control of the Senate), it was largely because of the lopsided support of newly enfranchised blacks.[13] In the southern section as a whole, blacks composed only about 20 percent of the active electorate, but they voted 90 percent Democratic, yielding an 18-point advantage to the Democratic party, according to Petrocik.[14] To offset that advantage, the Republican party had to carry at least 65 percent of the white vote. Republican victories in the South over the past three decades have depended on just such margins. In 1984, for example, the Republicans won a U.S. Senate race in Mississippi even though 30 percent of the voters were black and they voted 80 percent Democratic, giving their candidate a 24 percentage point advantage. The Republican candidate won by garnering 81 percent of the white vote. But these lopsided race-aligned majorities could not make the Republicans secure; their losses in the 1986 southern U.S. Senate races revealed the difficulty of offsetting the black Democratic vote even with large white pluralities.

Table 6.1. Southern Democratic Victories in 1986
U.S. Senate Races Despite Large White Republican
Pluralities

	BLACKS AS % OF VOTERS	% BLACK DEM. VOTE	% BLACK DEM. ADVANTAGE	% WHITE REP. VOTE
Senate races				
Alabama	21	88	19	61
Georgia	24	75	18	59
Louisiana	29	85	25	60
North Carolina	16	88	14	56

SOURCE: *Petrocik (1987b:49 and table 4).*

The third column of table 6.1 shows the black Democratic advantage in these races, and the fourth column shows the huge white pluralities with which the Republicans nevertheless lost.

Petrocik concluded that the "Republicans lost the Senate races in the South not because the realignment [among whites] of the past two decades was reversed, but because the parallel effort to effectively enfranchise southern blacks has been successful."[15] Moreover, southern black registration levels did not yet equal white levels. Of all groups in the country, black southerners were the most likely to overreport registration. Mississippi was a case in point. Blacks in that state reported to the Census Bureau/CPS in 1984 that they were registered at the extraordinary level of 86 percent (the national black reported rate was 66 percent). However, in a special study of Mississippi, Lichtman reported that the actual black registration level in 1984 was only 54 percent, compared to a 79 percent white rate.[16] The full impact of the southern black vote, in other words, was still to be felt.

In sum, the one-party South was history. The southern pillar of the New Deal inherited from the system of 1896 had crumbled. Meanwhile, deep cracks appeared in the northern pillar as well.[17]

Dealignment and Demobilization in the North

Unless the Democratic party could compensate for eroding support in the South by strengthening its base elsewhere, the breakdown of the sectional accommodation that had been part of the system of 1896 threatened to be fatal to the party's grip on national power. But instead of deepening and enlarging, the party's support in the North became weaker and more uncertain, even as the dimensions of its southern problem unfolded.

The evidence was apparent as early as the 1960s. The main problem was that the American working class was changing, and the Democratic party was not. The old white male working class based in the mass production industries was declining relatively and absolutely. A new working class, concentrated in the service sector, more geographically dispersed, and resting heavily on women and minorities, was emerging. But as the recomposition of the working class swiftly proceeded, the Democratic party and its mobilizing apparatus of unions and local parties lagged behind. Their failure to enlist the ranks of a recomposing working class was not much noticed, however. Instead, commentators directed their attention to a second problem: the rising tide of defections among the old industrial working class. Because this latter process generated so much discussion, we will consider it first.

PARTY FRAGMENTATION AND RISING CONFLICT

During the 1940s, the Democratic party commanded overwhelming majorities among industrial workers. That support wavered during the Eisenhower elections of 1952 and 1956, then rallied again in the elections of 1960 and 1964, but it was not being sustained (table 6.2). A main line of explanation attributed these defections to weaknesses in the American party system itself, which was said to be undergoing a process of "fragmentation" or long-term dealignment. The evidence summoned in support of this diagnosis included the rising numbers of independents, increasing volatility in partisan identification or voting, and the trend toward split-ticket voting. According to Pomper, one-third to two-fifths of the electorate had come to disclaim ties to the parties, and the proportion of the electorate voting on purely partisan grounds had declined markedly, from 42 percent in 1960 to 23 percent in 1972.[18] Jensen said that the percentage of "strong" partisans dropped from an average of about 36 percent between 1952 and 1964 to 24 percent in later years, while independents rose from 15 percent in the 1940s to about 40 percent in 1974. Using different measures, which

Table 6.2. Percentage of White Major Party Voters
Who Voted Democratic for President by Union
Membership, Class, and Non-South

	UNION MEMBER	WORKING CLASS	NON-SOUTH
1944	67	64	—
1948	79	76	—
1952	53	52	39
1956	50	44	36
1960	64	55	46
1964	80	75	65
1968	50	50	42
1972	40	32	33
1976	60	58	46
1980	48	44	36
1984	50	42	37

SOURCE: *Extrapolated from Abramson, Aldrich, and Rohde (1986: figures 5–2, 5–3, and 5–4). Based on National Opinion Research Center polls, which are susceptible to substantial overreporting of voting.*

showed a less extreme trend, Norpoth and Rusk reported a decline in partisanship during the 1964–76 period from 75 to 63 percent.[19] And the proportion of ticket-splitters rose from about one-fourth of voters in 1940 to two-thirds in the 1970s.[20]

Everyone more or less agreed that partisanship was eroding; the debate was about why.[21] Some analysts attributed it to the long-term decline of party organizations in the United States—Burnham, for example, traced the decline to the "anti-partyism" and electoral fragmentation he thought were ushered in by the system of 1896[22] (Subsequent "reforms," Burnham thought, only worsened these trends.)[23] Others thought the decline of parties and partisanship originated more recently. Thus Pomper contrasted the plight of the parties, particularly at the state and local levels, with the legitimacy, resources, and control over candidate recruitment which they commanded at the end of World War II.[24] And Jensen thought that 1968 was the Democratic Party's "last hurrah," because it was the last nominating convention that party leaders were able to control.[25]

Dealignment was said by others to be the result of the intense conflicts that swept through American society in the 1960s and 1970s. "Issue polarization over Vietnam, the racial question, law and order, new life styles, and moral questions have prompted large-scale voting defections to George Wallace in 1968 and Richard Nixon in 1972," according to Norpoth and Rusk.[26] Converse pointed to similar "chaotic" political events in trying to account both for voter volatility and for the lower sense of efficacy reported in survey data.[27] These explanations were not, of course, mutually exclusive. It was reasonable to suppose that the decline of party organization and the diminishing ability of the parties to orient voters and command their allegiance had left the electorate more exposed to the currents of disturbance generated by specific conflicts.

The parties were weaker, at least in the sense that their hold on the loyalties of voters was weaker.[28] And sharp political conflicts were precipitating voter defections, probably the more so because partisan allegiances had weakened.[29] Two sources of conflict were usually emphasized in accounting for voter volatility generally, and defections from the Democratic party in particular. The first was the spread of racial conflict to the North, which probably followed inevitably from the growing numbers of blacks (and Hispanics) in the northern cities and their new influence in the Democratic party. The growing electoral weight of northern black voters created, we think, the electoral context for the emergence and successes of the civil rights movement in the South. But blacks in the North, and Hispanics, had deep grievances of their own, arising from the poverty and discrimination they confronted. By 1963, in the wake of the confrontations in Birmingham, and even while the massive March on Washington was being planned, blacks in the northern cities joined in demonstrations to demand decent jobs, integrated schools, community control of schools, better housing code enforcement, and an end to the demolition of black neighborhoods by urban renewal. Protests escalated from demonstrations and marches and sit-ins, emulating the southern movement, to rent strikes and riots, and to intermittent street warfare and riots.

The national Democratic party, and especially Democratic presidents, responded to these troubles in the heart of its northern base with a series of new social welfare programs under the auspices of the Great Society. But if concessions to urban blacks could no longer be avoided, they were nevertheless costly, for they aroused the ire of big-city Democratic leaders and provoked resentments in the white working class. The rest of the story is familiar. The national Democratic strategy to win and hold the political allegiance of the new urban minorities became mired in racial conflict. As the 1960s drew to a close, the issues of school busing, affirmative action, and crime in the streets generated mounting resentment among white working- and middle-class Democratic constituencies in the cities. The forces that drove "the lower middle class" away from the Democratic party, Galston says in a thinly veiled allusion to the race problem, included "a deep seated antipathy to many of the party's efforts on behalf of the disadvantaged."[30] The results of the election of 1968, held in the wake of several years of urban rioting and federal concessions, reflected this antipathy as many of the white working-class urban voters most exposed to the race conflict in the North began to defect from Democratic columns.

Another line of argument blamed the intense conflicts of the period and their fragmenting or "dealigning" consequences for the Democrats on the rise within the party of middle- or upper-middle-class activists who championed such New Politics issues as peace, the environment, and racial and gender equality. Schneider wrote regretfully that in the old days, "a political party was a big tent, with room inside for all kinds of people. The Democratic Party included southern white racists, blacks, urban bosses, and liberal reformers." These good old days were gone, however; the tents had gotten smaller, much smaller, and the reason was the "liberal activists, union organizers, and radical nuns" who administered "litmus tests" in order to certify that political candidates were of the true faith.[31] Their lofty causes notwithstanding, the new activists were often charged with less than noble motives. They presumably represented an enlarging "new class" of educated professionals who had a self-interested stake in the expansion of government bureaucracies that employed them, and especially the federal bureaucracies, which supposedly accounted for their alliance with minorities, and for their diverse "causes"—such as environmental regulation or social welfare expansion.[32]

As the story was usually told, this elite stratum of activists both promoted and benefited from the McGovern reforms adopted in 1970, which elevated them in the party and put their causes at the center of the party agenda at the expense of old-style union and party leaders, and at the expense of older New Deal-style issues to which working-class voters responded.[33] As a result, the so-called new class and its causes brought disarray to the Democratic leadership, and prompted disaffection among the Democratic rank and file.[34] The New Politics activists certainly did alienate many party regulars, and probably many members of the old working class as well.[35] Still, the use of the term "elite" to describe them was misleading. The activists drew their influence from the increasingly restive ranks of minorities, women, and youth in the electorate, many of whom were employed in the expanding service sector, and especially in public agencies. Their leaders were, as is to be expected, often middle class and educated, drawn into politics by the civil rights, antiwar, environmental, and feminist movements.[36] But they surely were not higher in the class structure than the regular Democratic power brokers, and many of those for whom they spoke were worse off than the old Democratic working class.

There is no question, however, but that the demands of the new activists caused fissures in the Democratic party. Their issues competed for attention and prominence with more traditional Democratic commitments, and their fights for internal party democracy weakened the control of traditional party leaders, including union-based party leaders. If the McGovern candidacy of 1972 is taken as the high point of the New Politics, it was also a low point in working-class Democratic allegiance. The Democratic ticket won only 32 percent of the working-class vote, and only 40 percent of the vote among union families, by far the most dismal showing since the formation of the New Deal coalition.

WEAKENING DEMOCRATIC PARTY TIES
TO THE WORKING CLASS

The usual focus on the flamboyant battles associated with race and the New Politics, however, turns attention away from another more important source of working-class defections: the Democratic party's

growing unwillingness or inability to respond to the economic aspirations of either the old working class or the new. During the long-
term postwar economic boom, the main basis for the party's appeal to
its core working- and lower-class voters was the promise of steady economic growth through international expansion and Keynesian macroeconomic management.[37] It was a formula consistent with the interests of the party's union constituency in the mass production
industries, and with the interests of those corporations that were
coming to be allied with the Democratic party. The dividends of the
tremendous economic growth of the two postwar decades thus made
possible a kind of business-labor accord.[38] American corporations
struck a truce with unions where they already existed, conceded wage
increases which at least maintained organized labor's share of an expanded economic product, and acquiesced in government policies
which ensured relatively low unemployment rates as well as modest
social welfare protections. In the 1960s, in the wake of demonstrations
and riots, major business leaders even went along with a new expansion of social welfare programs, and some actually took the initiative
in efforts like the Urban Coalition, which sought to bring peace to the
cities through modest concessions for blacks. Living standards improved for the great majority, and so long as economic growth continued, the New Deal coalition was viable.

But when the trend of rising real wages and government spending
became problematic in the early 1970s, the political accommodations
based on them faltered and then collapsed, and dealigning tendencies
intensified. The first signs of economic trouble were evident in the late
1960s, when U.S. corporate profits began to decline. Investment in
new plant and equipment soon followed suit, and so did overall
growth rates. Analysts dispute the reasons for the ensuing period of
slow growth and economic instability, or even whether the problems
which the conventional indicators described are real.[39] But whatever
the reality and the reasons for it, by the early 1970s, especially in the
wake of the price shocks generated by the Arab oil boycott, the pie
seemed to have stopped growing, and corporate America announced
that it was no longer willing to live by the business-labor accord.

The subsequent turnabout is by now legendary. American business became much more resistant to wage increases, despite the infla-

tion triggered by the Vietnam war. Nonunionized workers were hurt first and most, and their numbers were enlarging, as more and more of the new jobs in the economy were concentrated in the lowest paid nonunion service sector. The wage differential between the old industrial working class and the new working class began to grow.[40] But the old industrial working class was not protected for long. As the decade wore on, corporations that had more or less accommodated to unionism and steadily rising wages mobilized to fight wage increases or improvements in working conditions, to demand wage givebacks, and to smash existing unions. The blame for economic malaise could not be readily fixed on the Democratic party (if only because Republican presidents presided over some of this troubled period), or indeed on anyone in particular. Even business leaders seemed exempted from blame, given their claim that survival in the international markets compelled them to take a tough new stance toward labor. But that is only to say that the Democratic party's promise of economic improvement grew increasingly hollow.

A parallel corporate mobilization emerged in politics, which Edsall described as "one of the most remarkable campaigns in the pursuit of political power in recent history."[41] The lobbying capacity of business, always formidable, became far more coordinated and proficient, achieving "the virtual dominance of the legislative process in the Congress" as the 1970s wore on.[42] Business won impressive victories under the Carter administration, foretelling the even larger steps that the ascendant business-Republican coalition would take after 1980. Corporate taxes, which had in fact been falling for some time, were cut again, along with capital gains taxes, while social security taxes were raised. Labor's efforts to promote a Labor Law Reform Bill were defeated.[43] And business also organized to reduce government regulation, including environmental regulation, and to increase military spending, which began to rise sharply in the closing years of the Carter administration. Meanwhile, the real value of the minimum wage, which directly affected about fourteen million workers whose earnings were pegged at or near the legal minimum, was falling steadily.[44] Finally, business pressed for reduced social program spending, by funding research and propaganda efforts to discredit social welfare programs and by lobbying to cut program funds. Business mobilized,

Table 6.3. Changes in Democratic and Republican
Voter Allegiance among Different Income Groups

INCOME GROUP	1952– 1958	1960– 1968	1970– 1978	1976– 1980
Bottom third	64–36	66–34	69–31	71–29
Middle third	63–37	65–35	64–36	63–37
Top third	56–44	58–42	53–47	53–47

SOURCE: *Edsall (1984: table 1.4). The first percentage in each column indi-
cates Democratic allegiance, and the second, Republican allegiance.*

in other words, to take back much of what labor, blacks, and the
poor—the old working class and the new—had won from the New
Deal coalition in the previous half century. During the closing years
of the Carter administration, a Democratic president and a good
many Democratic congressmen more or less went along. And after
1981, under a Republican president, Democrats in the Congress simply
gave way in the face of an even larger business offensive. In sum, as the
economy faltered and the business-labor accord collapsed, the Democratic party forfeited its claim to be the party whose macroeconomic
policies would ensure steady growth. Worse, under the combined
pressures of slow growth, rising prices, and a mobilized business class,
the party reneged on the political terms of the business-labor accord.[45] And as the Democratic party steadily gave ground to the political demands of business, working-class allegiance to the party eroded.

DEMOBILIZATION

The extent of working-class voter defections and volatility notwithstanding, a potentially more serious but less noticed difficulty for
the New Deal coalition outside of the South was the decline of voter
turnout, especially among the bottom third of the population, where
Democratic preferences were overwhelming. Indeed, while partisan
identification was shifting to the Republicans among the somewhat
better off, among the bottom third of the population Democratic
preferences were actually increasing, as shown in table 6.3. But the
changing ranks of the worse-off were not being enlisted in the electorate.

Table 6.4. Presidential Turnout Percentages, 1948–1980

	SOUTH	NON-SOUTH	NATIONAL
1948	25	62	53
1952	38	71	64
1956	37	70	62
1960	41	73	65
1964	46	69	63
1968	52	66	62
1972	46	61	57
1976	49	58	56
1980	50	57	55

SOURCE: *Burnham (1981c:100, table 1). Based on total of all citizens legally eligible to vote, aliens excluded.*

Postwar turnout peaked in the 1950s. Then it began to slide. Between 1964 and 1980, the national rate of voting dropped 8 points, from 63 percent to 55 percent, and the rate outside the South dropped 12 points, from 69 percent to 57 percent (table 6.4). One reason for the decline was the enlarged proportion of young people in the electorate, particularly after the voting age was lowered to 18 years before the 1972 election. Most analysts think that about one fifth to one quarter of the turnout decline is due to the incorporation of this huge youth cohort,[46] leaving most of the decline to be explained.

Lower-class groups, which were potentially the strongest Democratic partisans, showed the greatest turnout declines (table 6.5).[47] Between 1964 and 1980, for example, voting by those with eight years of education or less was down by 16 percentage points. The unemployed voted less by 16.8 percentage points. Regional differences are striking: all of the national decline was centered in the North and West, where voting fell off by 13.6 percentage points, with whites falling 12.3 percentage points and blacks falling 19.2 points. Intensified competition for voters in the South after the passage of the voting rights legislation of the 1960s kept the South from joining the downward national trend: black turnout rose by 4.2 percentage points, helping to offset a drop of 2.1 points among whites.

Various measures reveal how class-skewed the electorate had be-

Table 6.5. Percentage Claiming to Have Voted in 1964 and 1980

	1964	1980	NET CHANGE
National	69.3	59.2	−10.1
White	70.7	60.9	−9.8
Black	58.5	50.5	−8.0
Male	71.9	59.1	−12.8
Female	67.0	59.4	−7.6
Employed	73.0	61.8	−11.2
Unemployed	58.0	41.2	−16.8
Not in labor force	65.0	57.0	−8.0
0 to 8 elementary	59.0	42.6	−16.4
High school			
1 to 3 years	65.4	45.6	−19.8
4 years	76.1	58.9	−17.2
College			
1 to 3 years	82.1	67.2	−14.9
4 years +	87.5	79.9	−7.6
North and West	74.6	61.0	−13.6
White	74.7	62.4	−12.3
Black	72.0	52.8	−19.2
South	56.7	55.6	−1.1
White	59.5	57.4	−2.1
Black	44.0	48.2	+4.2

SOURCE: *Census Bureau/CPS Series P-20. In 1964, 8.6 percent more people claimed to have voted than did, and the inflation in 1980 was 7.6 percent (Series P-20, no. 405, table H).*

come. In 1972, for example, turnout among white male laborers with a grade school education was 41 percent, but 86.6 percent of those in managerial occupations with a college degree voted. The same skew appeared in 1976: among white males, 6 percent of the propertied middle classes reported never having voting compared with 13.5 percent of white collar and salaried workers, 20.2 percent of craftsmen and service workers, and 30.4 percent of lower-working-class occupations.[48] Burnham remarks that "While race differences are most often commented about in discussions of turnout in America, in fact class differences are greater."[49]

The strong correlation between declining turnout and the falling rates of registration among lower-strata groups suggested that the absence of Democratic party attempts to enroll new voters was important. Overall, registration fell 7.4 percentage points between 1968 and 1980 (table 6.6).[50] The largest declines were by education and unemployment status. Registration fell among those with less than a high school education by 13.9 percentage points. Registration among the unemployed was down by 10 points. The decline was greater in the North and West (down by 8.6 points) than in the South (down by 4.4 points). Black registration in the South rose slightly.

As we emphasized earlier in this chapter, the problem of low turnout among the strata who were potentially more Democratic existed from the beginning of the New Deal realignment. In 1934 and 1936, the potential reservoir of support in the South remained untouched, and the remobilization in the North was far from complete. Then, as the 1930s drew to a close, the combined power of resurgent business interests and the southern congressional wing ensured there would not be many new initiatives oriented toward the poor and the working class. Moreover, with the ebbing of the protest movements of the decade, the task of reaching and activating the poor and working class and helping them surmount registration obstacles came to fall entirely on the unions and local big-city Democratic organizations. For different reasons, each proved to be unable or unwilling to reach out to the pool of nonvoters.

The point is often made that the capacity of the unions to mobilize their members and ensure their allegiance to the Democratic party diminished after World War II. One explanation attributes this long-term decline of Democratic voting among union members to the increasing prosperity of the rank and file. The New Deal coalition is thus said to be the victim of its own achievements. The policies, so successfully propounded, that brought prosperity, homeownership, and even a life in suburbia to many of the have-nots of the 1930s worked in time to bring about changes in their interests and, inevitably, in their partisan preferences. Galston's comments typify this view:

The New Deal brought together Americans of low and modest income against the coterie of the wealthy that FDR ringingly labelled "economic royalists." Until well after the Second World War, this coalition of disadvantage was a clear majority. But in the next two generations, real incomes rose sharply. Homeownership soared. Tens of millions of Americans moved into the middle class, and their children did even better.[51]

There may be truth in the notion that prosperity, as well as aging and mortality, changed the political orientation of unionized workers. But this diagnosis misses the heart of the problem. Whether or not the unions' grip on those who were moving up in the class structure was loosening, it was the failure of the unions to reach the cohorts of new workers, especially minority and women workers employed in the new industries in the Sun-belt and in the rapidly expanding service sector, that made for the larger problem. In short, the recomposition of the working class was proceeding, but the recomposition of the unions lagged behind.

In part the diminishing ability of the unions to organize new cohorts of workers (public sector workers being an important exception), and to reach and enlist new voters, resulted from the increasingly comfortable and oligarchical character of union leadership, as well as from white male union members' resistance to the inclusion of new groups. But the stasis that overtook the unions was also ensured by the steady retreat of a Democrat-controlled national government from the support of labor. As normal politics was restored after the 1930s, accommodations by the party leadership to business interests, as well as to the southern congressional delegation, became the rule. During the 1930s, most American business, including most heavy industry, had virtually declared war on the New Deal and its labor and social welfare policies.[52] The advent of World War II moderated that antagonism. The tremendous increase in production and profits spurred by war demand, and the large concessions ceded industry by the War Labor Board, encouraged more accommodative relations between heavy industry and the Democratic party (symbolized by the appearance in Washington of the "dollar-a-year" corporate executives who joined the top command of the war economy).[53] With this rapprochement, the party's prounion tilt was reversed. In the mid-1940s, the National Labor Relations Board established under the Wagner Act

Table 6.6. Percentage Claiming to Be Registered, 1968 and 1980

	1968	1980	NET CHANGE
National	74.3	66.9	−7.4
White	75.4	68.4	−7.0
Black	66.2	60.0	−6.2
Male	76.0	66.6	−9.4
Female	72.8	67.1	−5.7
Employed	76.6	68.7	−7.9
Unemployed	60.3	50.3	−10.0
Not in labor force	71.3	65.8	−5.5
0 to 8 elementary	64.6	53.0	−11.6
High school			
1 to 3 years	68.5	54.6	−13.9
4 years	77.7	66.4	−11.3
College			
1 to 3 years	82.9	74.4	−8.5
4 years +	87.0	84.3	−2.7
North and West	76.5	67.9	−8.6
White	77.2	69.3	−7.9
Black	71.8	60.6	−11.2
South	69.2	64.8	−4.4
White	70.8	66.2	−4.6
Black	61.6	59.3	−2.3

SOURCE: *Census Bureau/CPS Series P-20. We estimate that overall registration claims are inflated by 7 to 10 percent, although the inflation by particular subgroups may be more, or less. See appendix A for a discussion of the biases in registration data.*

was reconstituted to eliminate its prolabor members.[54] The Smith-Connally Act in 1943 and the Taft-Hartley Act in 1947 legislated as national policy many of the antilabor policies which had been enacted by the states.[55] Smith-Connally authorized the federal takeover of struck industries and banned direct political contributions by unions. Taft-Hartley outlawed secondary boycotts, and required anticommunist oaths of union officials. Most important in the long run, Section 14(b) of Taft-Hartley legitimated state right-to-work laws, which hampered efforts to organize the South where new manufacturing was locating. A less sympathetic National Labor Relations Board also made it more difficult for new organizing drives to use the protections which the Board ostensibly provided. Southern and business opposition, together with the union fratricide precipitated by the Cold War anticommunist campaign, combined to shatter the CIO's "Operation Dixie," a much-heralded postwar campaign to organize the South. Finally, while the unions served as partisan mobilizing vehicles, they were not political machines. They had difficulty reaching and holding even their own members in the electorate and in Democratic columns unless the party offered strong rhetorical and programmatic appeals. And even apart from labor policy, the national Democratic leadership made little effort after World War II to improve or expand the programmatic initiatives of the 1930s. American workers never got a government health care program, for example, and other social welfare programs languished, falling far behind the initiatives of the European democracies.

The significance of weak party appeals and hamstrung unions has to be understood in the context of the restrictive registration apparatus inherited from the system of 1896. In the absence of mobilizing efforts, turnout did not continue to rise after the 1930s, and eventually began to slide. Meanwhile, the recomposition of the New Deal working class of the 1930s had begun in World War II, when millions of blacks and women joined the ranks of industrial workers. Davis reports a preelection survey of United Automobile Workers locals in Detroit as early as 1944 showing that a bare 30 percent of the membership was registered to vote. And in the late 1950s, the director of the Committee on Political Education (COPE), the AFL-CIO successor to the Political Action Committee (PAC), reported that less than 40 percent of members of affiliated unions were registered, while a survey by the Amalgamated Clothing Workers (with its larger proportions of women and minorities) found as few as 20 to 30 percent of their members registered.[56] But the full impact of a crippled unionism on electoral participation at the bottom began to tell in the 1970s, when the economy was changing more rapidly, and working-class recomposition was proceeding apace. As jobs in the old manufacturing industries shrank, as Sun-belt and service sector jobs expanded, and as a "contingent" workforce of part-time, temporary, and homeworkers grew, the reach of the unions into the working class narrowed. Moreover, the business campaign to slash wages and worsen working conditions in the 1970s was accompanied by the spread of union-busting efforts that harkened back to the era before the New Deal. Ferguson and Rogers report on the scope and intensity of the antiunion campaigns:

> The number of charges of employer violations of section 8(a)(3) of the Labor Management Relations Act, for example, which forbids employers to fire workers for engaging in union activity, doubled from 9,000 to 18,000 over the 1970–80 period. The number of workers awarded reinstatement or back pay by the NLRB rose from 10,000 to 25,000. By 1980, the number of illegal discharges for union activity had risen to about 5 percent of the total number of pro-union votes in representation elections before the Board. Put otherwise, by that time American workers faced a 1 in 20 chance of being fired for merely favoring unionization.[57]

Not surprisingly under these conditions, unions began to lose a majority of collective bargaining elections, and the losses were concentrated in the biggest firms.[58] The unionized share of the work force continued to drop, from 25.7 percent to 20.9 percent over the decade, as new organizing drives failed, and as existing members were lost through decertification elections.[59] However limited their effectiveness, the unions had been one of the main mobilizing mechanisms of the New Deal coalition. As their connections to the working class diminished, so did voter turnout.[60]

There was no vehicle to compensate for the growing incapacity of the unions. The other major agency of voter mobilization in the New Deal coalition was the big-city Democratic organization. In principle, the local parties functioned to reach potential voters, including the waves of newcomers who have successively populated American cities. In the post–World War II period, this task of integration was immense. The big-city parties were confronted with the vast immigration of blacks displaced from the South, and Hispanics displaced from Mexico and Puerto Rico, at the very time that millions of older urban residents were leaving the central cities for the suburbs. The enormous turnover in population was bound to cause political repercussions, simply because large shifts in population always threaten to undermine established patterns of political organization.

In the past, the machines used their control over municipal government resources to minimize the disturbances associated with population shifts, enlisting successive generations of new voters and holding old voters with favors or friendship or intimidation. These clientelist exchanges muted both class and ethnic conflict in the polyglot and changing cities. However, as a result of municipal reform campaigns, the resources of city government came to be controlled by bureaucracies which were at least somewhat insulated from direct control by partisan leaders.[61] Bureaucratization meant that the jobs and services which had earlier been used to cultivate allegiance among newcomers were no longer easily dispensed to new groups. The resources of the city agencies had become fenced in by civil service regulations, and later by union contract provisions. It was not that the bureaucratization of the goods, services, and honors controlled by city governments had depoliticized municipal administrations. Rather, bureaucratization provided a set of devices by which groups who already benefited from municipal largesse could protect their stakes, and thus impeded the use of municipal resources to integrate newcomers.

Moreover, the very fact of bureaucratization worsened the potential for conflict, which was in any case intense, between the older ethnics and the new minorities. Who got what in the more bureaucratic politics of the cities was no longer a matter of morseled and private exchanges between party organizations and their constituencies, as it had been in the clientelist system. Political allocations were now matters of public policy, and the process of allocation was therefore exposed to intense intergroup competition and animosity.[62]

The first main response of the national Democratic party to the political problems generated by population shifts in the cities was the urban renewal program. In its conception, the program provided something for everyone, including allocations for public housing which could reasonably have been oriented to the newcomers. But in fact urban renewal was implemented in ways that suited the interests of big-city mayors trying to ward off the disturbances associated with the new constituencies, and the interests of downtown businessmen with whom the mayors were allied. Very little public housing was built, but federal subsidies were used to acquire land in "blighted" central city areas which was subsequently resold to private developers for commercial and high-priced residential development. Downtown businessmen and mayors could unite around a program that would return better-off customers and taxpayers to the urban core. At the same time, urban renewal, which came to be known as "black removal," would remove the newcomers whose enlarging presence threatened to accelerate white flight and cause deepening fissures in local political organizations. There was even reason to hope that the destruction of the housing and neighborhoods of the minorities would stanch the flow of new migrants. However, given the powerful forces that were combining to generate the population shifts that were transforming the cities, urban renewal was not equal to its task of halting the recomposition of the urban electorate. Indeed, in the end, renewal exacerbated the political problems of the Democratic party, and especially of the national party.[63] On the one hand, renewal did not reverse the migration flows that were paralyzing the big-city political organizations. On the other hand, renewal itself became another source of grievance to the black and Hispanic populations who were being displaced, and this during the very period that urban black voters were becoming activated and volatile over the southern civil rights issue and poverty.

The political repercussions of these events could be seen in the election of 1956, for blacks either defected from the Democratic party, or sat out the election. Defections tended to be related to the civil rights turmoil in the South. As Moon remarked at the time, "the closer the Negro lived to the resurgent terror, the sharper was his defection from the dominant party. . . . In 1952 [Stevenson] carried the Atlanta Negro precincts by better than 2 to 1, but four years later he received less than 15 percent of the vote in those same precincts."[64] Overall, Stevenson's share of the black vote in 1956 was only 60 percent, down sharply from the 80 percent he received in 1952.

The problem in the North was different, and it revealed the conflicts that were paralyzing the ability of the local parties to enlist the newcomers:

There was a sharp decline in balloting [in 1956] in many Negro districts throughout the country, but particularly in Northern industrial centers from which, in previous years, the Democrats received huge majorities. This, despite an increased Negro population in most of these cities. . . . In Philadelphia, 27,000 fewer votes were cast than in 1952 for a loss of 14.7 percent. Voting in Negro wards of Kansas City, Mo., was off a fifth for a decline of 5,900 in the number of ballots cast. The percentage loss was even higher in Boston where the vote was down 28.5. The Negro vote declined 19 percent in Atlantic City; 15.6 in Toledo; 15.4 in Pittsburgh; 12 in Chicago; 9.3 in Brooklyn; 9.1 in Youngstown, Ohio; 6.4 in Cleveland; and 5.9 in Harlem.[65]

If 1956 was not enough to signal the significance of trouble for the national party in the big-city organizations, Kennedy's narrow victory in 1960—a victory that could not have been won without the huge northern urban black pluralities—underscored the point. Despite low levels of registration, the numbers of blacks in the cities were growing, so that the total votes they contributed mattered increasingly in determining the outcome of presidential races in the industrial states:

It had been Kennedy's great strength in the great Northern cities to which Southern Negroes had migrated that produced hairline victories for the Democrats in the eight states experts consider crucial to success in any close election—New York, Illinois, Pennsylvania, Michigan, Maryland, Missouri, Minnesota, and New Jersey. All but one—Missouri—went to Eisenhower in 1956. All eight went for Kennedy in 1960, on the strength of the big-city vote. The Republican National Committee, using Philadelphia as a laboratory, made a precinct-by-precinct study of why this happened. The study revealed, among other things, that their candidate won only 18 percent of the Negro vote, leaving 82 percent for Kennedy.[66]

In a word, while local Democratic political leaders protected their incumbency by excluding the newcomers, the political fortunes of the national Democratic party, especially its presidential wing, hinged on turning them out to vote. With southern support diminishing, the northern cities were all the more crucial to winning and holding national power. What had emerged was a profound conflict of interests over the black vote: it was a source of jeopardy for local Democratic incumbents, and a source of strength for the presidential wing of the party. From the perspective of national Democratic leaders, something had to be done to firm up black support, especially since the national party was still trying to avoid taking action on civil rights. And as protests in the cities escalated into riots, the need to reach out to blacks became imperative.

What emerged, at first gropingly under the Kennedy administration, and then in rapid-fire order under the Johnson administration, was a series of federal service programs for the "inner city," a euphemism for the ghetto neighborhoods that the programs were designed to reach. The tactics recalled those of the old political machine. Local agencies were created, many of them in storefronts. They were staffed by professionals who offered residents help in finding jobs, in obtaining welfare, or in securing other public services. Neighborhood leaders were sought out and hired as "community workers" to draw large numbers of people into the new programs, and in that way to spread the federal largesse. It made little difference whether the funds were appropriated under delinquency-prevention, mental-health, antipoverty, or model-cities legislation; in the ghettos and barrios, the programs looked very much alike.

In short, the national administration was revivifying the traditional strategy of urban politics: offering jobs and services to build party loyalty.[67] But it was not altogether as simple as that. To field these programs, the federal government had to take a unique initiative. It had to establish a direct relationship between the national government and the ghettos, bypassing both state and local governments. That state governments were ignored by national Democratic administrations hardly requires explanation. A number of northern states were controlled by Republicans, and in the South the controlling Democrats could hardly be expected to cooperate in new programs for blacks. But administrations in many of the big northern cities, traditional Democratic strongholds, were also bypassed, at least in the early years of the Great Society, a clear mark of the concern felt by national leaders over the rising number of blacks and Hispanics in the cities, and the failure of urban political organizations to incorporate them.

This was not the first time that shifting political alignments in the United States prompted federal action to undercut established relationships among levels of government. Federal civil rights legislation, for example, restructured the political order of the Old South despite the resistance of southern state and local governments. The New Deal Democratic administration had also sometimes bypassed recalcitrant state governments in order to channel grants-in-aid directly to the party's urban strongholds. But in the sixties it was these very Democratic strongholds that had become recalcitrant. Federal officials viewed city government as an obstacle to be gotten around if the new funds were to reach blacks and Hispanics. Therefore, the money was given to a host of intermediaries, including new antipoverty community action agencies in the ghettos (75 percent of the antipoverty programs were conducted by private agencies, according to the Advisory Commission on Intergovernmental Relations). And even when funds were funneled into regular city agencies, specific guidelines were imposed on their use.

Little of this was mapped out in advance, but neither was it random. Federal officials were feeling their way, step by step, casting about for a means of dealing with political problems in the cities. When controversies flared, the federal government generally retreated, especially in cities where white ethnic political organizations were still firmly entrenched. Some of the controversy over the Great Society programs grew out of the feature of the programs which bypassed local government, for local officials were hardly happy to have the substantial patronage and publicity of the new programs escape their control. They became outraged, however, when the new agencies then began to use federal funds to put pressure on regular municipal agencies in an effort to redirect benefits to the ghettos. Community workers and legal services attorneys were hired to badger housing inspectors and to pry loose welfare payments. Later the new federally funded agencies even began to organize the poor to picket welfare departments or to boycott school systems.[68] Local political leaders depended on the distribution of these services to traditional white constituents in order to maintain their coalitions. That they reacted with indignation to federal efforts to reorganize city politics was hardly startling.

Just as disturbing to big-city politicians, "nonpartisan" voter registration drives were launched in the ghettos under the first of the programs, inaugurated in 1962 under the Juvenile Delinquency and

Youth Control Act. More black voters meant larger pluralities for the national Democratic party, but they presented local white incumbent politicians with a new and threatening constituency. To such local leaders, voter registration in the ghettos seemed an incredible way to deal with juvenile delinquency or mental illness or poverty, and they were quick to say so. But as a device to promote a modest shift in the political balance between voting constituencies, it was not incredible at all.

Most revealing for our argument, local politicians prevailed in the contest over voter registration. The flagship of the Great Society was the Economic Opportunity Act of 1964, and it inaugurated a series of programs for the ghettos, including legal services, community action, job training, and Head Start. In short order, however, a coalition of big-city mayors and their congressional allies secured legislative language explicitly prohibiting voter registration activities in federal poverty programs (and also ceding greater control over the programs to local officials). As a result, the "war on poverty" programs did virtually everything and anything. But one thing they did not and could not do was voter registration. Fearful of local political challenges, Democratic and Republican mayors alike lobbied Congress for explicit prohibitions on voter registration activities by antipoverty agencies. Instead of serving as mobilizing vehicles for the national party, in short, the local parties kept the gates closed, and they used the apparatus of voter registration to do it. Nor did things much change once the turmoil of the 1960s subsided. Local Democratic organizations (including local Democratic organizations run by black mayors who commanded secure majorities), continued to resist the conflict and uncertainty associated with new voters. And as the growing suburbs became more important than the central cities in Democratic calculations, and inner-city protests and riots ended after 1968, national Democrats lost interest in mobilizing the new minority voters as well.

The Democratic apparatus to sustain voter participation was not working. The unions did little to enroll new black and Hispanic voters, or the poor and working-class women who were entering the work force. Nor did the local Democratic parties.[69] Instead, local officials who presided over voter registration used these procedures to maintain a narrow and reliable electorate, a pattern brought to light in the course of the voter registration war that emerged in the early 1980s and is described in the next chapter. Even black mayors, once they were in office, relied on restrictive procedures to maintain the electorate that had put them there.

True, during the 1960s, civil rights protests and litigation had resulted in the elimination of de jure tests of eligibility: poll taxes, literacy tests, and residency requirements exceeding thirty days before an election. The formal right to register was won, conditioned only on people being citizens, of age, domiciled, and free of felony convictions. Through the 1970s and 1980s, however, de facto administrative barriers remained, and state and local party officials defended them. There was still only one registration office in many counties, and these offices rarely remained open after working hours. Few election boards were willing to set up satellite registration centers in poor neighborhoods. These arrangements created obstacles to registration that of course were far more difficult for poorer and less educated people to surmount.

In sum, the New Deal electoral coalition splintered in the postwar years, in part because it was constructed on the foundations inherited from the system of 1896. Eventually, those foundations began to give way. Party competition was restored in much of the country, and restrictions on the franchise were weakened. There will never again be a national party system predicated on the one-party oligarchy that governed the feudal political economy of the Old South. Nor will there ever again be a Democratic party politics predicated on the industrial political economy of the North. But the party apparatus inherited from the past remains fixed: it is unable to stop the hemorrhaging of its old constituencies, and it is both ill-placed and unwilling to enlist a new electorate from the enlarging reservoir of nonvoters in the new working class. We concluded that the problem of low voting by poorer and minority people resulted from the combined effect of deterrents and demobilization.

Part Two

Experiment in Democracy

(With the assistance of Jo-Anne Chasnow)

CHAPTER SEVEN

The Welfare State and Voter Registration Mobilization

*T*he remainder of this book is about a project we began in 1982, with the goal of making registering to vote a part of the application process in social agencies serving poorer people: Whether at day care centers or public assistance agencies, human service workers would, as part of their regular duties, offer to register their clients to vote. We chose an organizational name to reflect that goal: Human Service Employees Registration and Voter Education, or Human SERVE. A decade later, Congress enacted and the president signed the National Voter Registration Act of 1993, which required the states to offer to register people at a range of agencies serving the poor and disabled, as well as when they get or renew drivers' licenses. It was this last provision that gave the Act its tag name, "motor voter." The Act also required states to allow people to register by mail. Finally, state officials were prohibited from purging people from the rolls for not voting.

The chapters that follow do not constitute a full legislative history of the Act or of the contributions made to its passage by a variety of voting rights organizations. Rather—and we emphasize this limitation—we concentrate on our own work at Human SERVE, and try to show how our experiences bear on certain suppositions regarding the process of reform. We treat Human SERVE's programs as a series of experiments guided by theories of political change, and try to assess whether theory is consistent with what in fact happened.

Registering Clients of the Welfare State

Reagan's election in 1980 was ominous for American welfare state policies. To be sure, Carter had already initiated measures to restrain program growth. But Reagan's agenda called for radical cutbacks in major social programs. As that became clear, the question was whether grassroots resistance would develop around the country.

In the late spring of 1982, we attended a national meeting of grassroots organizers called by the Food Research Action Center (FRAC), which worked to expand participation by poorer people in federal nutritional programs, especially food stamps. FRAC evolved out of the Great Society's community action and antipoverty legal services programs, and maintained close contacts with antipoverty activists throughout the country.

During the two days of discussions, organizers reported on their efforts to resist cuts in social programs. Welfare rights organizing in one place, tenant organizing in another place, a hunger coalition in still another, and so on. The descriptions and discussions were spirited, but none of the projects struck us as having the potential scale needed to turn back the Reagan initiatives.

But then, over lunch, Sanford Newman, a former antipoverty legal services attorney, described an organization he had formed several years earlier called Project VOTE!, which recruited and trained volunteers with clipboards to register people to vote on the lines in unemployment and welfare offices, or at check-cashing facilities where vouchers were exchanged for food stamps, or on lines at churches (which sometimes stretched for several blocks) where mainly women with children waited to be given federal surplus cheese as part of Reagan's effort to reduce federal agricultural surpluses. Newman marched up and down between the luncheon tables, passed out leaflets, gave a running rap about how benefits were going to be cut, and distributed clipboards, pens, and registration forms while exhorting everyone to sign up and vote in order to save the social programs. Project VOTE! was using this method to register thousands.

Newman's strategy interested us because he was registering recipients of the means-tested programs by warning them of threats to their benefits. A typical leaflet read like this:

POLITICIANS ARE CUTTING
Welfare
Food Stamps
Unemployment Benefits
Medicaid
Social Security
Disability
Legal Services
Housing

REGISTER AND VOTE
TO SAVE THESE PROGRAMS

Still, we thought the strategy was limited. To be sure, social program sites were full of unregistered people. But to register millions of people in welfare and unemployment waiting rooms would have required many more volunteer canvassers than could possibly be found. Here the Christian Right clearly had the advantage; it had an institutional infrastructure, a network of thousands of churches, through which to mobilize new voters.

Was there a comparable infrastructure to mobilize the beneficiaries of the social programs? The answer seemed obvious to us: the welfare state itself. Public workers could register their clients in welfare, food stamps, Medicaid, and unemployment agencies. Workers in the tens of thousands of private social agencies—settlement houses, day care and senior centers, family planning agencies, community health centers, and diverse community-based organizations—could do the same. The nonprofit social service sector alone had a scale commensurate with Christian Right church networks. As voter registration sites, the social programs in both the public and private sectors had the scale to help compensate for the Democratic party's failure to reach out to the recomposing working class.

Would human service workers be motivated to participate? The new class war threatened the values and material interests of human service personnel. Groups so threatened would surely want to fight back, especially if the fight-back strategy was as readily within reach as arranging for voter registration forms to be filled out in waiting rooms or at reception desks.

That left the question of whether human service workers had the authority to register clients. Even without the sanction of department heads, the tens of thousands of public workers in welfare, unemployment, and hospital settings were within their rights if they registered clients on their own time: before the doors opened, or in waiting rooms during coffee or lunch breaks, or on compensatory time, and even at their desks, if no one in charge seemed to mind. All sorts of workers could participate: elevator operators in hospitals, eligibility specialists in welfare, counselors in unemployment agencies. The only restriction was that the registration process had to be nonpartisan so that public workers would not risk violating the Intergovernmental Relations Act (the Hatch Act).

But what most interested us at the time was the possibility that the private agency sector could be mobilized, and mobilized rapidly. We thought the leaders of prominent nonprofit agency networks—day care, family planning, family and children's services, settlement houses—would react favorably to the proposal that they build an electoral defense of the welfare state by registering their clients to vote at reception/intake desks. The most important women's social service network, the Planned Parenthood Federation of America (PPFA), was already doing it. The national office was distributing to clinic affiliates voter registration manuals, posters, and buttons that had been prepared by Linda Davidoff, vice president for public affairs. President Faye Wattleton

> urged affiliates to intensify existing efforts to register voters. Nonpartisan voter registration is a public service of value both to the community and to the affiliate. . . . In 1982, the New York City affiliate registered 4,000; the Ohio affiliate registered 1,000. Dutchess-Ulster and Granger-Sullivan affiliates in upstate New York registered 300 in September."[1]

The packet also contained a legal opinion from private counsel that voter registration activities would not jeopardize the nonprofit tax status of clinics, provided that the activity was scrupulously nonpartisan, an opinion that was confirmed when the Maryland affiliate obtained a similar ruling from the Internal Revenue Service.

We thought that this dual strategy—public workers and nonprofit agencies—might gain important support from organizations with which many human service workers identified, or to which they belonged. Why wouldn't national human service associations, such as the National Association of Social Workers, the American Public Health Association, and the American Public Welfare Association, urge their members to participate? With its government contracts and grants in jeopardy, the nonprofit sector needed allies, and the population they served was a good place to find them. And why wouldn't public sector unions urge their members to participate, once the ease of agency-based registration was explained? Public sector unions faced not only cutbacks, but also the threat of privatization and union-busting. So the unions too needed allies, and again the people who depended on public services seemed logical recruits. If the leaders of nonprofit organizations and unions endorsed and promoted the strategy, it seemed to us that their more activist members would find ways to make it happen.

It also seemed likely that women's and civil rights organizations would support the strategy because it suggested a way to get women and minorities more fully registered. The growth of the welfare state converged with the movement of middle-class women into the occupational world and with their growing politicization. Indeed, more than half of the employed middle-class women in the early 1980s worked in the health/education/welfare complex. This meant that there was a large overlap between the women workers in the social agencies and the membership of women's organizations. For example, Alice Rossi, past president of the American Sociological Association, analyzed the first National Women's Conference at Houston in 1972 and found that 72 percent of the delegates were employed either by government or by nonprofit social welfare organizations in the education, health, and social service sectors.[2] Given the Republican assault on women's rights—reproductive rights in particular—it seemed to us that the leaders of women's organizations would welcome a strategy of "women registering women" in the human service agencies where so many of their members worked.[3]

The growth of the welfare state had also provided an important avenue of employment and upward mobility for blacks and Hispanics, especially in the years after the protests of the 1960s. We guessed that these workers made up a large fraction of the membership of civil rights organizations, such as the NAACP. Given the Republican hostility to civil rights, we expected these organizations to want to encourage their members in social service agencies to sign up the huge numbers of minority clients. And if black human-service workers took the lead, many white human-service workers would follow. In sum, if leaders in social welfare, in service sector unions, and in civil rights and women's groups all beamed the message to public workers and voluntary social agencies that they should register their clients, we thought there was a reasonable chance that they might do it.

In 1983, we incorporated Human SERVE and began raising money to finance organizers in the most populous states to promote "agency-based" voter registration. Our goal was to mobilize staff members to register their clients to vote in tens of thousands of agencies and even to make voter registration a routine part of the application/intake process. Hulbert James, a black activist from the civil rights movement, whom we first came to know when he headed the New York City welfare rights movement in the late 1960s, agreed to become executive director.

Above all, the moment seemed right to attempt a mobilization. It was not just that human service workers had the institutional capacity and authority to register millions. It was also that Reagan's reelection was spurring activism on the right and the left, and much of that activism was being channeled into canvassing among the unregistered. Indeed, something like a voter registration war was breaking out.

Voter Registration War

The 1982 recession converted the usual election-year skirmishing over voter registration into all-out campaigns. In response to the highest unemployment since the Great Depression, midterm turnout rose for the first time in two decades, reaching sixty-four million, or ten million more than in 1978, and swelling the Democratic House vote by six million. The additional voters were mainly blacks, Hispanics, and industrial workers, and the rise in turnout was greatest in the Midwest and South. Republican governors were replaced with Democrats in the large industrial states of Ohio, Michigan, New York, and

Texas, as well as in Wisconsin and New Mexico; a number of black mayors were also elected; and Republicans lost enough economically hard-hit congressional districts to give the Democrats a midterm net gain of twenty-six House seats.

Many pundits read the returns to mean that a broad upsurge was underway among what the *Congressional Quarterly* called have-not voters. "The question [for 1984] and the rest of the decade is whether this upsurge in the 'have-not' vote will continue."[4] Virtually every major political strategist predicted that overall turnout would rise sharply in 1984, by as much as ten million, and that the groundswell would be made up largely of members of "marginal groups."[5] The *New York Times* political columnist James Reston said that "what Reagan is in the process of doing is to scare the voters and wake up the dropouts, and encourage them to register and vote. This, no doubt, is a contribution to democracy and the Democrats, but not necessarily what the President had in mind for the Republican Party."[6]

Conservatives were alarmed, to say the least. Kevin Phillips, the strategist of the "emerging Republican majority," warned that the latent voting power of poorer and minority people was the single most important force that could potentially deter a Republican realignment, and that the economic hardship inflicted by Reagan's conservative economic program could bring that force to the polls:

> To protect transfer payments and government spending programs, low-income and minority turnout has the potential to surge. These voters could come to the polls to protest conservative economic policies tailored to redistribute income toward upper rather than lower income groups. *Of all the trends that will affect the 1980s, this could be the most important.*[7]

The Christian Right saw the danger. A Christian Right voter registration effort had begun after the 1964 Goldwater defeat, and it grew during the 1970s, spurred by the formation of national religious/political organizations, including Jerry Falwell's Moral Majority in 1979. Registration and voting levels among evangelicals had been low, partly because they had traditionally spurned secular political action in favor of social change through mass religious conversion.

After 1964, the Christian Right consciously adopted the tactics of the civil rights movement by making the church the staging area for voter registration drives and political education, and even for mass demonstrations and civil disobedience over issues such as reproductive rights.[8] Fundamentalist clergy began registering people in church auditoriums, called upon them to vote, and told them for whom to vote, in Sunday sermons, television broadcasts, talk radio, and direct mail. Moral Majority claimed that cooperating churches registered four to eight million white evangelicals in the pre-1980 election period. A Harris poll gave a figure of between one and two million.[9]

The threat the have-nots posed to Reagan's reelection led Gary Jarmin, legislative director of the lobbying group Christian Voice, to warn religious leaders that they would have to register two million fundamentalists in 1984 "just to stay even" with the anticipated surge on the left. To do so, conservative religious leaders launched a national umbrella organization, the American Coalition for Traditional Values—an entity that included the Moral Majority; Christian Voice; and televangelists such as Jimmy Swaggart, Jim Bakker, and Rex Hubbard. The Christian Right strategy included mass mailings to clergy in three hundred cities in twenty-five states about how to organize registration drives—for example, by forming "good government" committees in their churches and by arranging to have church members deputized as voter registrars. The press reported some three hundred training sessions with clergy and laypersons were held in roughly two hundred cities. And Republican Senator Paul Laxalt wrote to thousands of fundamentalist ministers in August 1984 asking that they help register Republican voters in their congregations.[10] Finally, leading evangelists in the "electronic church" urged their audiences to register and vote, and the Christian Coalition purportedly supplied thousands of churches with thirty million "voter guides."

Where the Christian Right saw danger, other groups saw opportunity. Civil rights organizations—such as the NAACP, the southern-based Voter Education Project, and the Southern Regional Council—intensified voter registration activity among blacks. In 1976, the National Coalition on Black Voter Participation was formed. Its voter registration arm, called Operation Big Vote, stimulated, funded, and coordinated drives among black organizations throughout the country. Similarly, in 1974, low rates of registration among Mexican-Americans spurred the formation of the Southwest Voter Education

Project, with the goal of registering Hispanics throughout the Southwest and in California. The Midwest Voter Education Project was created in Chicago in 1982 to reach Hispanics, and the National Puerto Rican/Hispanic Voter Participation Project was formed in 1983. Canvassing efforts gained momentum from analyses concluding that the number of unregistered blacks in a number of key states far exceeded Reagan's margins in 1980 and from evidence that the surge of blacks and other "have-nots" to the polls in 1982 had been decisive in key congressional and gubernatorial races.

Many campaign organizations, such as the Churches' Committee for Voter Registration, sponsored by northern Protestant denominations, and the NAACP adopted Project VOTE!'s strategy of registering the unemployed and welfare recipients. Because so many of the beneficiaries of social welfare programs were unregistered, this strategy was far more efficient than traditional and labor-intensive door-knocking drives. Furthermore, volunteers felt safer in agency waiting rooms than in slum and ghetto neighborhoods, where residents also felt unsafe opening their doors to strangers.

Voter registration also attracted grassroots organizations that were attempting to build mass-based permanent organizations among minorities and lower-income whites. ACORN, which had grown out of the welfare mothers movement in the 1960s, is one example. It focused mainly on registering poorer and minority people in the slums and ghettos of such industrial cities as New York, Detroit, St. Louis, and Bridgeport. The Citizen Action network, which focused on white working-class and lower-middle-class constituencies, also launched registration drives in about ten northern states.

The United States Public Interest Research Group (PIRG) and the United States Student Association targeted college students. Some peace and environmental groups joined in registration drives. The Women's Vote Project, representing over sixty organizations, kicked off a national voter drive in 1984 on Susan B. Anthony's birthday with the slogan "Its a Man's World, Unless Women Vote!" After Geraldine Ferraro was nominated by the Democrats as the first female vice-presidential candidate, enthusiasm among women's groups for voter registration soared.

Perhaps because many of these left organizing efforts had roots in the protest movements of the 60s, they sometimes acquired a movement spirit. ACORN mounted direct action and civil disobedience campaigns against obstructive voter registration officials in Bridgeport and St. Louis who refused to deputize volunteer registrars. In Cincinnati, a female Project VOTE! organizer who was canvassing in a welfare waiting room was arrested and strip-searched, setting off a furor. The NAACP mounted an "Overground Railroad" march under the banner, "Bury Voter Apathy," which began in Richmond on August 20, 1984, and ended in New York City on Labor Day. Some 35,000 people were reportedly registered in urban black neighborhoods along the way.

Human SERVE developed two similar campaigns. Although we were most focused on mobilizing public workers and voluntary agencies, we wanted to exploit the potential of other cause-oriented social movement organizations that had caught the registration fever. Consequently, we organized two national campaigns in which people could participate by volunteering to canvass in welfare and unemployment offices on the Project VOTE! model. One initiative, called the "Freedom Summer '84 Voter Registration Campaign," was undertaken jointly with the United States Student Association (USSA), under the direction of Penny Von Eschen of Human SERVE. USSA enlisted sixty students who in turn recruited volunteers for ten-week drives in unemployment and welfare offices in sixty-three cities in twenty-three states, and Human SERVE raised money from donors to provide them with $1,500 stipends. We persuaded graduate schools of social work to recruit and finance another thirty-one students and we enlisted local YWCAs, Planned Parenthood agencies, churches, grassroots community groups, NAACP chapters, unions, and cooperating voter registration campaigns to provide the student coordinators with free offices and telephones, and lodging. These Freedom Summer student coordinators organized local voter-registration coalitions or staffed existing ones; recruited hundreds of volunteers to canvass in welfare state waiting rooms; and generated local publicity celebrating the twentieth anniversary of Mississippi Freedom Summer while drawing the media's spotlight to persisting voter registration barriers. By the end of the campaign, they had signed up 230,000 people, often by flamboyant tactics, as when they called themselves "freedom riders" and registered thousands of people on transit authority buses serving the poorer districts of Houston.

Human SERVE also launched an "October 4 National Day of Voter Registration" under the banner "Millions More October 4." The idea was to encourage social movement organizations to recruit their supporters to spend October 4 registering people in unemployment offices, welfare centers, food stamp offices, hospital outpatient waiting rooms, public housing projects, and transportation stops serving poorer neighborhoods. The supporters would also be encouraged to write to ten of those they had registered urging them to vote and to call them with reminders a day or two before election day. "Register 10, Write 10, and Call 10." The proposal was quickly endorsed by some eighty-odd national organizations (student, religious, civil rights, environmental, peace, women, labor, and grassroots groups), and meetings were held in Washington, D.C., during the summer of 1984 to deal with the logistics by which these different organizations could activate their constituencies. The National Organization for Women, for example, sent out a letter to its chapters announcing that "NOW has joined 56 peace, environmental, and other progressive groups for a last minute blitz to register a million more October 4."

On October 4, an editorial in the *New York Times* commented approvingly that "thousands of volunteers are fanning out today all over the country to register voters." The Democratic Socialists of America organized their affiliates under the slogan "Last Chance Voter Registration Mobilization." The slogan was also used by the San Francisco Nuclear Weapons Freeze and the Bay Area Central American Peace Campaign. In New York City, PIRG organizers and students took the lead and, together with human service volunteers, the Gray Panthers, and peace organizations (such as the Women's International League for Peace and Freedom, the Committee in Solidarity with the People of El Salvador, Mobilization for Survival, Freeze Vote '84, and Women's Action for Nuclear Disarmament), they completed 62,000 cards in a single day, causing the head of the elections board to complain in the *New York Times* about registration "fanatics." On the same day, social work faculty and students from the University of Indiana/ Purdue, together with local human service workers, joined with the Indianapolis Citizen Action chapter to bus 4,000 low-income and minority people to the elections office. When the doors closed at midnight, the thousand or so still unregistered jammed in, forcing the office to process applications until 4:00 A.M., and producing a spate of front-page publicity about Indiana's archaic registration laws.

As election day approached, the war heated up. In a last-minute warning, Falwell mailed out a "1984 Election Alarm" because "America may be just days from disaster" at the polls. He enclosed an Associated Press story about the October 4 campaign ("Plans are being made by 70 national groups to send 100,000 volunteers into the streets of America to register millions in a single day at work sites, unemployment and welfare offices, day care centers, schools, hospitals, universities, subway and bus stops and housing projects."), and he called attention especially to "how many they plan to register in *one single day*."[11]

The *Congressional Quarterly* thought that this was a time of "potentially historic significance" for the Democratic party: "With the possible exception of fundamentalist Christians, [the Republican party] has no new, reliably Republican voting bloc to mobilize. The likely GOP voters, for the most part, have already been voting."[12] Nevertheless, the Democratic National Committee did nothing except issue press releases announcing multimillion-dollar registration campaigns that never materialized. Key politicians in the Democratic Leadership Council had rushed to define the 1980 election as evidence of a "sea change" in public opinion, a shift to the right that the Democratic party could ignore only at the peril of precipitating a Republican realignment. Downplaying the association of the Democratic party with labor, minorities, and women was a crucial part of the defensive strategy that developed. Moreover, party leaders feared that registering more blacks and Hispanics would help Jesse Jackson's candidacy in the presidential primaries, and endanger Mondale. Jackson made this threat seem real enough by making voter registration a centerpiece of his campaign rallies, and his efforts received wide publicity. But even after winning the nomination, Mondale decided against a registration strategy despite a 250-page study written by his aides which concluded that "the only way Mondale can win is by pitching his appeal to the white working class and minorities, not the middle class."[13] Mike Ford, Mondale's field director, argued that a Mondale victory "is nearly impossible with the current electorate. . . . We must consider dramatic and perhaps high-risk strategies," and he urgently recommended that $12 million be spent to register five to six million new black, Hispanic, and union voters.[14] But these recommendations were spurned in favor of a get-out-the-vote campaign among the existing electorate, mainly the middle class and suburbanites. Democratic party leaders thus turned away from the possibility of mobilizing a mass opposition among the less-well-off. They did not raise issues that would attract them, such as denouncing widening inequalities. And they did not organize voter registration and get-out-the-vote campaigns to bring in new voters.

The Republican party, however, did not sit on its hands, its historic preference for low turnout elections notwithstanding. For one thing, the party was now allied with the Christian Right movement, and the insurgents from that movement had penetrated the party to become its activist wing. Much as the Democrats had been pushed by the movements of the 1930s and 1960s, so were the Republicans pushed to mobilize. They were also no doubt disturbed by the extravagant claims made by the Democrats about their registration drives and by the pundits who warned that a have-not tide was running.

Even so, the Republicans had to be very selective in their mobilizing efforts. Republican pollster Lance Terrance had warned that the downward tilt of the unregistered pool meant that "for every new voter the Republicans pick up, the Democrats pick up two."[15] Helen Cameron, head of the Reagan-Bush registration effort, complained that even in heavily Republican areas, telephone surveys found only 10 to 18 percent of the unregistered were Reagan supporters.[16] Traditional registration methods, such as setting up tables in shopping malls, could thus boomerang, producing more Democratic than Republican registrants. Democratic strategists crowed that while the Republicans were registering the "needles," Democrats were registering the "haystack."[17]

However, given the huge amounts of money available to them, Republican organizers could turn to computer technology and phone banks to solve the problem of finding the needles. The chairperson of the Ohio Republican party announced that $455,000 would be spent before the 1984 election in "43 of 83 counties, the ones that are at least 40 percent Republican":

> We have computerized lists in the precincts, and every nonregistered voter is called. Forty phone callers ask three questions: Is the country going in the right or wrong direction? Are you for President Reagan or not? And do you consider yourself philosophically more Republican or Democrat? And if they answer these three questions right, we send out canvassers to sign them up.[18]

Republicans also merged and purged computer tapes from DMVs and from boards of elections to identify people who owned late model cars but weren't on the voter registration lists. And they matched tapes to identify unregistered people who subscribed to financial magazines or lived in affluent neighborhoods. These upscale unregistered voters were then called by phone banks, and if they identified themselves as Republicans, paid or volunteer registrars visited them.[19] By the 1984 election, Republican strategists claimed to have recruited 55,000 volunteers who made 2.5 million phone calls and follow-up visits to homes, with somewhere between 1.7 and 2 million new registrants, at a total cost of $8 million.[20] Costs in some states ran as high as $5 to $7 per registrant. High-tech pinpointing, Edsall and Johnson remarked in the *Washington Post*, had become "a 1984 version of the American political machine."[21]

Our point for now is simply this. The 1984 presidential campaign provoked the largest voter registration mobilization in American history, whether measured by the money spent, the number of organizations engaged, or the variety of innovative approaches employed. Analysts and activists everywhere concluded that voter registration was the key not just to Reagan's fate, but to the future of American politics.

Mobilizing Voluntary Social Agencies

This political context encouraged us to believe that human service workers could be persuaded to register their clients. To succeed, the strategy had to be disseminated rapidly to workers across the country. Frank Reissman published a short version of the plan in the December 1982 issue of his *Ideas for Action* newsletter, which reached many human service activists.

VOTER REGISTRATION:
AN OLD STRATEGY WITH NEW PROMISE

Many groups, as they cast about for ways to resist the corporate/New Right/ Christian Right/Republican alliance, are turning to voter registration. But the problem is that these groups cannot recruit enough volunteer registrars to make a serious political difference.

There are millions of low-income and minority people who are beneficiaries of the social welfare programs. A huge proportion of them is not registered to vote. They interact regularly, however, with tens of thousands of human service workers in public and voluntary social agencies. We think this interaction provides an unprecedented opportunity to reach and register these nonvoters.

The objective would be to mobilize thousands of professional and clerical workers to conduct voter registration in the waiting rooms and on the lines, and at reception/intake desks of the social agencies where they work— hospitals, family service agencies, welfare centers, agencies for the disabled, settlement houses, day care centers, unemployment offices, public housing projects, community health clinics, senior centers, planned parenthood offices, and kindred social welfare settings. By this means, it should be possible to register substantial numbers before the 1984 presidential election.

The organizational connections between human service workers and beneficiaries can also be used to promote voter turnout. As the election approaches, waiting rooms can be converted to voter education projects with nonpartisan materials available on the voting records and policy positions of candidates, and on polling places. Staff members can also urge beneficiaries to exercise their democratic right to vote.

Reissman also sent out a press release announcing that we had written a full version of the plan which would appear in the Winter 1983 issue of his *Social Policy* magazine. On January 2, in a front-page article in the Sunday *New York Times* under the headline "New Voter Drive Aims at Unemployed and Welfare Recipients,"[22] Robert Pear referred to the upcoming article and treated the strategy as if it were already underway: "Social workers and civil rights groups are organizing a nationwide voter registration drive designed to encourage greater political participation by the millions of people who are unemployed or who receive government benefits such as food stamps and welfare." It contained these quotes:

Cloward and Piven: "The welfare state agencies aggregate large numbers of nonvoters who are otherwise dispersed and difficult to reach, and it is a strategic time to register them because the Reagan administration's policies raise issues of urgent concern to large numbers of nonvoters."

Mary Ann Quaranta, president of the National Association of Social Workers and Dean of the Fordham School of Social Work: "This imaginative campaign for empowering poor people will be supported by workers and supervisors of numerous public and private welfare agencies."

Mitchell I. Ginsberg, former Welfare Commissioner of New York City: "I support the plan by Cloward and Piven, but I doubt that it will work."

Lawyers at the Merit Systems Protection Board, a Federal agency that interprets the Hatch Act: "Federal employees, and state and local employees paid in part with federal funds can engage in voter registration provided it is nonpartisan."

Joseph Madison, national director of voter registration for the NAACP: "When people are standing in line to get cheese and butter or unemployment compensation, you don't have to tell them how to vote. They know how to vote."

George W. Strake, chairman of the Texas Republican Party: "There are not a lot of Republicans on the welfare lines."

Reactions were quick in coming. On the one side, Howard Phillips of the Conservative Digest called Piven to complain that if nonprofit social agencies registered their clients, it was nothing more than a ploy to help the Democratic party, to which she replied, "Shouldn't Democrats have a chance to register?" That nonprofit agencies would even contemplate registering clients was, Phillips subsequently said in an editorial in the *Conservative Digest,* the fault of David Stockman, Reagan's Management and Budget director, who had not issued "regulations which would prevent the assignment of public money to non-profit elitists heavily immersed in ideological advocacy and organizing."[23] This was an opening salvo by the Republican right wing in what would be a continuing campaign to "defund the left" by enacting severe restrictions on advocacy and lobbying activities by nongovernmental agencies if they wanted to preserve their nonprofit tax status and their federal grants.

On the other side, we received a letter from Sherrod Brown, the Ohio Secretary of State who had been elected on the 1982 upsurge for the Democratic party:

> I have read with growing excitement the account in the *New York Times* of January 2 about your plan to use social service agencies to register people to

vote. . . . I would like to explore with you the possibility of using Ohio as a
laboratory to try an intensive voter registration and get-out-the-vote campaign. Ohio demographics would seem to make it an excellent test; Ohio laws
make the project feasible; sponsorship by the Secretary of State would assure
nonpartisanship and could resolve many of the problems about government
employees being registrars.

In New York City, Horris Morris, the black executive director of
the Greater New York Fund and United Way, a confederation of 371
nonprofit social service agencies in the metropolitan area, wrote to say
that he would make his mailing lists available to us, and he then wrote
his members that "the offer of voter registration services in tens of
thousands of agencies across the nation may be the most important
way in which we can build support for the social and health programs."[24] Victor Gotbaum, head of District Council 37-AFSCME,
with its locals of human service workers, obtained an opinion from
James A. Krauskopf, head of the city's Human Resources Administration: "Employees are permitted during their free time to assist in
nonpartisan voter registration drives in waiting rooms and on lines
with willing client listeners." Jack John Olivero, Executive Director of
the Puerto Rican Legal Defense Fund, and chair of the board of directors of the Community Service Society (CSS), the oldest, wealthiest,
and most prestigious voluntary social service agency in New York
City (or for that matter, in the country), arranged for some initial financial support from CSS. David Hunter, executive director of the
Stern Family Fund and the leader of the foundation world's small left
wing, agreed to begin funding the strategy, as did Richard Boone at
the Field Foundation and Colin Greer at New World. Bernard Shiff-
man, executive director of the Community Council of Greater New
York, also a confederation of hundreds of voluntary social service
agencies, offered to open a bank account so that we could receive tax-
deductible funds.

Given these favorable responses, we incorporated Human SERVE
in 1983, and began trying to enlist the support of national organizations of human service workers and agencies that we thought would
be crucial to legitimate and disseminate the strategy in their newsletters and conferences. We held two Washington, D.C., meetings attended by forty different human service organizations. We met indi-

vidually with organizational presidents and executive directors, and they sometimes invited us to speak at board meetings. Our message was simple: to protect social programs, it was necessary to build an electoral defense by "helping to enlarge the political influence of social welfare beneficiaries."

Key organizations quickly authorized their presidents or executive directors to join Human SERVE's board of directors:

Council on Social Work Education
American Public Health Association
National Association of Social Workers
Affiliated Leadership League of and for the Blind
American Orthopsychiatric Association
National Board of the YWCA
Children's Foundation (an organization of family day care
     workers)
Wider Opportunities for Women
Planned Parenthood Federation of America
National Assembly of National Voluntary Health and Social
     Welfare Organizations
Columbia University School of Social Work

Dozens of other organizations signed on as supporters—such as the American Coalition of Citizens with Disabilities, the Child Welfare League of America, the American Nurses Association, the National Family Planning and Reproductive Health Association, and the National Abortion Federation.

These national organizations, in turn, ran dozens of stories and editorials in their newsletters about the legitimacy and importance of doing voter registration routinely in agencies as a public service. Human SERVE national staff worked closely with their publicity directors to help tailor the voter registration message to different membership constituencies.

Several national organizations assigned staff to promote the strategy among affiliates: Debra Livingston was assigned by the National Association of Social Workers; Rich Gilbert by the American Public Health Association; Linda Davidoff by the national Planned Parenthood Federation. The national organizations arranged for us to speak at their regional and national conferences. When schedules were already firmed up, Human SERVE staff called the plenary speakers, explained the strategy, and asked them to say something supportive during their time at the microphones. Many did. Sometimes there was an unexpected plenary opening. The American Public Health Association had invited the Democratic candidate, Walter Mondale, to address their 1984 convention attendees. At the last minute, Mondale, in the thick of a difficult campaign, dropped out. Association officials asked Frances Piven to fill in. So, carefully instructed, she marched to the speaker's platform to the accompaniment of a color guard and brass band and tried to persuade the thousands of assembled public health professionals that every community health center and family planning and hospital clinic in America should become a voter registration site. "The polls show dramatically," she said, "that the strongest support of health and welfare services is among low-income and minority women. And if we want to register these women in large numbers, we have to use health clinics and battered women's shelters and day care and family planning clinics."

Audiences often seemed dumbstruck. Sometimes they erupted as if at a rally. Overall, there seemed to be a current of excitement, that here was something human service workers could do, hopefully with agency approval, that might make a difference to the fate of the welfare state.

A typical Human SERVE leaflet, reproduced in dozens of national human service newsletters, read this way:

WILL BENEFICIARIES REGISTER?
YES because they've been badly hurt by unemployment and program cuts.
WILL NEW REGISTRANTS VOTE?
YES because first-time registrants turn out more, not less, than long-time voters.
YES because human service workers can help increase turnout by reminding beneficiaries to vote and by distributing lists of polling places.
YES because a wide variety of groups—churches, civil rights groups, civic groups, political parties—will be publicizing the importance of voting in 1984.

THE POSSIBILITIES ARE STAGGERING

"**IF JUST 5,000 OF THE 45,000** graduate and undergraduate social work students each register 200 beneficiaries in field agencies, that's 1,000,000 more on the rolls."

> Arthur Katz, Executive Director
> Council on Social Work Education

"**IF JUST 5,000** (1 IN 20) of the 100,000 members of the NATIONAL AS-SOCIATION OF SOCIAL WORKERS each registered 200, that's another 1,000,000."

> John E. Hansan, Executive Director
> National Association of Social Workers

AND IF JUST 1 IN 20 of the thousands of local health, family planning, and disability agencies register 500 monthly at intake for a year, that would be millions more.

IS AGENCY-BASED REGISTRATION ETHICAL?
PROFESSIONAL? LEGAL?

"**YES** it is ethical to help empower people by encouraging them to exercise their democratic rights. But it wouldn't be if we coerced them or influenced their votes."

> Sara-Alyce P. Wright, Executive Director
> National Board, YWCA

"**YES** voter registration is a professionally sound way to help people over-come their sense of powerlessness."

> Marion F. Langer, Executive Director
> American Orthopsychiatric Association

"**YES** it is permissible under IRS codes for voluntary 501 (c) (3) not-for-profit agencies to register people, provided we do not advocate parties or can-didates."

> Linda Davidoff, Vice-President
> Planned Parenthood Federation of America

"**YES** it is permissible under the Hatch Act for public workers to conduct nonpartisan voter registration on their own time in waiting rooms, or at in-take and at their desks."

> Ira Glasser, Executive Director
> American Civil Liberties Union

Meanwhile, Human SERVE's field staff expanded to cover thirteen states. Organizers were hired in New York, New Jersey, Massachusetts, Pennsylvania, Florida, Ohio, Michigan, Texas, California, and Ore-gon; Human SERVE contributed toward the costs of a Citizen Action organizer already working with local groups in Illinois who agreed to help mobilize voluntary agencies; and it reimbursed the expenses of volunteer organizers in Connecticut, Tennessee, and West Virginia. The field organizers concentrated on forming local coalitions of agencies, especially those affiliated with the national organizations that had endorsed the drive.

To sum up, human service agencies probably registered four or five hundred thousand, not the four or five million we had hoped for. Two national human service organizations actually monitored their affiliates: Planned Parenthood reported 30,000 registered, and the YWCAs 100,000. There were human service voter registration coalitions in a number of cities, including New York, St. Louis, Detroit, San Diego, San Francisco, Los Angeles, and Seattle. At a 1984 rally in Minneapolis, for example, representatives of 125 agencies from across the state announced that 19,500 people had been registered. We would guess that 1,500 agencies participated, although many thousands could have.

Of all the human service groups, social work faculty and students were probably the most active. The two of us personally telephoned all eighty-nine graduate deans of social work in the country, and many of the more than four hundred undergraduate directors, to describe the idea and to ask them to sponsor community-wide meetings of faculty, students, and agency personnel and to pay our expenses to attend as speakers. Many did. Some schools encouraged students who interned in social agencies to try to persuade agency executives to establish application/intake voter registration systems. However, it is our impression that what students mostly did was register people waiting on lines. In March 1983, Kenneth Grossinger, Human SERVE's first staff member, recruited twelve Columbia University School of Social Work students to work the lines with the minister of Harlem's Antioch Baptist Church, who was distributing surplus cheese on a Saturday morning. They registered 1,875 people in four hours, a feat to which the *New York Daily News* devoted a full front-page picture and a full-page article in a Sunday edition. Similarly, social work student groups in such varied places as San Diego, Chattanooga, and Normal, Illinois, each claimed 5,000 or more new registrants, found mainly by canvassing surplus cheese lines. A number of schools of social work were also active in the FREEDOM SUMMER '84 and OCTOBER 4 campaigns which together produced a half million registrants, almost all of them from waiting rooms and lines, but not at reception/intake desks.

Given these relatively bleak results, Human SERVE abandoned the voluntary agency campaign after the 1984 election, except for a renewed effort a decade later after the Republicans had won the House, ending forty years of Democratic dominance. Higher turnout by the Christian Right was apparently one of the reasons (although there is some disagreement about that). With Republicans waving the banner "Contract With America," welfare state programs were again subject to assault. However, the NVRA had become law, and we thought that would legitimate a new effort to mobilize the voluntary sector, so we had another go at it during the 1995–96 presidential campaign, this time with the campaign name ENFRANCHISE AMERICA. We essentially replicated the 1983–84 campaign, with the same results: well-attended Washington, D.C., meetings of representatives of national organizations; dozens of organizational endorsements; many newsletter articles and editorials; much speechifying at meetings and conferences. And again, few were registered.

In sum, the strategy was not implemented. One possible explanation is that it was not communicated widely. We kept track of articles and editorials in newsletters, and it appeared to be a blitz. But in a huge and sprawling field, many local agency personnel may not have noticed.

However, our work in New York City, to which we devoted more organizing resources than elsewhere, suggests that awareness of the strategy was not the problem. The city had something like a social democratic tradition: a large public sector of human service institutions, a dense union movement, and a rich tradition of private sector social service agencies. If the strategy could succeed anywhere, it would be in New York City.

During the 1983–84 effort, Human SERVE had organized many human service meetings, distributed "how-to" leaflets and kits with advice on how agencies could get started, and trained agency staff to be voter registrars. Many agencies endorsed the plan, including the Greater New York Fund and United Way and the Community Council of Greater New York. The Federation of Jewish Philanthrophy in New York City asked all affiliates to develop registration programs:

Federation agencies are not excluded from the effects of government spending cuts. . . . It is imperative we let our legislators know our position. . . . We need your concrete support to achieve our mutual goal of increasing the number of registered voters among those who use your services, but also families and friends of those using your services.[25]

The Federation of Protestant Welfare Agencies sent out the same message:

This year's election will be of particular importance. . . . Major issues such as economic decline, unemployment, the welfare of the poor and social agency financing will be debated. Your agency can participate by offering voter registration services at your reception desk or at intake.[26]

Bruce Vladeck, director of the United Hospital Fund of New York, wrote members that since human services are "highly affected by decisions of our elected officials, I think it is particularly important that hospitals adopt the Human SERVE plan and make voter registration available in our facilities." The League of Disabled Voters and the Interagency Council of the Disabled urged their consortium of agencies to register the disabled and help get them to the polls. The Gray Panthers agreed to stimulate registration in senior centers in poorer and minority neighborhoods. Prominent Democrats on the left of the party, whose careers depended on cross-class coalitions of white middle-class liberals and minorities, spoke out for the agency-based strategy: Ruth Messinger and Ed Wallace, members of the city council; Herman Badillo, the senior Hispanic political leader; Congressman Major Owens and his campaign manager, Bill Lynch; and Carl McCall, New York State Commissioner for Human Rights.

The *Human Services* newsletter, distributed throughout the New York metropolitan region with the motto of "Keeping Human Service Professionals Informed," carried lengthy stories with such headlines as "N.Y. Voter Registration Campaign Launched by 50 Organizations."[27] At one rally, James Farmer, former director of the Congress of Racial Equality and a hero of the civil rights movement, delivered a rousing speech to an audience of three hundred human service workers who *Newsday* reported were "Lining Up Jobless Votes."

Some forty thousand people were registered during this 1983–84 campaign in New York City. All but a few thousand were registered by volunteers who worked with Human SERVE to canvass on lines. Some volunteers were welfare recipients who set up tables in waiting rooms; some were individual human service workers; some were activists in the peace, environmental, or women's movement; some of the most devoted canvassers were from the old left, such as the members of the Women's International League for Peace and Freedom who systematically covered the unemployment offices right up to the election. This unusual influx of volunteers reflected the upsurge of activism across the political spectrum in the 1983–84 period.

But few agencies participated. A string of thirteen family-planning clinics said they had registered about a thousand; eight community health centers made the same claim; visiting nurses completed several hundred forms; Henry Street Settlement, the leader in its field, reported one hundred registered; and so on. Perhaps a hundred agencies made registration a part of their service.

Human SERVE made some subsequent efforts to spur greater participation by agencies in New York City. In 1987, for example, New York staff persuaded executives of the key social service networks to call a one-day conference to discuss agency-based registration. The letter was individually signed by the head of Greater New York Fund/ United Way, the Community Council of Greater New York, the United Jewish Appeal, Federation of Jewish Philanthropies, the Jewish Board of Family and Children's Services, Catholic Charities, Day Care Council, State Communities Aid Association, the Association of Puerto Rican Executives, the Children's Aid Society, United Neighborhood Houses, and the Community Service Society (where the conference was held). About one hundred staff attended, but we could see little evidence that much resulted.

Nor did the agencies in New York City do any better when Human SERVE revived the voluntary agency strategy nationally in advance of the 1996 election. Again, there were many well-attended meetings, many organizational endorsements, much publicity, but little to show for it. In a word, communication was not the problem.

Why were the agencies such reluctant partners? We have thought about that question often. The strategy we proposed seemed to us to require little of their energy and resources and at the same time offered the possibility, at least, of protecting them from an ongoing political assault.

But it was not so simple as that. For one thing, there were currents of opposition in the human service community. Some objected that clients might get the impression that registering was a condition of service. Others felt that registration activities were demeaning and unprofessional. There was also concern that the not-for-profit tax status of the agencies might be jeopardized. And some human service workers were ambivalent about their clients as political allies.

Concurrent with these objections was a pervasive worry about the repercussions of registering clients for the agencies themselves. Directors were often afraid they might antagonize local politicians who influenced their grants and contracts. In New York City, for example, many nonprofit agencies with minority constituencies relied on city subsidies, and they shied away from participation for fear of appearing to take sides in the simmering conflict between Mayor Koch and minority political leaders. For similar reasons, voluntary agencies in Republican districts rarely felt free to participate.

Finally, we ran afoul of federal prohibitions on voter registration, a legacy of the 1960s. A good many agencies that contacted us because they wanted to do voter registration, including antipoverty community action agencies, Head Start, Legal Services, job training, and community health centers, were explicitly prohibited from doing so by federal regulations. As we explained earlier, these laws were demanded by indignant mayors and congressional representatives after some of the early antipoverty programs began mounting voter registration campaigns in poor neighborhoods. On January 4, 1988, the Community Action Agency of Los Angeles issued a special bulletin on "prohibited practices" to remind its various affiliates of the prohibition:

> The purpose of this bulletin is to remind all of the Community Services Block Grant providers of Federal requirements which prohibit agencies from engaging in "any activities to provide voters and prospective voters with transportation to the polls and to provide similar assistance in connection with an election or any voter registration activity.

Still, we think the biggest obstacles were rooted in organizational calculations of risk and advantage. It was all very well for national human service leaders to endorse a voter registration campaign tied to the big political goal of changing the electorate. The directors of particular agencies, however, had reason to hold back. For one thing, the big political goal required a huge campaign, dependent on the efforts, even if they were minimal efforts, of many dispersed organizations. It was easier, and safer, to endorse the campaign and then wait and see if others carried it out. This is, of course, the much talked about "free rider" problem, and we think it was fatal to our campaign.

There are periods when people are so seized by indignation and enthusiasm that the narrow calculus of the free rider is overcome. But we misread the political temperament of the human service organizations to which we were appealing. We imagined something like a social movement. The executives of thousands of human service organizations were not ready to join a social movement.

Moreover, there is a sense in which the organizations were right, and we were wrong. We predicted dire consequences for the human service field after Reagan's election. But while the Reagan administration's rhetoric was overheated, the actual cuts in programs were gradual, selective, and targeted at the poorest and most marginal groups rather than at the programs with a broader constituency and less contested moral claims. In any case, the provider groups we were relying on to be the agents of the voter registration campaign were themselves usually spared direct assault. Indeed, as the years passed, some of them even prospered from the expansion of welfare-to-work programs and the new funds that became available.

The Unions

The idea of agency-based voter registration was not entirely novel to leaders of the public sector unions. In 1982, Josiah Beeman, director of Political and Legislative Affairs of the American Federation of State, County and Municipal Employees (AFSCME), had sought a legal opinion "as to whether government offices handling such programs as welfare, unemployment compensation, food stamps, social security, veterans benefits, etc. could handle voter registration as part of their intake process."[28] He was assured that there was nothing in the statutes to prevent this, so long as program officials agreed to the voter registration activity. But so far as we have been able to determine, AFSCME did nothing.

Our own experience with the unions began with the New York campaign in 1983, where we first tried to enlist the local unions to recruit members who worked in the relevant agencies to register clients, on the job where possible, or as volunteers if agency heads did not approve. The unions participated regularly in the meetings of our "New York Voter Registration Campaign" coalition. But there was virtually no actual voter registration by union members in the agencies.

At first we were not discouraged. We remained convinced that the public sector unions and their members would leap to take political advantage of the agency-based strategy if only we could get their attention. Accordingly, we pursued the unions zealously, meeting with the leadership on the national, state, and local levels, and occasionally with the heads of local chapters, with union stewards, and sometimes even with membership. But most of our efforts were directed to union leaders, whose backing we thought was essential.

As early as 1983, we met with Gerry Clark, National Political Action Director of AFSCME, to make the case for a union drive to promote agency-based registration among their members. By 1985, we had made similar approaches to the national leadership of Service Employees International Union (SEIU) and invited John Sweeney, then head of SEIU, to join our board (Sweeney declined). In New York and New Jersey, where the Communication Workers of America (CWA) represented significant numbers of welfare staff and supervisors, we pursued CWA leaders, and recruited Jan Pierce, a high official, to our board.

We were always encouraged. Our meetings produced a steady stream of cheering letters, proclamations, resolutions, and articles in union newspapers heralding the new voter registration campaign. In August 1984, Gerald McEntee, national president of AFSCME, and the secretary-treasurer, William Lucy, cosigned a memo to the presidents of all AFSCME hospital and human service locals, calling on them to mobilize their members to register citizens who receive public services, on the job where employers permitted it, or as volunteers during coffee breaks or lunch hours or after work. The memo was quite specific:

> Get some of your state's mail registration forms. Put them in the hands of your stewards and activists, and encourage them and other members to begin asking clients, "Are you registered to vote? Would you like to be?"[29]

But these efforts did not result in much registration activity by union members. During the 1984 presidential campaign, SERVE's California organizer succeeded in enlisting SEIU local 660 in Los Angeles and 535 in San Francisco, and some activist members staffed tables in welfare waiting rooms. But that was not much to show for all the proclamations.

We should have understood what was wrong from the experience of the New York campaign. When it became clear that the unions were not producing voter registration cards, we met with Victor Gotbaum to try to persuade him to activate his members. Gotbaum's response was that he had no influence with his members (much as Gerry Clark of national AFSCME had complained that he had no influence with Gotbaum and his union). So, we asked him if he had influence with Governor Cuomo, enough to persuade him to order voter registration at agency intake. Gotbaum assured us that was possible, and in fact he and his political action director, Norman Adler, did produce the first New York executive order, as we explain in the next chapter.

Our experience with unions elsewhere was similar. They did not recruit their members to do agency-based registration, although they sometimes allowed us to speak to their locals and make our appeal. In New Jersey, where county officials had responded to publicity about agency-based registration by endorsing it in their agencies, SERVE's New Jersey organizer, Jo-Anne Chasnow, began a minicampaign to enlist CWA locals to help make the process come alive. But for the most part, union participation was limited to proclamations and, in some cases, participation in the coalitions we created to lobby first for executive orders, and later for state legislation.

In 1984, we were so intent on recruiting the unions as partners that, strapped for funds though we were, we usually stressed that we were not asking for money, which the unions were accustomed to giving, but for active union participation. As time wore on, and serious union participation seemed less and less likely, we retreated and simply asked the unions to help us by providing printing and other in-kind services, and cash. And we did get modest levels of support of that kind. But even after passage of the NVRA had smoothed the way for a union effort to spur members to implement the new law vigorously, the unions hung back.

Why were the unions such reluctant partners? We ponder that question too. Our conclusions are not dissimilar to our conclusions about the social agencies. Organizational preoccupations simply trumped big political goals, including the goal of enhancing the political prospects of the union movement. Instead, union leaders were preoccupied with more immediate issues, such as contract negotiations or dealing with internal dissension. And the free rider problem applied here too. If a mass registration effort could improve the political future of the unions, well, then, wait and see if anyone else does it.

The constant problem of internal dissension, worsened by the fact that union gains were lagging, relates to another reason that union leadership was quick to endorse our campaign but reluctant to appeal to their members who, as Victor Gotbaum as much as said, were not inclined to listen to an appeal from leaders that involved "more work," especially at a time when the leadership was doing little to reverse the decline in real wages and benefits. Indeed, when the coalition organized in Massachusetts by Robin Leeds of Human SERVE succeeded in persuading Mayor Flynn of Boston to permit registration in a number of municipal agencies, it was SEIU Local 285 that aborted the compromise by insisting on job upgrades for workers who did voter registration. And finally, the de facto political alliance we were proposing between working-class union members and their clients ran smack into the antagonisms that workers often felt for the poor people they served. As one union organizer said to us flatly, "They don't like the clients." Only a confident and determined leadership with large aspirations could make persuasive arguments about the political potential of such an alliance.

Voter Registration Stalemate

With the 1984 election, the voter registration war was over. The scale of Reagan's victory disheartened left activists. In the Republican presidential primaries of 1980, candidate George Bush had accused Reagan of engaging in "voodoo economics" when he promised simultaneously to cut taxes, escalate military expenditures, and balance the budget. Voodoo economics was a political success, however. Taxes on the rich were cut, and military expenditures did indeed jump. True, the budget deficit ballooned, but the result was a debt-led economic boom at the start of 1984 that ended the 1982 recession by dramatically shrinking unemployment and putting a walloping five percentage points of additional income in people's pockets by the following November. The result was a reelection sweep.

The Christian Right was, of course, delighted. They planned to distribute millions of "voter guides" through their church networks from election to election. But the left was disheartened. The activist moment had passed. At Human SERVE, this meant that there was little prospect that public workers and voluntary agencies could be mobilized. That strategy seemed a dead end.

The left voter registration effort was also weakened by reports on the numbers who were added to the rolls. Just days before the 1984 election, the press was filled with stories based on official state statistics that the national voter registration rolls had jumped by 12 million, or 3.2 percent. By historical standards, that was a substantial increase. However, Curtis Gans of the Washington-based Committee for the Study of the American Electorate, a widely respected research organization, announced that voter registration campaigns—all of them, on both the left and right—could be credited with adding only 4 million. This flew in the face of the claims by left voter registration organizations that they had registered over 2 million, or by Jesse Jackson who claimed another 2 million, as did both the Christian Right and the Republican National Committee. And then there were the numbers reported registered by dozens of smaller voter registration groups. Adding up all the numbers, the grand total was 10, 12, even 14 million. It was impossible to evaluate these claims. (Some years later, for example, it was revealed that the Christian Right had "printed millions of voter guides that the coalition leaders expected would never be distributed." David Welch, former national field director of the Christian Coalition, said that "state affiliates took stacks of them to recycling centers after the election.")[30]

Shortly after the election, Gans was invited to present his findings to members of the Voter Registration Network in Washington, which consisted of representatives of the left voter registration organizations. They protested that the estimate seemed too low, given their experience in the field. Gans agreed that although all the campaigns, taken together, had registered many more than 4 million, he argued that they had nevertheless added only a *net* of 4 million to the rolls. The problem, Gans said, was that canvassers enroll anyone who is willing, including those who are already registered and those who would have registered on their own. The voting age population had increased by 9.5 million between 1980 and 1984. Based on past experience, Gans estimated that 70 percent of this group, or roughly 6.6 million, would have registered anyway. In this sense, hands-on voter registration campaigns are inefficient. The actual numbers registered will always be much larger than the net increase. During this dispute, Human SERVE had found a methodological error in the Gans report, which he acknowledged, raising his estimate of the net increase attributable to voter registration campaigns from 4 million to 5.6 million,[31] although the higher figure didn't mollify anyone.

A much more important lesson was that the registration war ended in a draw. The Current Population Survey division of the U.S. Census conducted its regular postelection survey and reported that registration rates rose equally among the less-educated and better-educated. Voter registration campaigns contributed to this stalemate. Campaigns targeting the poor and minorities were counteracted by the combined resources of the Republican Party and the Christian Right. Bruce E. Cain and Ken McCue, researchers at the California Institute of Technology, conducted a study in Los Angeles, where voter registration organizations were required to record their names on all completed registration cards, which were then computerized by election authorities. With computer printouts in hand, these researchers concluded that the drives had registered as many Republicans as Democrats, making for "a wash."[32] Why it was a wash, and not just in Los

Angeles, was clear enough. Republicans had the money to finance technologically sophisticated registration drives among upscale constituents. The Christian Right had an infrastructure through which to mobilize its constituency; a postelection national poll by Peter D. Hart Research Associates of first-time registrants showed that 28 percent were fundamentalist Protestants. And there was every reason to think that left voter registration drives would be similarly neutralized in future election cycles.

In sum, volunteer voter registration campaigns were not equal to registering the vast numbers of unregistered. The numbers reached depended not on the vastness of the pool but on campaign resources, and campaigns among the better-off attracted more resources. Consequently, campaigns could not lessen class and racial skews. The conclusion followed that to register minorities and the less-well-off en masse, an institutional solution was needed. The private agency strategy appeared to be a dead end; so did trying to mobilize public workers as volunteers. The strategy question to which we then turned was whether public officials, such as governors, county executives, and mayors, could be persuaded to make voter registration a regular service in state, county, and municipal agencies.

CHAPTER EIGHT

Party Competition
and Electoral
Mobilization

*I*n the 1983–1984 period, Human SERVE tried to persuade a few Democratic governors in the big industrial states to make voter registration part of the application process in public assistance and unemployment agencies. By 1980, the Democratic party had lost the presidency three times in four elections, and the Republicans had won the Senate. The voting and poll data made clear that Democratic prospects would improve were the party to exert itself to mobilize new voters from the bottom. Public assistance recipients were a Democratic constituency. They were (1) less educated, poorer, younger, unmarried black and Hispanic women, (2) working women and men who received food stamps and Medicaid to supplement their low wages and lack of health benefits, and (3) less-well-off elderly, mainly women, who were receiving federal Supplementary Security Income benefits and were also eligible for state-administered food stamps and Medicaid. However, our reading of party history made us skeptical that electoral competition would be enough to spur the party to mobilize. Our skepticism was reinforced by Mondale's refusal to enlist voters in 1984. New voters could put party incumbents at risk, and masses of new low-income voters would also threaten existing party coalitions and policy agendas.

Still, we thought we might find some allies within the loose and decentralized network of the Democratic party. In particular, we thought that some of the governors who had been elected on the surge of have-not voters in 1982 might be open to registration reform. In particular, we had high hopes for Tony Anaya in New Mexico (the first Hispanic governor); Richard Celeste in Ohio (formerly with the Peace Corps); Mario M. Cuomo in New York (who got huge black and Hispanic pluralities); and Mark White in Texas (where Hispanic turnout was up sharply, almost all of it going to the Democrats).

However, state constitutions vested control over voter registration arrangements in legislatures, where suburban and rural representatives with little interest in expanding voting among the lower strata often held sway. We thought there was a way around this roadblock. Democratic governors could issue executive orders requiring application/intake workers in welfare and unemployment agencies to offer to register people as part of their regular duties. This raised a "separation of powers" question, and Republicans were sure to raise it. They would go to court defining executive orders as infringing on constitutionally delegated legislative prerogatives. We consulted Arthur Eisenberg at the New York Civil Liberties Union. He did not think Republican challenges would succeed. It was his opinion that making forms available in state agencies would be taken by the courts as consistent with the grand legislative language about government's role in expanding democracy that typifies election codes. This judgment turned out to be right. When several governors did subsequently issue executive orders, state Republican parties sued and lost.

There were precedents for voter registration in government agencies, especially in DMVs. The Michigan legislature, spurred by Richard Austin, the first black secretary of state, enacted the first motor voter program in 1975. In his 1984 annual report, when interest in reform was growing, Austin reported that there were 266,273 new registrants and 505,888 changes of name and address, for a total of 772,161 voter registration transactions that year.[1] The system was also administratively simple and cheap—$0.17 per registrant or reregistrant. By 1983, four additional states allowed people to register to vote when they obtained or renewed drivers' licenses (Maine, Ohio, Arizona, and Oregon). Moreover, the public seemed to approve of motor voter, a form of one-stop shopping, as two referenda showed. Arizona's motor voter referendum passed in November 1982 by 51 percent, following a string of failed attempts to win reform measures in the legislature, and despite full page ads in local newspapers by opponents (including election officials) warning that this measure would open the door to fraud. More than a quarter of a million people registered to vote during the next three years, and the Arizona secretary of state reported that the state registration level, which had fallen by nine percentage points between 1972 and 1980, then jumped by nine points between 1980 and 1984 (from 57 percent to 66 percent).

Later, in November 1984, 61 percent of Colorado's voters approved a motor voter initiative. Spurred by the local chapters of the League of Women Voters, Common Cause, and the U.S. Public Interest Research Group, a coalition of thirty groups formed to sponsor the initiative. This action also followed a series of failed efforts to secure legislative action. Colorado had no postcard registration, no deputization, no registration at county elections offices except between the hours of 9 and 5, and it systematically purged voters who missed a single federal election. The state's registration level ranked thirty-fifth in the nation. In the first year after the program was begun, 175,000 people were registered to vote: 144,000, or 82 percent, were new registrants, and they represented 11 percent of Colorado's already registered voters.

A number of other states had also passed motor voter legislation—Pennsylvania in 1976; Minnesota and Ohio in 1977; Oregon and Tennesee in 1983—but didn't implement it (except partially in Ohio). In some cases, other agencies were also included, as in the Pennsylvania statute: "Secretary of the Commonwealth shall request the proper governmental agency to make an official registration application card available to all persons applying for or changing address for drivers' licenses, library cards, senior citizen transportation passes, entry to all schools and institutions of higher education." All of these were signs of growing acceptance of this method of reform.

What troubled us at the time was that poorer and minority people, especially in inner cities, were less likely to have licenses than better-off whites. Without voter registration in voluntary agencies and in public assistance and unemployment agencies, motor voter perpetuated class and racial inequalities. That, at least, was how we saw it in

1983. We changed our minds a few years later when we realized that driver rates were rising rapidly, especially among the poor and minorities; by 1990, 90 percent of the electorate had licenses or nondriver identification cards.

In the meanwhile, Human SERVE concentrated on social agencies. If the courts allowed governors to make voter registration available in public assistance agencies, we saw no reason why county executives and mayors could not do the same in county and municipal agencies serving poorer and minority people. Big-city Democratic mayors, including a growing number of black and Hispanic mayors, could themselves produce millions of new registrants. By the same reasoning, county and municipal legislatures could also order agencies under their jurisdiction to offer to register voters without infringing on the powers of state legislatures.

We thought we had a versatile strategy. If a governor wouldn't issue an executive order, perhaps a big-city mayor would; if a state legislature wouldn't authorize agency voter registration, perhaps a city council would. The strategy could take advantage of the fragmentation of the American state structure, both the decentralization of public authority in the federal system and the dispersion of power among the branches of government. If registration services could not be won at one level or by one branch, they might be won at another level or by another branch, including the judiciary.

Between March and September 1984, Human SERVE succeeded in winning six gubernatorial executive orders. As we had hoped, the governors of Texas, Ohio, New York, and Montana directed that voter registration services be established in various human service agencies and in DMVs. The governors of New Mexico and West Virginia ordered voter registration in state human service agencies only. In addition, the governor of Minnesota issued a letter to department heads saying he favored agency registration, but left it to their discretion. The California secretary of state urged county welfare directors to implement registration. The Michigan secretary did the same. The secretary in Washington state obtained legislation authorizing a range of state agencies to make deputized staff members available to register voters.

Then the political fireworks began. The media were quick to predict that the outcome of the 1984 election might be determined by voter registration in welfare and unemployment offices in key industrial states. The *Chattanooga News-Free Press* editorialized that "tieing voter registration to the handout lines" is a plan to "add all sorts of people getting government payments" to the registration rolls so that "they can vote themselves richer." The *Detroit News* complained of "ham-fisted intimidation" because, it claimed, welfare and unemployment recipients who refused to sign up "could get into trouble with their government social workers, the reverse of the situation in the South a couple of decades ago when the poor who tried to register got into trouble with the sheriff."[2] The *Dallas Morning News* was critical of William Greener, communications director of the National Republican Committee, because he "professes not to care that government social workers will be doubling as voter registrars, hoping to register 5 million beneficiaries for the 1984 presidential election." Furthermore, "Greener claims that no one benefits more than the poor from Reagan's reduction of inflation. True, but he surely knows that the poor who will be registered aren't likely to vote for Reagan, since he cut the budgets of programs that benefit the poor."[3]

Officials who opposed registration reform mobilized. What became evident is the familiar process by which a decentralized and fragmented state structure provides not only multiple opportunities to promote reform, but also multiple points to nullify reform. A fragmented state structure works both ways. An institutional reform mounted by one group of officials for partisan reasons can be blocked by another group of officials for their partisan reasons.

PARTISAN CLEAVAGE. In early 1984, Human SERVE's California organizer, Barbara Facher, noticed a section of the election code that said public agencies may "authorize and assign officers and employees to serve as deputy registrars of voters and to register qualified citizens on their premises during regular working hours." Facher then persuaded Common Cause and the League of Women Voters to join in urging March Fong Eu, the Democratic secretary of state and chief elections officer, to press for implementation in county welfare agencies. The Secretary issued a press release on February 29, 1984, that ran as a major story across the state, announcing that she had sent a letter to the fifty-eight county welfare directors urging them to make voter registration a regular service. "County welfare workers come in daily contact with hundreds of thousands of unregistered eligible voters. By offering nonpartisan voter registration services, large numbers of social service recipients will be brought into the political arena for the first time." She also urged Governor Deukmejian, a Republican, to issue an executive order covering a range of government offices, including welfare. He demurred on the ground that "such a policy would undermine confidence in the state work force."[4]

The public controversy between the secretary of state and the governor created a dilemma for the few welfare department directors who were favorable to the plan; the governor was much more powerful than the secretary, and they worried about political repercussions. The Contra Costa county welfare department resolved the dilemma by rejecting the idea that employees should routinely offer to register clients, or what it called a "worker initiated" system. It proposed instead a "client initiated" system. Registration cards would be available in the lobbies with signs saying "You Can Register to Vote Here. If You Need Assistance, See _____, _____, _____," these being the names of employees who would be available to assist.

INTERNAL PARTY CLEAVAGE. The New Mexico order was stimulated by national news articles describing the Human SERVE strategy. Joseph Goldberg, a professor of social welfare who had taken leave to head the the state department of human resources under the new Hispanic governor, wrote Human SERVE to say that a plan for welfare agencies was in the making, the first step in extending registration services to a wide range of public agencies.[5] When Governor Anaya issued an executive order in June 1984 covering public assistance agencies, the reactions were explosive. Republicans, many Democrats, and most editorialists and political cartoonists in the state charged that the program was nothing more than a ploy to register poor Hispanics. Some typical comments:

> At this point in the year, when Walter Mondale is on the verge of getting the Democratic nomination for president and Governor Anaya is Mondale's No. 1 fan in New Mexico, the smell of partisan politics in this plan is pungent.
>
> It's another example of the Anaya administration trying to politicize

state government. Obviously they are registering a select group who will be more likely than others to support their policies and political objectives.

Welfare workers who owe their jobs to the Democratic party will coerce aid recipients into registering as Democrats as the price of their benefits.[6]

In short order, the attorney general, a member of the traditional wing of the Democratic party, which Anaya had bested, declared that the order violated the state constitution, which says that "all elections shall be free and open and no power, civil or military, shall at any time interfere to prevent the free exercise of the right of suffrage." As the controversy boiled up, the governor's advisors cautioned against defying the attorney general, and Anaya rescinded his order.

A similar Democratic party cleavage appeared in Michigan, where the Democratic governor, Jim Blanchard, was fighting off a tax revolt in the spring of 1984. Human SERVE had no hope that he would issue an executive order. Instead, Roseanne Handler, Human SERVE's Michigan organizer, persuaded the secretary of state to write to human service department heads: "Human SERVE, a newly formed coalition of human service workers, is conducting a nationwide effort to provide voter registration access to recipients of health and human service programs. To the extent that you can, according to Michigan and federal statutes, I urge your involvement."[7] Handler also persuaded the heads of departments of mental health, social services, services to the aging, public health, and labor to circulate a letter signed by all of them saying simply: "We endorse the efforts of Human SERVE to promote nonpartisan voter registration in human service agencies."[8]

Although these gestures were merely symbolic, since no follow-through could be expected, they nevertheless provoked the Michigan House to pass an amendment to an appropriations bill in March 1984 prohibiting these departments from offering voter registration and expressly enjoining them from cooperating in any way with Human SERVE. Republicans unanimously supported the amendment; so did a decisive number of Democrats. The *Detroit Free Press* criticized the legislature in an editorial entitled "Human SERVE's registration drive should be allowed to continue."[9]

ONE BRANCH NULLIFIES ANOTHER. In New York, Human

SERVE worked closely with Victor Gotbaum and Norman Adler of District Council 37-AFSCME. They were crucial in persuading Governor Cuomo to issue an order in July 1984 covering a range of agencies. Within 72 hours, the state Republican party persuaded a state supreme court (New York's lowest court) to issue an order of restraint. The court accepted both the claim that the governor had invaded the legislature's constitutionally granted power over voter registration, and the claim that the Republican party would be "irreparably harmed" because state employees would try to bias new registrants toward the Democratic party. However, the appellate division lifted the restraining order and unanimously rejected the charge that the governor had infringed on legislative prerogatives, as did the New York State Court of Appeals (the highest court). They held that the legislature, in enacting postcard legislation some years earlier, had intended that registration forms be widely accessible, and that the governor was doing nothing more than carrying out that intent. Arthur Eisenberg made this argument in an amicus brief on behalf of a number of voting rights organizations. However, the Republican party also won: it succeeded in persuading the courts that state employees should be prohibited from asking citizens whether they wished to register, and from answering questions, assisting in completing forms, or collecting completed forms; the courts limited the agencies to making the forms available. This was a big limitation on agency registration and on executive discretion.

A similar suit was filed by Ohio Republican party leaders against Governor Celeste's order, issued in July 1984, but the court ruled against them. The court began by noting "a disturbing discrepancy between the number of Ohio citizens eligible to vote and those registered to do so," and went on to declare that "it is a situation mandating action." In turn, the court found that Celeste's action to make registration services available in agencies was "within the powers and duties of the Governor" and that the executive order was "constitutional and valid."

FEDERAL GOVERNMENT NULLIFIES STATES' RIGHTS. One of the arguments Republicans used in the congressional debates leading up to passage of the NVRA in 1993 is that it violated states' rights, since states had traditionally controlled voter registration procedures. Just a few years earlier, however, a Republican president had also tried to override state control over voter registration. The controversy over executive orders provoked the Reagan administration to try to block the governors by invoking the 1970 Intergovernmental Personnel Act (the Hatch Act), which prohibits state employees involved in administering federal grants from engaging in "partisan political purposes and . . . from using their official authority for the purpose of interfering with or affecting the results of an election." We had anticipated this sort of attack by distributing excerpts from a federal government pamphlet defining the "Political Do's & Don'ts for Federal Employees," including state employees paid from federal funds, which stated that they "may engage in nonpartisan voter registration drives."

Nevertheless, on September 27, 1984, Donald Devine, director of the Office of Personnel Management (OPM) threatened Governors Celeste, Cuomo, and White that the Reagan administration might cut off federal grants-in-aid, on the ground that the Hatch Act would be violated if human service workers registered citizens in the course of their regular duties:

> It has come to our attention that your state is using its employees to ask individuals if they are registered to vote. . . . If they express some interest in registering, state employees are used to help the individual to become registered. The concern has been raised as to whether this use of state personnel interferes with or affects the results of the election this November 1984.

The OPM letter went on to imply that Celeste, Cuomo, and White were forcing state personnel to influence people to register as Democrats. It ended by demanding that the governors forward all materials pertaining to their registration programs.

The OPM letter created an opportunity for political theatrics which no one involved let pass, beginning with a rhetorical shooting match between the governors and the Reagan administration. In Ohio, Governor Celeste called Devine's action "blackmail"; in New York, Governor Cuomo complained of "a transparently political attempt to curtail the access of United States citizens to the ballot box"; and in Texas Governor White convened a press conference in a state agency waiting room and distributed voter registration cards, declaring that he was going to begin a vigorous program to implement his executive order throughout all state agencies (which, as it happens, he never did). All three governors rejected the allegation that state employees were being compelled to engage in partisan activities. Celeste and White made the point that voters in Ohio and Texas did not register by party. And Cuomo made the point that New York's program, as a result of the Republican law suit, was not "staff-active"—state employees were doing nothing more than making registration forms available on tables in waiting rooms. In Florida, however, where the legislature had authorized state-agency voter registration in 1984, officials in the executive branch declined to implement the program, citing fear of federal reprisals.

In response to this controversy, hearings were held by the House Committee on Government Operations, chaired by Barney Frank (D-MA), which ended with a bipartisan conclusion that Devine had made "selective application and misuse" of the Intergovernmental Personnel Act with the intent, in the chairman's words, to "intimidate three Democratic governors of large states from continuing to encourage voter registration in the critical two week period before the books closed for the presidential election."[10] Devine was subsequently denied reconfirmation by the Senate, in part because of this affair, and also because of the opinion in Congress that he had politicized the Office of Personnel Management. Since the controversy gave the impression that the Republican party was attempting to discourage poorer and minority people from registering and voting, the Republican-dominated Senate passed a ballot-waving "sense of the Congress" resolution praising democracy and urging every citizen to go to the polls. Much to our delight, the Senate declared that "Voter registration drives should be encouraged by government at all levels; and voter registration drives conducted by state governments on a nonpartisan basis do not violate the provisions of the Intergovernmental Personnel Act." Then, in September 1985, the Reagan administration retreated altogether and wrote the governors: "We conclude that no substantial evidence of a pattern of misuse of state employees in violation of federal statutes has been found. This constitutes our final judgment in the matter and no further action is planned."

Another Reagan administration strategy to head off the Democratic governors was to declare that the use of federal grants-in-aid money for voter registration was not legislatively authorized and thus was a misuse of funds. Whether for this reason or for their own reasons, the governors limited their agencies to making registration forms available on tables in waiting rooms, refusing to allow staff to distribute them along with routine agency forms, to answer questions, or to collect and deposit completed registration applications with election officials.

The issue first arose in Texas where Lafe Larson, a former ACORN organizer who represented Human SERVE in the Southwest, brought together a coalition of unions, civil rights, human service organizations, and religious groups. Together with the active support of John Fainter, the Democratic secretary of state, the coalition succeeded in persuading Governor White to issue what was the first executive order, in March 1984. However, the director of the Employment Commission balked, and instead wrote to the U.S. Department of Labor asking whether it would be proper for federally funded state personnel to hand out voter registration forms. The Labor Department not unexpectedly replied that permitting employees to ask unemployment applicants whether they were registered and to answer questions about how to fill out the forms would be improper, and it distributed this opinion to all state employment directors. Human SERVE complained about inconsistency: the Texas Department of Labor and the Selective Service were encouraging federally funded state job training officials to act as "uncompensated registrars" for Selective Service, so that applicants for job training could register for the draft.

But the U.S. Department of Labor did concede that it would not object if registration forms were merely placed on tables. At Human SERVE, we thought that this concession opened up another possibility to which the Department would probably not object, since the cost would be negligible—namely, to insert registration forms in agency application packets—and we encouraged state officials to take that tack.

The issue of using federal funds for agency-based voter registration was a vexing one. It didn't arise in DMVs, which were largely state-financed; it arose in unemployment and public assistance agencies that received federal matching grants. Human SERVE was stymied unless it could find a way around this prohibition. We turned to the American Public Welfare Association (APWA), an organization mainly of state and county welfare directors, in the hope that it might see a solution. At that time, the APWA membership was still rooted in the New Deal/Great Society tradition, and was heavily Democratic owing to the predominance in those years of Democratic governors. Leon H. Ginsburg, the APWA president and director of the state department of human services in West Virginia, strongly supported agency registration and set an example by obtaining the governor's approval to begin voter registration in welfare agencies in his state.

After extensive discussions with Human SERVE staff, Edward T. Weaver, APWA executive director, issued a "guidance memorandum" to state welfare directors entitled, "Alternative Ways for Government Human Service Agencies and Personnel to Participate in Voter Registration." It began by saying that state welfare directors could "permit and encourage staff to use personal time (lunchbreak, etc.) to volunteer to engage in voter registration in the agency's public reception room." However, allowing staff to register clients on the job "would be likely to jeopardize federal matching funds." The exception was receptionists who "generally serve an information and referral function," and could therefore "ask each inquirer if they want to register to vote, and refer them to a staff member regularly assigned this duty who is paid with state funds, but not federal matching funds." Most important, states could "overmatch, paying for voter registration costs from the excess state match." The Michigan secretary of state reported that the computerized system of voter registration in DMVs cost $0.17 per registrant. Even if a noncomputerized system in public assistance cost a dollar of staff time per registrant, the overmatch funds needed would be miniscule. Human SERVE publicized this memorandum widely among public officials.

The gubernatorial executive orders came late in the 1984 presidential campaign and were immediately embroiled in controversy. Relatively few people were in fact registered before the election. What could be said is that when the smoke cleared, the public agency strategy had survived challenges in the courts and by the Reagan administration. All of a sudden voting rights activists were debating the merits of something called "agency-based" voter registration, and politicians in both parties at different levels of government were exchanging political epithets over it.

On the other hand, as political columinist David Broder wrote in the *Washington Post,*

> Why the grudging cooperation from elected Democrats to making voter registration available in agencies serving minorities and poorer people? The answer that both experience and Human SERVE give is that people in power, whatever their party label, really don't want to rock the boat. Enlarging the electorate, especially enlarging it from the bottom, changes the basic political equation. It empowers new people, with new demands. It threatens the old arrangements, and is too dangerous for the Democrats to take on.[11]

In the same vein, the *Wall Street Journal* quoted a member of the Massachusetts legislature as complaining that Democrats are "reluctant to change the system for fear they'll lose."[12]

CHAPTER NINE

Barriers or Mobilization? The Debate over Nonvoting

*I*f more people were registered, would they vote? If not, why reform the system? In the 1980s, a renewed controversy broke out among the experts over this question, and the press paid close attention. Support for reform depended importantly on the outcome of this debate.

When we formed Human SERVE in the early 1980s, we thought that low voting among poorer and minority people was the result of both persisting barriers to registration and the failure of the Democratic party to mobilize them. As we observed in chapters 7 and 8, the party was not helping to register poorer and minority people and it was not encouraging them to vote by appealing to their interests and mounting get-out-the-vote campaigns.

The question, then, was whether registration reform would, in the absence of party mobilizing efforts, raise voting. If people were only helped to register—no "political education," no party appeals, no get-out-the-vote campaigns—would they nevertheless go to the polls? The prevailing view was that they would not. Get-out-the-vote efforts were considered essential. Edsall and Johnson reported in the *Washington Post* just before the 1984 election that the American Coalition for Traditional Values was appealing to Christian Right pastors in North Carolina to divide their congregations into groups of fifteen families, asking everyone in each group to make calls to parishioners on election day, right up to poll closing. In effect, Edsall and Johnson concluded, the Christian Right was "trying to set up a system of church-based precinct captains."[1]

We didn't disagree. In 1983, just as we were initiating the voluntary agency campaign, we wrote that perhaps only one in five registrants would vote. We drew in part on a report circulating in the nonpartisan voter-registration community that only 20 percent of those registered in welfare and unemployment lines by campaign volunteers had voted in an earlier election. However, we argued that agency staff could improve that ratio by putting up posters, passing out leaflets, and utilizing their direct contact with clients, all calling attention to the upcoming election, the issues at stake, and the importance of voting.

During the 1983–84 period, however, we began to change our minds on the question of whether voter registration reform, taken alone, would raise voting. For one thing, we learned that the report that only 20 percent of those registered in welfare and unemployment offices had voted was based on a special election to replace a congressman who had died in office, an election in which only 30 percent of all eligible voters had gone to the polls. With this clarification, welfare and unemployment registrants had voted at relatively high rates. Indeed, a great deal of competent evidence was produced in this period showing (1) that a high proportion of people who are registered do in fact vote, including previous nonvoters registered by campaign organizations, and (2) that persisting barriers helped explain why more weren't on the rolls. Study by study, experience by experience, we began giving more weight to the role of legal/institutional factors in deterring voting.

This was a longstanding debate. When it was revived in the 1980s, it was in the context of a secular decline in voter turnout of 10 percentage points between 1960 and 1980 (down from 63 percent to 53). Nor did the 1983–84 voter registration war, with its huge 3.3 percent net rise in the registration rolls since 1980, reverse that trend. Voting rose by a mere 0.7 percent, perhaps because the outcome of the Mondale–Reagan campaign was a foregone conclusion.

Many of the groups that participated in the voter registration war were not concerned with the turnout decline as such. If those who voted were a random sample of the electorate, what difference would it make whether a few or many voted? The result for governance and public policy would be the same. The voter registration war was mainly about class and racial differentials in voting, and the resulting bias in governance and public policy toward a white and upscale electorate. Some groups fought to reduce that bias, and others fought to maintain or increase it.

Part of the fall in voting was attributed to the Twenty-sixth Amendment, which lowered the voting age to eighteen beginning in 1972. According to the Census, "Between 1964 and 1980, 34 million persons 18 to 44 years were added to the voting-age population: about 12 million because of the lowering of the voting age to 18 in all States, and the remainder because of the maturing of the large baby-boom cohorts." Analysts generally agreed that the addition of younger persons to the voting age population explained between one-quarter and one-third of the turnout decline, since younger people register and vote less, particularly in the low-turnout United States.

As for the rest of the decline, there was no agreement. One side said voting was down because registration rates were falling; the other side said voting was down because fewer and fewer of those who were already registered were bothering to vote. Both sides invoked authoritative evidence. The reformers drew on the U.S. Census studies showing that registrants vote at high levels and that what explained the turnout decline was that fewer and fewer people were registered. The skeptics about reform drew on the registration and voting statistics provided by state election officials showing consistently high levels of registration, and argued that what explained the turnout decline was that fewer and fewer registrants were bothering to vote. The two sets of government statistics led to opposite conclusions; one set suggested that raising registration rates would raise turnout, and the other that it would not. The prospects for reform partly turned on the question of which body of evidence was more trustworthy.

Registrants Will Vote

In the 1960s, the Census began conducting interviews in large samples of households (typically 50,000 or more) after each federal election to determine how many Americans were registered and had voted. The Census is a competent research organization, and its findings were consistent over time. "Unlike the overall voting rate, which declined 10 percentage points between 1964 and 1980, turnout among persons who were registered declined slightly from 91 percent in 1968 to 89 percent in 1976 and 1980," or by two percentage points. This led to the conclusion that people "overwhelmingly go to the polls" if they are registered.[2] By contrast, registration rates had "declined . . . in a manner parallel to that of voting"—from 74 percent in 1968 to 67 percent in 1980, or by seven percentage points.

The main bias in the Census data is that people, in deference to democratic norms, overreport both registering and voting. The Census estimated that the inflationary bias ran between 5 and 15 percent.[3] We adopted 10 percent, which meant that the reported registration rate of 67 percent in 1980 was probably only 61 percent.

However, when we calculate the percentage of registrants who vote, the inflationary biases in voting and registration claims probably cancel each other out. It is therefore likely that Census statistics on the percentage of registrants who vote are relatively unbiased by overreporting.

This conclusion was supported by the University of Michigan's National Election Study (NES), which conducted a small sample survey of households (under 3,000) after each federal election. The NES went a step further than the Census, actually consulting election records to verify whether interviewees were reporting accurately. When false registration and voting claims were eliminated, they found that 84 percent of registrants had gone to the polls in 1980 and similarly high proportions in earlier elections, which is roughly what the Census had reported.

The Census findings were featured in a widely publicized symposium, "Voting for Democracy," sponsored by Harvard University and ABC News in 1983. The participants, who represented all points of view about nonvoting, included prominent journalists and academics, representatives of good government and civil rights groups, corporate leaders, the heads of the Republican and Democratic national committees, as well as former Presidents Ford and Carter. A report was issued in 1984, and ABC News produced an hour-long television documentary focusing on the causes of low voting and potential remedies.

During the proceedings, Carter explained why his election-day registration bill failed in 1977:

> In spite of a strong and well organized campaign [to enact this bill], we were unsuccessful. The conservatives, Democrats and Republicans, almost to a person opposed this legislation. I was taken aback that many of the liberal and moderate members of the Congress also opposed any increase in voter registration. . . . The key [source of resistance was] "incumbency." Incumbent members of the Congress don't want to see additional unpredictable voters registered. I'm speaking in generalities and there were obviously some exceptions. But I tell you that what I say is true. The more senior and more influential members of the Congress have very safe districts. To have a 25 or 30 percent increase of unpredictable new voters is something they don't relish. . . . I would suggest to you that this is the single most important obstacle to increasing participation on election day.[4]

What appeared to impress participants most were cross-national comparisons provided by David Glass, Peverill Squire, and Raymond Wolfinger. A comparison of voters as a proportion of the voting age population (table 9.1) showed that the United States was at the bottom. In democracies where voting was high, just about everyone was registered. Census figures showed that voting was also high among those in the United States who were registered (table 9.2): "By this measure the United States looks better than most countries and nearly as good as any country," is the way Glass, Squire, and Wolfinger put it. They therefore recommended that "money, energy, and political capital" should be devoted to getting people registered, "on the amply documented assumption that once people register, they vote."[5] The implication followed that if the United States adopted one of the European systems of near-universal registration, voting would reach European levels. Consequently, the symposium recommended (although not unanimously) that instead of the traditional system of voter registration in the United States, with its time and place barriers, people be permitted to register to vote at the polls on election day.

The symposium report did not go unnoticed. For example, on June 27, 1984, Al Swift (D-WA), chair of the Task Force on Elections of

Table 9.1. Voter Turnout Percentages in Democratic
Nations (Most Recent Major National Elections
as of 1983)

1.	Belgium	95
2.	Australia	94
3.	Austria	92
4.	Sweden	91
5.	Italy	90
6.	Iceland	89
7.	New Zealand	89
8.	Luxembourg	89
9.	West Germany	87
10.	Netherlands	87
11.	France	86
12.	Portugal	84
13.	Denmark	83
14.	Norway	82
15.	Greece	79
16.	Israel	78
17.	United Kingdom	76
18.	Japan	74
19.	Canada	69
20.	Spain	68
21.	Finland	64
22.	Ireland	62
23.	**United States**	**53**
24.	Switzerland	48

SOURCE: *Harvard/ABC News Symposium (1984:7). Turnout for the United
States is based on the voting-age population; for other countries, it is based
on registered voters. Apart from the United States, registration is more or
less universal, so these comparisons are roughly correct. Low voting in Swiss
federal elections, it should be noted, is a unique case. The federal government there plays a minor role compared with the cantons, and there is little
political competition at the national level. See Jackman (1987:409) and
Powell (1982:119).*

Table 9.2. Voter Turnout in Democratic Nations as a Percentage of Registered Voters (Most Recent Major National Elections as of 1983)

1.	Belgium	95
2.	Australia	94
3.	Austria	92
4.	Sweden	91
5.	Italy	90
6.	Iceland	89
7.	New Zealand	89
8.	Luxembourg	89
9.	West Germany	87
10.	Netherlands	87
11.	**United States**	**87**
12.	France	86
13.	Portugal	84
14.	Denmark	83
15.	Norway	82
16.	Greece	79
17.	Israel	78
18.	United Kingdom	76
19.	Japan	74
20.	Canada	69
21.	Spain	68
22.	Finland	64
23.	Ireland	62
24.	Switzerland	48

SOURCE: *Harvard/ABC News Symposium (1984:7).*

the House Committee on Administration, opened a hearing by noting that "today's hearing stems in part from the symposium that was sponsored jointly by ABC and Harvard University last fall . . . which concluded that our present registration system is a significant barrier to voting and that easing the means of voter registration should have the highest priority."

Some symposium members did not support this conclusion. They thought that historic barriers had, on the whole, been abolished, and they doubted that barriers any longer much deterred registration. The Voting Rights Act (and subsequent amendments) had transformed practices in the South. In many northern states, people could register by mail. The implication was that day-of-election registration and comparable reforms would have no effect. The question, then, was whether there was credible evidence that significant barriers still existed.

Barriers

Controversy over the impact of time and place restrictions on registration intensified in the early 1980s. For one thing, the Voting Rights Act was up for renewal, and opponents said it was no longer needed because southern states had liberalized their procedures. To help counter that claim, the League of Women Voters organized its chapters in Georgia and Alabama to conduct a study of voter registration procedures in these states between December 1981 and September 1982. Among the findings:

- Registration rates among blacks were consistently lower than among whites.
- Many counties had no satellite registration sites, which meant people had to drive as much as forty miles to a county seat.
- Deputization was severely restricted. Some elections officials boasted that they could throw up enough obstacles to "outlast" the groups demanding to be deputized.
- Registrars were often hostile and threatening to blacks. Sometimes they interrogated them "abrasively" about felonies and parentage.
- Registration offices were commonly located in courthouses, which blacks avoided because they symbolized oppression.

The nonpartisan voter registration groups in the 1983–84 period also contributed to this debate by showing that obstructive practices by elections officials were widespread. Barriers persisted not just in Virginia and Georgia, but in Massachusetts, Connecticut, Michigan, Illinois, and other northern states. Equally important, advocates of reform presented instance after instance showing that politicians and election officials were using these restrictions to keep registration down among poorer and minority people.

As the 1983–84 registration war heated up, elections officials were besieged by groups demanding that they be permitted to conduct voter registration. In sixteen states, people still had to appear at a central office to register; eleven states had deputization laws and procedures, but they allowed very few to be deputized. A typical justification of this restrictivenesss was that people who weren't sophisticated enough to figure out where a local office is or who weren't interested enough to travel to it (which might have been halfway across a county or to a downtown office in a big city) didn't deserve to vote. The time and resources required to mount campaigns under these conditions were formidable. Steve Kest of ACORN complained that his organization had no time for political education activities in Bridgeport, Connecticut, because the organizing staff had spent months raising money to bus 7,000 people from public housing projects to the elections office, which refused to deputize organizers. On October 5, 1984, the *New Haven Register* reported that election officials had ordered a minority-oriented voter registration organization as well as the Central Labor Council to cease registering people altogether, because of alleged irregularities which they refused to specify. Apparently Republicans had complained that Democrats were being disproportionately registered.

Boards that did deputize often did so selectively. They would deputize members of the League of Women Voters or the Moral Majority, but not members of the NAACP, ACORN, or human service agencies. A Catholic registrar in New Haven, for example, refused to deputize staff members from Planned Parenthood. Gracia Hillman, director of the National Coalition on Black Voter Participation, testified before a congressional committee in 1984 about voter registration barriers in Bedford, Massachusetts:

> There were no minority deputy registrars nor sites within the minority community where one could register. We encountered vehement resistance from the director of elections when we approached him about these problems. He would not appoint minority members as deputy registrars, nor would he expand the list of satellite sites.

An editorial in the *Boston Globe* referred to a "survey by the Massachusts PIRG chapter showing that Massachusetts has the most restrictive voter registration procedures in the nation."[6]

Moreover, volunteer deputies were often told that some locations were off-limits—such as welfare and unemployment offices, or public housing projects. The Richmond, Virginia, board revoked the deputy status of NAACP volunteers who were canvassing on federal surplus cheese distribution lines. In Massachusetts, elections officials were presumably required by state law to dispatch their own employees to sites of "principal activity" at a designated time if petitioned to do so by ten registered voters. However, the Worcester and New Bedford town clerks, when petitioned to designate welfare centers, unemployment offices, and community health facilities, simply denied that these facilities were places of principal activity.

Local boards also obstructed registration campaigns logistically by hobbling them with restrictions: "Pick up the forms after 9:00 a.m., and return them by 4:45 p.m. Late forms will be voided." Some boards required volunteers to repeat the burdensome application and training process over and over again. In Indianapolis volunteers were given only twenty-five forms at a time. In order to get additional forms, they were required to repeat the entire process by which they were initially deputized: they again had to secure permission from representatives of one of the political parties and the county registrar and again undergo training, after which they again received only twenty or twenty-five cards. A complete inventory of these obstructions would fill a small book. Needless to add, volunteers often gave up in frustration.

Similar problems arose in states that permitted people to register by mail. Boards of elections often frustrated registration campaigns by keeping few forms on hand, demanding that registration organizations pay for printing additional forms, or limiting the number of forms given out to twenty-five, with the result that volunteer registrars spent as much time traveling as registering. West Virginia required that every registrant appear before a notary public, which presented a well-nigh insuperable logistical problem for large-scale campaign efforts.

These obstructions were particularly onerous for Human SERVE, since social agency personnel were often unable to get deputized or to get ample forms. In Detroit, for example, applicants for deputy registrar status were required to attend a two-hour training session to learn how to fill out forms (which were, it should be added, the most complicated in the country). They were also required to repeat the training process and to be redeputized each time registration was closed, as it always was during December and January and before primaries and elections, including school elections. This meant that to offer registration services social agencies had to arrange for staff members to be retrained about six times each year. Some social agency staff went through the process several times but got worn down by it. Registration efforts in the state were also stymied by the fact that Michigan has 1,500 boards of elections (25 percent of the total in the United States), and anyone deputized by a particular board was allowed to register only people who resided in the same tiny jurisdiction. Social agencies thus had to send staff to be deputized in all the jurisdictions from which they drew clients. Few agencies went to the trouble.

Restrictive local boards created something of a farce in Connecticut. Human SERVE had tried to persuade the governor to issue an executive order. He decided instead to direct department heads to submit plans showing how they would make it easy for volunteers to canvass for new registrants in waiting rooms (e.g., by making tables available, etc.). Every department sent in detailed plans, some of them enthusiastically. Then agency administrators throughout Connecticut waited over the summer of 1984 for volunteer registrars who never appeared because they could not get deputized. The farce was repeated in Massachusetts, where Governor Dukakis, after considerable pressure from a voting rights coalition organized by Human SERVE, agreed to permit canvassing in state agency waiting rooms. However, the local boards of elections declined either to deputize volunteers or to send their own employees to staff tables.

Campaign organizers responded to these obstructions in a variety of ways. The older voter registration organizations tended to treat board procedures as a more or less fixed feature of the political environment and tried to work within the procedures or to negotiate limited exceptions to them. But newer campaign organizations—not having yet been worn down by struggles with the elections clerks—reacted with outrage. Not only were the boards unwilling to mount outreach efforts themselves, but they were preventing others from doing so.

One particularly galling practice was the refusal by government officials to permit access to agency waiting rooms. Project VOTE! went to court, claiming that government agency waiting rooms are public places (like sidewalks) where First Amendment rights may be exercised, including registering people, provided that these activities did not interfere with the work of the agencies. The courts agreed flat out. During the 1983–84 period, Project VOTE! won suits in federal court (in two cases, within several days of filing) against four governors, all Republicans (Rhodes in Ohio, Orr in Indiana, Thornburgh in Pennsylvania, and Bond in Missouri) who tried to bar its volunteers from registering voters in public offices.[7]

In early 1984, Human SERVE asked Ira Glasser, executive director of the ACLU, to host a meeting at the ACLU's national headquarters in New York City to launch a simultaneous barrage of suits against elections boards in various states and initiate hearings in Congress on time, place, and deputization restrictions. In addition to ACLU, the participating organizations included the NAACP Legal Defense Fund, the Lawyers Committee for Civil Rights Under Law, the Lawyers Guild, and representatives from groups participating in voter registration campaigns, such as Project VOTE!, the Atlanta-based Voter Education Project, the U.S. Public Interest Research Group, and Planned Parenthood Federation of America (which at the time was suing Waterbury, Connecticut, elections officials who had refused to deputize their staff members). The first meeting was chaired by Hulbert James of Human SERVE, and subsequent meetings were co-chaired by Lani Guinier of the NAACP Legal Defense Fund. This emerging coalition named itself the National Emergency Mobilization on the Right to Vote, and Human SERVE acted as its staff.

After several months of meetings, the National Emergency Mobilization went to court. The Associated Press reported on May 29 that

civil rights lawyers go to court in St. Louis today in the opening round of a planned legal assault against at least 15 states, including Michigan, accused of discriminating against poor and minority voters. The suits, charging that state and local rules impede voter registration drives, mark the latest attack in a movement to sign up eligible voters—many of them poor and minorities—in time for the fall presidential election.

The article quoted Hulbert James as saying "Established political leaders don't want new voters, particularly if they are of a different class and color." And Arthur Eisenberg said that "although defendants and charges differ, all the suits will claim barriers to registration violate the U.S. Constitution and, in some case, the Voting Rights Act." Lani Guinier defined the goal: "We are suing to place the burden of registration in the hands of the government instead of on the shoulders of the voter."

Two weeks later, on June 13, the Emergency Mobilization staged a Citizen Hearing in the U.S. House of Representatives Office Building, with a tribunal consisting of members of Congress and national legal rights leaders, including former Assistant U.S. Attorney General Roger Wilkins and Eleanor Holmes Norton of the Georgetown Law Center. Hulbert James announced that the purpose of the hearing was to "request that legislators pass laws in their states to alleviate restrictive registration practices, and to strongly urge governors to make voter registration services available in state agencies." Testimony on voter registration barriers was given by leaders from virtually all of the major civil rights and grassroots groups: Geraldine Thompson from the Atlanta Voter Education Project; Juan Andrade, Midwest Voter Education Project; Rolando Rios, Southwest Voter Education Project; Gracia Hillman, National Coalition on Black Voter Participation; Joseph Madison, NAACP; Sanford Newman, Project VOTE!; Cora Tucker, Citizen Action; Joanne Howes, Women's Vote Project. During the session, Congressman John Conyers (D-MI) announced the filing of H.R. 5815, a bill to extend mail registration nationally. Sherrod Brown, secretary of state in Ohio, and Peter Shapiro, executive of Essex County (Newark, New Jersey), each described dramatic plans in his jurisdiction to make registration available in social agencies. A surprise appearance by presidential candidate Jesse Jackson, tailed by a herd of reporters and TV cameras, capped the day. In a summary article in the *Washington Post,* Thomas Edsall announced that "across the nation, liberal to radical organizations are attempting to make barriers to registration the political cause of the 1980s."[8]

Registrants Will Not Vote

Results from the Census and NES surveys do not become available until long after election day, when press interest has waned. The only timely data are supplied by county and state officials. Just before election day, state officials tally up the reports from county officials on the numbers registered, and on election day they tally up the vote. These statistics get the big play in the press for the simple reason that they are available at election time, when the question of why turnout has been falling is national news. Furthermore, these numbers are taken as valid, since they appear to be straightforward counts of the registration lists and of those who voted. What state statistics showed in 1980 is that voting by registrants had dropped six points, from 81 percent in 1968.[9]

However, data from the Census and NES studies contradicted this conclusion. As we have noted, the Census showed voting by registrants falling by only two percentage points, from 91 percent in 1968. Instead, it was registration levels that had fallen, by seven percentage points, from 74 percent in 1968.

Curtis Gans of the Committee for the Study of the American Electorate prepared detailed press releases a few days before and after each presidential or midterm election, using the statistics provided by state election officials. In the preelection release, he reported how many people were registered; in the postelection release, he reported how many registrants had voted. Because his reports were so timely, the media relied on his heavily. His findings appeared in hundreds of newspapers and editorials. Gans also maintained close relationships with elections officials and was knowledgeable about local elections policies and practices.

Walter Dean Burnham, arguably the nation's leading electoral analyst, dominated academic interpretations of falling turnout. In an important way, Gans and Burnham were a working team; Burnham was a Committee board member, and Gans often quoted him. Following every election, they delivered a one/two punch, first in the media and then in academic sources. Most people were registered, they said, but voting by those who were registered was in a free fall.

After the 1984 election, Gans reported that fewer and fewer registrants were bothering to vote, thus "destroying the myth . . . that increased voter registration will automatically increase voter turnout." The press gave wide coverage to his statistics. Citing his 1984 postelection press release, the *New York Times* said editorially that "The percentage of registered voters who do vote has steadily declined—from 85.3% in 1960 to 80.5% in 1968 to 72.6% in 1984."[10] In other words, only three out of four registrants were bothering to vote. It is a measure of the power of this view of low voting that one pundit, David Osborne, in a widely noticed article, misread these statistics as saying that only one in four of the registered vote.[11] And when voting by registrants fell again in the 1988 election, Gans minced no words in his press release: "It is becoming incandescently clear that it is the will to vote . . . that is at the heart of the turnout problem."

In the same vein, Burnham wrote in academic publications that "three-quarters, more or less, of the adult citizenry were registered" in 1984, but that nonvoting by registrants "rose very substantially."[12] These expert opinions encouraged the view that registration reform wasn't necessary.

Doubts about registration reform were also expressed in a report commissioned by a consortium of foundations that had invested millions in nonpartisan voter registration drives during the 1983–84 period. The organization chosen to conduct the evaluation, called INTERFACE, specialized in studies of public education. The key staff were educators, including a former chancellor of the New York City schools, and perhaps that is why they emphasized motivation and expressed skepticism about whether registering people would raise turnout. They insisted on "the importance of . . . consciousness raising or other activities broadly grouped under the heading of voter education if sustained voter participation is to be achieved."[13] INTERFACE therefore recommended that funding priority be given to voter registration organizations "which allow opportunities for instruction or discussion"—for example, organizations that conducted "door-to-door registration, which permits more personal contact and opportunity for voter education." In the same vein, they said that get-out-the-vote campaigns were key to raising turnout among poorer and minority people. As for Human SERVE's approach, the report concluded that just registering people en masse in welfare agencies would not raise voting. Upon publication of the INTERFACE report in July 1985, the editorial writers at the *New York Times* readily picked up the message: the task now, they said, is to "lead eligible voters all the way" to the voting booth.

This perspective troubled us for several reasons. For one thing, it appeared to be contradicted by postelection studies. Peter D. Hart Research Associates verified from 1984 election records that voting by a national sample of 833 first-time-ever registrants (reregistrants were omitted) "closely approximated the turnout for registered voters." The figure was 77 percent, and it did not vary much by age or class. Project VOTE! also verified from election records that 70 percent of a sample of those whom its canvassers had registered in unemployment and welfare waiting rooms had gone to the polls. Bruce Cain and Ken McCue verified from Los Angeles election records that 75 percent of all new registrants had voted—80 percent of the Republicans and 69 percent of the Democrats. Moreover, since registration campaigns in Los Angeles were required to put their organizational names on each registration card, the study was able to estimate that slightly more than 70 percent of those registered by campaigns focusing on poorer and minority people went on to vote.[14] We were very impressed by this particular piece of research. Since Cain and McCue were working entirely with computerized records of those who had been registered by drives, we could not see any significant methodological biases. The conclusion that registrants voted had to be taken seriously.

Finally, when the 1984 Census and NES surveys appeared months later, both showed high voting by registrants (Census, 87 percent; NES, 84 percent). And registrants turned out in high proportions despite differences in race, income, and education. Here are the 1984 Census comparisons between those at the *extremes* of education— eight or fewer years versus college/postgraduate:

- 79.1 percent of the highest educated voted but only 42.9 percent of the lowest educated, a spread of 36 points.
- The spread narrows to 14 points when *voting by registrants* is

compared—94.4 percent of the highest educated registrants went to the polls, and so did 80.3 percent of the lowest educated registrants.

The opinions of seasoned politicians provided another body of contradictory evidence. Although many academics thought poorer and minority people wouldn't vote if they were registered, most politicians thought they would, or at least saw no reason to take chances by going along with reform. The voter registration system was so highly politicized because variations in rates of registration could potentially determine electoral outcomes. The goal of protecting incumbency thus governed considerations of every rule change. The politicians who set voter registration policy asked one question: Who would lose, and who benefit? That county election officials resisted deputizing outside groups to canvass was evidence that politicians wanted the contours of the active electorate to remain as they were. That was certainly Human SERVE's experience with executive orders. Incumbents in both parties saw worrisome risks. With a surge of excitement in the ghettos provoked by Jesse Jackson's run for the Democratic presidential nomination in 1984, Governor Cuomo, in deference to Mondale's candidacy, delayed issuing his executive order to establish voter registration in welfare and unemployment offices until after the state Democratic presidential primary in June. State Republican parties challenged executive orders in New York and Ohio. The Reagan administration reacted to executive orders as if they could change the outcome of the 1984 election. And the durability of time and place restrictions, put in place and kept in place by election officials with partisan purposes, was another source of evidence on the views of politicians. The data were unambiguous; politicians thought that once they were registered, people would vote.

We thought Gans and Burnham were being misled by an unacknowledged bias in the aggregate state statistics on which they relied. We were suspicious of these data in part because of the experiences of Human SERVE field organizers during the 1983–84 campaign. They had noticed that local registrars of voters were forever complaining about how difficult it was, as they put it, to keep their rolls "clean." Removing the names of people who had died or moved was a continuing and costly problem. Localities had the power to purge anyone who failed to vote; some localities could purge anyone who had failed to vote in a two-year period, although most had to wait four years. In many places, they were first required to go to the expense of sending out nonforwardable postcards to determine that nonvoters were no longer at their addresses of record. This took time; a person who had moved could remain on the rolls for as long as five years. Human SERVE staff came away from these experiences convinced that official voter registration levels were grossly inflated. We began referring to "deadwood registrants" and set out to estimate the scale of the deadwood problem.

One clue was reported by Squire, Glass, and Wolfinger who were interested in how high levels of residential mobility inflate registration rates. Some 530,000 registered voters in Rhode Island were mailed information pamphlets by the Secretary of State about an upcoming election in the fall of 1981. More than 100,000—or almost 20 percent of the state registration list—were returned by the post office marked "addressee unknown." Squire, Glass and Wolfinger explained this high rate of return by analyzing residential mobility patterns in the United States, and they concluded that some 30 percent of the electorate changes addresses between presidential elections.[15]

Beginning in 1985, Human SERVE began collecting more evidence on deadwood. We asked the elections clerk in Essex County, New Jersey (which contains Newark) to give us the results of the annual mail checks to verify addresses, as well as of the annual purging of people who had not voted in four years. The registration rolls contained 385,166 names in 1980; by 1984, 192,444 names, or 50 percent of the rolls, had been struck off. The point is that if election officials were slack about cleaning the rolls, as many were, deadwood built up rapidly. In 1986, the California chapter of the League of Women Voters, using volunteers to check samples of addresses of registered voters, concluded that the Sacramento County deadwood figure was 18 percent. The Sacramento County Registrar of Voters, Ernie Hawkins, said he thought that figure was about right, and related this series of experiences. When he completed the regular address verification procedure in March 1987, 5.8 percent of the nonforwardable postcards had been returned. But Hawkins completely mistrusted that result, believing the post office failed to return many undeliverable forms. Consequently, he negotiated with postal officials to verify the addresses of an additional special list of 5,000 names. By summer, 10.7 percent had been returned, leading Hawkins to conclude that "The deadwood level could be as high as 18 percent." The point is that to eliminate deadwood, local elections officials would have to conduct mail-check purges almost monthly, at great cost, so none did.

Based on these reports, we estimated that the 128 million names on the 1984 registration rolls contained the names of 20 million deadwood registrants, or 15 percent, who had died but whose names had not been purged from the rolls, or who had moved and reregistered elsewhere but whose names remained on the lists where they previously lived, so that they were counted *twice* in national totals.

Deadwood explained why it appeared that voting by registrants was low. Gans and Burnham treated millions of deadwood registrants as if they were *actual* registrants who abstained from voting. Subtracting deadwood, the true level of registration in 1984 was probably 63 percent, not 73 percent as Gans and Burnham claimed. And the true level of voting by registrants in 1984 was probably 88 percent, not 72 percent.

As the debate developed, Burnham reversed himself. In a review in the *New Republic* of the first edition of this book (1988), he endorsed our claim that deadwood was obscuring the fact that registrants voted at high (if slightly declining) levels, and that registration levels were falling. He abandoned the use of state aggregate data and endorsed the Census as "the best of surveys"[16] and he adopted the Census conclusion that "the overwhelming majority—somewhere between 85 and 90 percent—of people who are registered actually do go out and vote, at least in presidential election years." Furthermore, he said that the decline in voting by registrants during the past two decades was "relatively small" and that registration levels had fallen more. He wrote us separately that

> You have performed a real service in reminding us all of the gross inadequacies of . . . state-generated aggregate registration data. And you and I would certainly agree . . . that by far the largest share of abstentions falls in the ranks of those who don't get registered in the first place.[17]

Gans also reversed himself. At a debate with us arranged by the national League of Women Voters in February 1989, he conceded that state data contain 10 percent deadwood, which was two-thirds of the way toward our estimate of 15 percent. Some years later, he went further: "With residential mobility rates running about 16 percent a year," the deadwood increase during a four-year election cycle "could be as much as 60 percent."[18]

In any event, after 1985 Human SERVE circulated two key statistical conclusions—that registration was only 60–63 percent, and that roughly 86 percent of registrants voted. We would see these numbers time and again in the media. They were also cited repeatedly in state legislative arguments over reform, especially in the congressional arguments over the National Voter Registration Act. As the debate over registration reform intensified, in short, we were able to raise enough doubt about the dominant view to help give institutional reform some legitimacy.

In sum, we came—experience by experience, and study by study—to give more credence to the legal/institutional explanation of nonvoting. Barriers still existed; if they were eliminated, voting would rise, especially among the less educated. After 1984, barriers, and the need for government agency registration to overcome them, were Human SERVE's constant themes.

This opened us to the charge that our perspective was too narrow. Burnham thought that universal voter registration would solve only "30 to 40 percent" of the problem of low turnout. In fact, that was an estimate we were glad to endorse. We did not assume that higher registration, taken alone, would produce European levels of voting. But we did think that the creation of a pool of registrants among the lower strata might set in motion a dynamic of mobilization by the Democratic party. Certainly the rapid movement of blacks into the electoral system, once registration barriers were weakened in the postwar period, did much to change the southern party system, not least by forcing Democratic politicians to campaign for the votes of minority people. We thought that registration reform might have a similar effect on the national Democratic party. If registration rates could be raised substantially in the northern big-city wing of the Democratic party, there was reason to believe that voting would rise. Such an upsurge might spur entreprenurial Democratic politicians to undertake more serious mobilizing campaigns among poorer and minority people. In this sense, we were both legal/institutionalists and party behaviorists. To our minds, an explanation of low voting depended on synthesizing these alternative explanations.[19]

Nevertheless, we singled out voter registration because we thought something could be done about it. The government agency reform seemed politically possible. Party behaviorists, who attributed depressed voting to broad societal conditions, had no similarly viable remedies to offer. Gans presented this inventory of causes:

> The only thing that is certain is that the political conditions which have undermined citizen will to vote and participate have gotten worse. Unless we begin to address some of these problems—the decay and misalignment of the political parties, the conduct of our campaigns, the lack of civility in political dialogue, the inadequacies of our educational system when it comes to training citizens, the fragmenting effects of the coaxial cable and computers, and our increasingly anti-engagement, anti-government, self-seeking and libertarian values, among other things—the nation which prides itself on being the best example of government of, for and by the people, will continue to drift towards a government of, for and by the interested few.[20]

As to how to begin to remedy these systemic problems, neither Gans nor Burnham gave the slightest clue. Indeed, Burnham thought that "the answer to this question is anything but clear," and that "it is far from clear that there is an answer."[21] There was, in short, nothing to be lost by pressing for registration reform. It might not work, but no one had a more feasible idea.

CHAPTER TEN

The States
as Laboratories
of Democracy

*A*fter the 1984 election we decided to concentrate on promoting
government agency registration reform. The 1983–84 registration war had settled the question of whether hands-on campaigns
could correct class and racial skews. It showed that campaigns directed toward lower-income and minority people would inevitably be
counteracted by better funded efforts directed at higher strata. We
thought the remedy was to reform registration procedures. But there
were competing reform proposals. The traditional proposals were to
permit people to register by mail, or at the polls on election day.

At Human SERVE, we had little confidence in mail registration,
taken alone. True, it overrode local restrictions on deputization, and
thus facilitated hands-on campaigns. A mail system, in addition, was
essential if public or voluntary agencies were to conduct registration.
Furthermore, it was politically viable. Many politicians supported it,
as shown by the way it was spreading. Three states enacted it in the late
1960s, seventeen in the 1970s, four in the 1980s, and five in the early
1990s (including South Carolina and Mississippi in the Deep South).

But mail registration by itself didn't raise registration rates. Human SERVE compared states with and without mail-in systems in
1984, and found no differences. The reason seemed obvious. State

mail-in laws did not contain provisions to get the forms into people's hands so they could complete and mail them back. As a result, most people still had to go to a county seat or downtown office in a big city to obtain a form. The government agency system solved that problem. It also solved the problem of movers; they could update their registration in the agencies with which they had regular contact. (This advantage was confirmed after the NVRA was implemented in the states beginning in 1995; more than 70 million people registered and updated their addresses, names, and party affiliations for voting purposes in social agencies and DMVs during the next four years.)

Another proposal circulating at the time involved the postal system. Whenever someone notified the post office of a change of address, postal authorities would be required to notify the local voter registration office to cancel the person's registration, and notify the election office at the new place of residence to enroll the person. Professor Raymond Wolfinger championed this method, with impressive supporting evidence from his studies showing that residential mobility in American society was quite high—one in three people move during a presidential election cycle. But this reform would do nothing to lessen class and racial skews. Moreover, on the basis of a long history of poor service in minority communities, civil rights groups simply did not trust the post office, and it was doubtful that the states or the Congress would enact voter registration legislation to which they strongly objected.

The reform method that was much preferred by the voting rights community, especially the civil rights groups, was election-day registration. Civil rights supporters in the Congress regularly introduced bills calling for this reform. It had the advantage, at one stroke, of overriding the whole system of time and place and deputization restrictions. Moreover, the 1983 Harvard/ABC Symposium had recommended it, as we said in the last chapter. So did two subsequent national commissions.

The Commission on National Elections—cochaired by Melvin R. Laird, a nationally known Republican, and by an equally well-known Democrat, Robert S. Strauss—convened after the 1984 election and issued a report in 1986. Its forty members were weighted toward national politicians, media personalities, and corporate executives. Although the commission was concerned with a range of problems in national elections, from the length of presidential campaigns, to the timing of primaries, to cost and financing, it was also concerned with the fall in voting. On this topic, its findings and recommendations paralleled those of the Harvard/ABC Symposium:

> Low voter turnout, which has placed the United States at or near the bottom of the list among democracies, can be largely explained by two statistics. Only about two-thirds of eligible voters are registered to vote. But the vast majority who are registered—87–89%—actually go to the polls in general elections. *Thus the inescapable conclusion is that this nation must do far more to enable every citizen to register* [emphasis in original].

Two recommendations followed. One was to "strongly urge that the President and Congress designate National Registration day, to be held each election year on a weekday in late September or early October, in order to promote both increased registration and public education about the importance of elections." The other was to urge political leaders to permit "election day registration at polling places."[1]

The Citizens' Commission on Civil Rights, chaired by Arthur Fleming, and directed by William L. Taylor, initiated hearings in New York City in November 1984; additional hearings were held elsewhere during the next year or two. A wide range of voting rights groups testified about obstructive registration practices. In April 1988, the Center for Policy Alternatives published the commission's report, *Barriers to Registration and Voting: An Agenda for Reform.* Mail and election-day registration were featured recommendations.[2]

In principle, we too favored election-day registration. Turnout rates in the few states that allowed it were higher on average by roughly 11 percentage points. But its political prospects were dim. Unlike mail registration, it was not spreading; politicians and elections officials were almost uniformly opposed to it. Only four states had enacted it: Maine, Minnesota, Oregon, and Wisconsin (and Oregon subsequently repealed it when a religious cult, followers of Bhagwan Shree Rajneesh, bussed in street people from other places to help vote out the incumbent county administration, with which it was feuding over religious tax-exemption and other matters). Public officials claimed to fear that this system would create logistical chaos on election day (two long lines instead of just one), especially in large urban centers. They also claimed that it would encourage fraud in states where illegal immigrants were concentrated. When an election-day bill was introduced in the California legislature in 1987, the state Republican Senate Committee sent out an "urgent call" to mobilize opposition to it:

> Tens of thousands of illegal aliens, many of whom cannot speak English, will cast ballots cancelling out your vote. Every year, hundreds of thousands of illegal aliens cross our border to take advantage of free medical benefits and higher pay checks. What would stop radical fringe groups—like Tom Hayden's and Jane Fonda's organizations—from picking them up by the busload and delivering them to key districts to vote time and again?

In short, we did not think day-of-election registration was politically feasible.

Government agency voter registration appeared to have the best chance politically because, as we will describe in this chapter, it was already spreading. After 1984, Human SERVE began to argue that government had an "affirmative obligation" to register the electorate, and that signing people up in public agencies was the way to do it.

We also thought that reform at the state and local levels was a crucial precondition for winning national reform. There was every reason to anticipate strong congressional resistance to government agency registration, to say nothing of a presidential veto during a Republican era. But we thought that opposition might be weakened if we succeeded in getting agency-based registration in at least some states. At the very least, proponents would be able to argue that the new system worked, that it was administratively feasible, cheap, and fraud free. Then too, if government agency registration were to spread, it would rob congressional opponents of the states' rights argument against federal action. Federal legislation could be defined as simply nationalizing a state innovation. But to get these precedents, Human SERVE needed to persuade more state, county, and municipal officials to test the system. A political scientist would say that Human SERVE needed states and localities to play their traditional role as the "laboratories of democracy."

States and Localities as Laboratories of Democracy

Human SERVE followed a two-part strategy to promote state and local government agency voter registration. National staff lobbied national organizations of relevant state and local public officials to endorse and promote the idea among their members. They haunted the annual meetings of public officials, arguing that barriers kept voting down and that government agency registration was the solution, and importuning them to pass resolutions of support. A number of these organizations did so, and Human SERVE distributed their resolutions widely.

1983: National Black Caucus of State Legislators declared that "agency-based registration represents a bold departure whereby millions can be registered systematically and routinely in agencies serving precisely those most underrepresented in the electorate."

1984 (AND AGAIN IN 1986): National League of Cities endorsed training city employees "to assist citizens who want to register to vote." December 1987 newsletter contained a four-page insert prepared by Human SERVE describing how cities were implementing voter registration.

1986: United States Conference of Mayors "encourages individual members to issue executive orders and support legislation requiring governmental agencies, including public health, hospitals, housing, social welfare, libraries, employment security, personnel, tax offices, and drivers' bureaus to permanently institute voter registration as an additional service."

1986: National Conference of Black Mayors urged that black mayors "issue executive orders and support legislation requiring voter registration by government employees, including public social welfare, health, employment security and drivers' bureaus."

1987: Council of State Governments adopted the Minnesota agency-based legislation bill as a model to be recommended to state governments.

As a consortium of the nation's chief election officers, the National Association of Secretaries of State (NASS) was the most important. Its members could promote reform with governors and legislatures. For a decade, Human SERVE staff attended NASS annual conferences, maneuvered themselves on to panels to talk up reform, and worked with interested secretaries to promote reform in their states.[3] As time went by, the secretaries warmed to government agency registration, not least because of the success of the Michigan motor voter program, which was featured in the report of the 1984 Voter Registration Task-force of the National Association of Secretaries of State, chaired by Alabama secretary Donald Siegelman.[4]

In the mid-1980s, Sherrod Brown, the Ohio secretary, took center stage (he had first contacted us, as we said in chapter 7, in 1984, and we worked closely with him). He had motor voter running in his state, and he promoted the idea tirelessly among other secretaries, and among voting rights groups. Later he took responsibility for a major NASS report endorsing government agency registration. Human SERVE and the Center for Policy Alternatives had proposed that NASS schedule a plenary session on voter registration reform in July 1986, with Arthur Fleming, former chair of the Citizen's Commission on Civil Rights, as the main speaker, a proposal that was accepted. Shortly after the plenary, also at the suggestion of Human SERVE staff, NASS president Jim Douglas, a liberal Republican from Vermont, wrote Brown inviting him to chair a task force on voter registration barriers.[5] In 1987, after meetings, studies, and hearings, Brown's Task Force on Barriers to Voting issued a report (drafted by Brown's deputy, Margaret A. Rosenfield) with this conclusion:

> Public agencies that have frequent contact with the general public provide effective and efficient locations for voter registration. Agency administrators and workers can easily incorporate nonpartisan voter registration services into the routine job activities within each office. The barriers must come down. Universal registration must be the rule.[6]

Our work with the secretaries appears to have had some effect, or at least they thought it did. In 1994, the year after the NVRA was passed, NASS conferred its annual award on Human SERVE for "your efforts over the years to enhance voter registration opportunities."

The award committee singled out Jo-Anne Chasnow, who was Human SERVE's main staff liaison with the secretaries, "for her ability, hard work, research, technical assistance and commitment," and they asked that she be designated to accept the award at the ceremony.

The second part of the strategy was to lobby state and local officials. Some Democratic governors might be persuaded; so might some county executives and mayors in heavily black and Hispanic inner cities. Some Democratic state legislatures might act; so might some Democratic county and municipal legislatures. To this end, Human SERVE's state organizers, along with Susan Kotcher of the national office, worked to develop lobbying coalitions, with limited success. Groups participated sporadically in Delaware, Florida, Indiana, Kansas, Louisiana, Maryland, New Hampshire, New Jersey, New York, Oregon, Rhode Island, Vermont, Virginia, Washington, and West Virginia. State chapters of the United States Public Interest Research Group were active in a few states; League of Women Voters and Common Cause chapters participated in a few others; and the American Civil Liberties Union, human service organizations, and labor unions joined with us here and there. Farley Peters of the Center for Policy Alternatives (CPA) was consistently helpful, which was important because progressive state and local political leaders depended significantly on CPA for advice on various policy reforms. In 1985, Human SERVE prepared a booklet on "Executive Orders" that CPA published and distributed to its state and local mailing lists. The booklet reproduced executive orders that had already been issued by governors, as well as a model executive order recommended by Human SERVE. And it contained copies of resolutions of support from national organizations of public officials. As it turned out, only four gubernatorial executive orders were issued after 1984: by Democrats Evans in Idaho (1985) and Kunin (1986) in Vermont, and by Republicans Bellmon in Oklahoma (1987) and Kean in New Jersey (1989).

We thought Democratic mayors, especially big-city mayors, would want to set up voter registration programs. The cities were suffering badly from domestic program cuts. Augmenting the city voting base would help strengthen the urban lobby. According to the Census report for 1984, rates of registration among renters, who tended to be concentrated in cities, were 26 percentage points lower than among those who lived in owner-occupied housing—53 percent versus 79 percent—suggesting that access to registration services in municipal agencies could produce millions of new voters. Once Human SERVE began promoting the idea, some mayoral executive orders resulted in the mid-1980s: for example, twenty-one cities in Ohio, five cities in New Jersey. Trenton, under Mayor Arthur Holland, was one. In addition, during his presidency of the U.S. Conference of Mayors in 1986, he helped obtain a resolution of support of government agency registration. San Francisco made forms available in one hundred locations and instructed employees to ask all clients whether they wish to register. The Minneapolis City Council, with the mayor's support, also passed a resolution. Mayor Koch issued an order in New York City. In Texas, more than nine thousand forms were distributed in municipal health clinics and courts in the City of Houston during the first six weeks of a program that began in the summer of 1987. The City of Austin distributed six thousand forms through city libraries, utility customer service offices, and neighborhood recreation centers between January and June 1987.

Human SERVE organizers worked actively with minority mayors who we thought might lead the way. Mayor Harold Washington of Chicago was persuaded to issue an executive order in September 1986, but implementation was delayed by the stringent deputization procedures in Illinois. A bill enacted by the legislature, which became effective in 1984, permitted representatives of qualifying "civic" organizations to be deputized to register voters. This meant that before municipal employees could be trained, deputized, and supplied with forms by the Cook County and Chicago elections authorities, they had to be certified as members of an appropriate civic organization or one of the city's municipal unions. The problem of released time for the training of deputies who were city workers also had to be settled before the program could be carried out. It finally went into effect for about two weeks before the registration cutoff for the mayoral primary in January 1987. City agency tallies show that roughly 1,000 persons a day were registered, mainly in multi-service centers serving low-income clients, for a total of 10,000.

In February 1987, Los Angeles mayor Tom Bradley issued a letter to department heads announcing the formation of the City Voter Assistance Program requiring "city employees who deal with the members of the public in the course of conducting city business to . . . ask those individuals if they would like assistance in registering to vote." Voter registration cards were made available in 350 locations in fifty city departments.

Registration services at fifty sites within ten departments began in San Antonio in August 1987 as the result of joint action by the city council and the city's Hispanic mayor, Henry Cisneros. Alabama's association of thirty-three black mayors endorsed the principle of agency-based registration, and about a dozen of the mayors said publicly that they would implement it. Human SERVE was sufficiently impressed by all this to invite Michelle Kourouma, executive director of the National Conference of Black Mayors, to join Human SERVE's Board in 1989. Still, as time passed, it became clear that most orders were never implemented, and others only haphazardly.

Human SERVE also succeeded in establishing precedents in a range of other government settings. The Texas Human SERVE organizer persuaded the Harris County Hospital District, which includes the City of Houston, to establish a voter registration program headed by a "Coordinator of Voter Registration." Between February and August 1987, hospital Medicaid eligibility workers—who certified 250,000 people annually for medical care—distributed 12,000 voter registration forms to Medicaid applicants and helped fill them out. In Texas, Human SERVE also worked with Willie Velasquez and the Southwest Voter Education Project to arrange for voter registration services in migrant health services. But not many were registered, nor did the programs last.

We also promoted the idea that parents should be registered to vote when they enroll their children in the public schools each September. One of our California organizers, Susan Philips, got such a program underway in several schools in Los Angeles in the late 1980s, but it collapsed after we were forced to close the California office for lack of funds. Human SERVE's associate director, Louise Altman, and New York City organizer Jordan Moss also got the program up and running in some schools in New York City, for a time.

The officials who worked for state reform were usually Democrats, although many Democrats remained aloof, or even opposed it.

(Rarely was there a Democrat who supported registration in social agencies.) In addition to those already mentioned, the secretaries of state who were important included Mike Cooney (MT); Frankie Sue del Papa (NV); Dick Molpus (MS); and Phil Keisling (OR), and his staff, Nina Johnson and Rick Hanson. Governors acted in about ten states, as did mayors in several dozen cities, northern and southern. Here and there, individual state legislators took the lead: Paul Ogren (MN); Ron Withem (NE); Miles Rapoport, both as a Connecticut state legislator and subsequently as the secretary of state. The main activists in the South were black state legislators who were elected as a result of redistricting: Bob Holmes (GA); Mickey Michaux (NC); Rodney Ellis (TX); Cleo Fields (LA), who was subsequently elected to the Congress. Some heads of election boards supported reform: George Russell (KY); Sandy Steinbach (IA); David Maidenberg (IN); Thomas Wilkey (NY); Cecilia Burke, Travis County (TX); Ion Sancho, Leon County (FL); Germaine Wong, San Francisco; Marlene Hager, Virginia Beach (VA); and Margaret Jurgensen, Douglas County (NE). Emmet Fremaux, highly respected by his peers, was the election director from the District of Columbia who not only created a model motor voter program but also gave endless assistance to congressional staff in framing the government agency bill; Cook County Clerk David Orr's strong support helped counter outspoken opposition among other election officials in Illinois.

Motor Voter

Social agency registration got short shrift everywhere. It was registration in DMVs that caught on, and that made us look more closely at its possibilities. Although we had been skeptical of such programs when we formed Human SERVE in 1983 because of class and racial biases in license rates, we gradually changed our minds because license rates were rising so sharply that these biases were diminishing. According to the federal Department of Transportation (DOT), which collects statistics from state DMVs annually, only 75 percent of voting age adults held licenses in 1969. The figure rose to 81 percent in 1977 and to 84 percent in 1983. Thereafter it rose by about a percentage point annually, reaching 87 percent in 1988,[7] and 89 percent in 1990.[8]

To this figure must be added nondrivers who apply for DMV

photo IDs. The DOT does not collect data on personal IDs, and many states do not either, so no national total was available. But a few states did collect these statistics: 2.5 percent in both Maryland and Michigan, and 8 percent in Louisiana, all of which suggested that perhaps 3 percent of the national voting age population had them. It appeared that roughly 90 percent of the age-eligible electorate had licenses or photo IDs in the late 1980s.

There were two sources of inflation in these figures. Some proportion of drivers maintain licenses in more than one state, so they are counted at least twice in national totals. No one we consulted at DOT had any idea how many that might be. Probably the more serious inflationary bias was interstate residential mobility. People who move to a new state are supposed to obtain new licenses within 60 days (or they have to repeat the drivers' test). In turn, the old licenses are returned to the state of issue to be canceled, which takes time. Meanwhile, at the end of each reporting year, people could be counted as holding licenses by two different states, thus appearing twice in national totals. They were "deadwood drivers," like deadwood registrants. Statisticians at DOT with whom we spoke thought this bias could be at least as high as 10 or 15 percent.

On the other hand, there was a major deflationary bias. In the late 1980s, there were approximately 10 million noncitizens in the United States.[9] All noncitizens must be subtracted from the voting age population, and those among them who drive must be subtracted from the DMV rolls. If all noncitizens hold licenses or IDs, the subtractions from the VAP and DMV rolls would be the same, resulting in a wash. But it was reasonable to think that noncitizens held licenses at a lower rate, if only because many undocumented aliens would avoid government agencies. The consequences of subtracting *all* ineligibles from the VAP but *fewer of them* from the DMV rolls is to raise the proportion of the eligible VAP who have licenses or IDs. In other words, the fewer the ineligibles who have licenses/IDs, the more the eligibles who do.

We assumed that these two major biases, one inflationary and the other deflationary, tended to cancel out, and we therefore took the DOT gross figures as probably correct. We thus settled on a combined license/ID rate of roughly 90 percent of eligible voters. Consequently, we began reporting that drivers' licenses and nondriver photo IDs were becoming almost as universal as social security cards, and that motor voter would go far toward reducing class and racial biases in registration rates.

In 1986, Human SERVE produced a booklet, "Motor Voter: Toward Universal Voter Registration," that we distributed widely to state officials. It featured the Michigan experience—the large numbers registering and updating addresses, and the low cost. It contained examples of motor voter legislation and Human SERVE's recommended model legislation, which included voter registration in public assistance and unemployment agencies. An updated version of this booklet in 1992 showed the stages through which the twenty-nine motor programs were evolving, from registration forms on tables to application forms that incorporated registration forms:

Forms on Tables
    Alaska
    Connecticut
    Hawaii
    Louisiana
    Mississippi
    New York
    Oklahoma
    Pennsylvania
    Vermont

DMV employees ask whether applicants wish to register
    Illinois
    Massachusetts
    Michigan
    New Jersey
    New Mexico

Driver's license application asks whether applicant would like a
    separate form to register to vote
    Arizona
    Nevada
    North Carolina
    Ohio
    Rhode Island
    West Virginia

Single form with both license and registration sections
Colorado
District of Columbia
Iowa
Minnesota
Montana
Oregon
Texas
Washington State

On the question of cost, Human SERVE's 1992 report contained this evidence:

ARIZONA: There were 116,191 voter registration transactions in DMVs between July 1987 and May 1988. Secretary of state reports that no additional staff were required.

COLORADO: 155,652 transactions in 1988. No additional staff required.

DISTRICT OF COLUMBIA: 35,569 transactions between January and October 1990, at a cost of $0.18 per registrant. No additional staff required.

IOWA: With half of all counties reporting during October–November 1989, 3,176 registrations of new drivers only.

MAINE: 25,000 transactions between August 1990 and July 1991 at a cost of $0.24 per transaction. Secretary of state estimates that it takes 18 seconds per transaction. No additional staff required.

MICHIGAN: Roughly 750,000 transactions annually, costing $100,000 or $0.17 per transaction. No additional staff required.

MINNESOTA: 200,000 transactions in 1988, costing $65,000 or $0.33 per transaction. No additional staff required.

NEVADA: 73,012 transactions in 1988, costing $19,004 or $0.26 per transaction. No additional staff required.

NORTH CAROLINA: 84,396 transactions between January and August 1990. No additional staff required.

The strategy some election officials who opposed NVRA followed was to inflate estimated costs. They are still the brunt of jokes, since actual costs were much below the estimates. On a MacNeil/Lehrer Newshour (February 25, 1990), Pat Roberts, Republican member of the House from Kansas, reported that his secretary of state, Republican Bill Graves, estimated that he would need "22 additional staff to handle" government agency registration programs, "not to mention what's going to happen at the county courthouse level just to put up with this." Ron Thornburgh, who became Kansas secretary of state in 1995, when the NVRA program began, told us that "There have been no additions to the State elections staff related to the National Voter Registration Act. And I'm not aware of any staff additions at DMVs or at the county levels." The main costs to the states were associated with computerizing their operations, which they should have been doing anyway. When Human SERVE began in the early 1980s, the New York City Board of elections was still conducting all processing by hand.

No Social Agency Programs

Although motor voter programs spread, agency-based voter registration did not. The comprehensive state agency registration bill enacted in Washington State in 1984 produced little effect; it exempted social agencies if they considered themselves overworked, and most climbed through that loophole. The legislator who introduced a motor voter bill in the Maryland legislature in 1984 was persuaded by a voting rights coalition organized by Steve Rivelis, public affairs director of Planned Parenthood of Maryland, to include other state agencies as well. The bill, passed in April 1985, provided that space, posters, and new statewide registration forms be made available in the departments of human services, health, and mental hygiene, as well as in DMVs. Maryland election officials reported that 25,472 people were registered in 240 state offices during the first ten months after registration services were established in state agencies in 1986, representing 18 percent of all registration forms filed in the state during this period.

In 1987, the Iowa legislature was considering a motor voter bill introduced by House Member Rod Halvorson (D-Fort Dodge), but Secretary of State Elaine Baxter, after consultations with Human SERVE, testified that citizens who did not own or drive cars, including many lower-income Iowans, might be denied the opportunity to register unless state offices with which they came in contact also provided registration forms and assistance. The provisions of the final bill mandated that registration services also be established in such agencies as the departments of human services, employment services, human rights, and the Civil Rights Commission, and that employees must routinely inquire whether people wished to register and assist them in doing so.

But these agency-based programs did not last, if they were implemented at all. Although Human SERVE succeeded in persuading a substantial number of public officials to issue executive orders or enact legislation, few people got registered. Governors, county executives, and mayors staged signing ceremonies with great flourish: they draped themselves in the flag and delivered speeches sounding like the Founding Fathers, while cameras rolled. But then they didn't follow through to implementation. Much rhetoric, few registrants. And no permanence. Peter Shapiro, executive of Essex County, New Jersey, issued an executive order in 1984 and his senior staff worked actively to implement it. But once the presidential election was over, they dropped it.

One deterrent was continued threats by the Reagan/Bush administrations that voter registration was not an authorized use of federal matching funds. In 1984, Paul Wellstone, then a political activist in Minnesota, formed a Human SERVE chapter and helped win model legislation in May 1987 requiring voter registration in all state agencies serving the public directly. (Wellstone was subsequently elected to the U.S. Senate, where he promoted the National Voter Registration Act.) This bill was designed to solve two other problems with which Human SERVE was struggling. One was how to get nonprofit social service agencies to do voter registration. The solution we advocated was included in the Minnesota legislation—namely, to require that "nonprofit corporations that contract with the state . . . shall provide voter registration services for employees and the public." Second, the bill required that Community Action Program agencies, which were prohibited by federal laws from engaging in voter registration, shall nevertheless provide registration services. Human SERVE's thinking was that this provision, if implemented, would provoke federal officials, and we were hopeful that Minnesota officials would stand their ground. If an uproar ensued, the national Republican administration would be portrayed as trying to keep voting down, and might possibly back off, freeing antipoverty agencies elsewhere in the country to conduct registration.

The Minnesota measure was signed by Governor Rudy Perpich, and Secretary of State Joan Growe made a public commitment to implement it effectively. Motor voter went into effect quickly. But when welfare and unemployment officials amended their intake applications to include voter registration and began routinely signing people up, they were warned by federal officials that matching-grant funds should not be used for voter registration. Minnesota officials decided not to resist, and the program was terminated.

Human SERVE had argued (as we noted in the last chapter) that states could ward off this threat by simply overmatching by an amount equal to the federal share of the cost of staff time for participation in voter registration. Such a provision could have been incorporated in legislation or executive orders. But despite the miniscule costs involved, state officials were unwilling to adopt this strategy. No state made voter registration an integral part of the application process in social agencies—by instructing staff to ask whether people wanted to register and helping them fill out forms, or by designing a single combined application/registration form. As fallback, we argued that registration forms could be included in the agency application packets without risking federal audit exceptions. But state officials were unwilling to do that either. The best we got was that forms were placed on tables in welfare and unemployment waiting rooms, or perhaps on counters.

But merely making forms available did not result in many registrations. After the courts finally approved Governor Cuomo's executive order in 1985, it was implemented in nine state agencies with 389 local offices in fifty-six counties. During the first six months of operation, 41,533 voter registration forms were completed, more than half of them in unemployment offices, and 8,763 in motor vehicle offices (which had so far claimed to be too busy to implement the program fully). Eight additional state agencies with seventy-seven local offices were subsequently added. In his 1987 State of the State address, the governor reported that state agencies had "facilitated the registration of up to 150,000 voters" in 1986. Considering that New York had some four or five million unregistered voters, this was not impressive. As to how the program looked on the ground, implementation was scatter-shot. Human SERVE surveyed rough samples of state motor vehicle and unemployment offices on three occasions. A fall 1985 survey of fifteen state office sites showed that registration forms were available in nine of them; of twenty-three sites surveyed in the spring of 1986, forms were available in six; of twelve agencies surveyed in the fall of 1986, eight had forms.

In sum, we were chastened by the gap between proclamation and implementation; we had thought that the incentives generated by electoral competition would move governors and mayors to act. We took some encouragement from the spread of drivers license registration. Nowhere, however, had we succeeded in getting registration in welfare and unemployment agencies implemented effectively, partly because of federal obstructions. Consequently, we continued to work at the state and local level, but we also turned toward the Congress after 1986, when the Democrats regained the Senate, hoping to win national legislation mandating both motor voter and social agency registration.

CHAPTER ELEVEN

Federal Reform

*T*he Democrats in Congress would not have sponsored voter registration reform on their own. True, a few Democrats regularly introduced legislation in the 1980s, as they had done in the 1970s, generally either for registration by mail or for registration on election day.[1] For example, John Conyers, the black representative from Detroit, introduced two bills in 1985, one for mail and the other for same-day registration. But no one expected them to pass, a conclusion that Margaret Groarke also reached in her study of the history of the NVRA.[2]

Three conditions made the National Voter Registration Act of 1993 possible. One was the growth of an influential national voting rights coalition committed to making government agency registration the law of the land.

A second condition was the rapid spread of motor voter programs in the states. When the NVRA was enacted in 1993, twenty-nine states had motor voter programs. Most were just starting up and had registered few people. Still, it mattered in the congressional debates that more than half the states had opted for this reform. John L. Sousa, chief counsel of the Senate committee that had jurisdiction over voter registration, would later say, "We wanted this voter registration reform bill to reflect what's already happening in the states."[3] When the National Voter Registration Act came up for consideration in the early 1990s, *Washington Post* political columnist David Broder remarked that "by building on the State experience, its sponsors have done something that is all too rare in Washington: They allowed the design to be field-tested before taking it national."

The third condition explaining why reform succeeded is ironic. Neither party thought that voter registration reform would change electoral outcomes. One report after another appeared in the 1980s concluding that nonvoters were "carbon copies" of voters.[4] It was not self-evident that the Democrats would benefit more; greater voting for the Democrats by the poor and minorities could potentially be offset by higher voting for the Republicans by young people.

This political situation was altogether different from the circumstances preceding the enactment of the Voting Rights Act of 1965. Then, the endangered southern Democratic political leadership fought tooth and nail to prevent the enfranchising of blacks, since new black voters would undermine the apartheid basis of the "Southern Democracy." It took massive turbulence—civil disobedience campaigns in the South and civil disorder in the northern cities—to force national Democratic leaders to override southern opposition. But nothing like that was necessary to win voter registration reform three decades later. No large political consequences were anticipated, and there was less resistance. Now, a voting rights coalition could have, on its own, the potentiality to succeed.

Consensus among Advocates

There could be no national reform unless a consensus was reached among voting rights groups on the method of reform. Lloyd Leonard, public affairs director for the national League of Women Voters, put the point this way: "The civil rights groups could kill a bill with which they disagreed. Labor could kill a bill, and so could good government groups. But together, we could pass a bill." The main division was between proponents of election-day registration, favored especially by the civil rights groups, and proponents of government agency registration, which became the coalition position.

The consensus evolved gradually, as the membership of the coalition changed. After 1984, the hands-on voter registration groups were superseded by legal organizations that demanded reforms, including registration in welfare and unemployment agencies, as remedies in suits against election officials. Then, by the late 1980s, the legal groups were superseded by voting rights organization lobbyists who were oriented toward legislative reform and the government agency method.

HANDS-ON. Traditional voter registration organizations were ambivalent about reform. If reform was successful, their projects would become obsolete, or they would have to shift emphasis. At the same time, however inadvertently, they had also contributed to the viability of government agency registration as the preferred reform since much of their canvassing activity was conducted in welfare and unemployment waiting rooms. If volunteers could do it in waiting rooms, why not workers at their desks? And their experience had also made barriers a public issue, spurring the litigators who became advocates of agency registration into action. At the same time, the poor results of the hands-on drives in the 1984 election eroded their credibility, especially among donors, as we noted in chapter 7. And then an episode in California caused them further hurt.

Senator Alan Cranston (D-CA), convinced that his narrow re-election victory in 1986 was owed to his hands-on voter registration campaign, made two decisions. He decided to champion a federal reform bill, as we shall presently note. More to the immediate point, Cranston also decided to finance a massive hands-on voter registration apparatus in California in advance of the 1988 presidential election. Because the effort was a failure—worse, it ended in scandal—it undermined the hands-on approach and encouraged support for reform.

Cranston had been persuaded by Marshall Ganz, a longtime grassroots organizer, to try to build political organizations in a number of poor and minority neighborhoods in California that would register, educate, and get out the vote. The plan was to put a paid coordinator in each neighborhood, with the goal of recruiting volunteers who would register a million people and then go on to organize their neighborhoods. "This mechanism," Ganz hoped, "would be created by developing the leadership potential of young people drawn from target communities who would be recruited not only for an election season of social activism, but for a lifetime."[5] Ganz was in effect proposing to construct an organization of precinct captains, no matter that they had no jobs, favors, or turkeys to hand out. Cranston was enthusiastic and raised $3.5 million to support the effort, more than had ever been available in a short period to any hands-on voter registration campaign. But the neighborhood coordinators did not succeed in recruiting volunteers to canvass for new registrants; they had to do it themselves. They signed up 350,000 people—at a cost of $10 per card.

There was no more money after the election, and the operation was shut down. Then the scandal broke. Cranston was accused of abusing his power as a senior member of the Senate Banking Committee. He had solicited nearly $1 million for the voter registration project from Charles H. Keating Jr. at the same time that he was intervening with federal banking regulators to save Keating's California-based Lincoln Savings Bank from collapse. (It did subsequently collapse, with a $2.5 billion debt.) The FBI investigated, and Keating and others who had milked the bank went to jail. As for Cranston, the Senate ethics committee, in November 1991, found him guilty of "improper and repugnant" behavior, citing a meeting in November 1987 in which $250,000 for the voter registration project was delivered to his Senate office by the Keating group at a time when federal regulators were beginning to raise questions about sham real estate deals, backdated files, and perilously high rates of risky investments by Lincoln Savings.

These events frightened the funders of nonpartisan registration campaigns, particularly the foundations. They were also put off by the high cost per registrant. The hands-on voter registration community lost credibility, and the case for legislative reform was strengthened.

LITIGATION. After 1984, Human SERVE redoubled its work with voting rights attorneys who were bringing suits against local officials who maintained time, place, and deputization restrictions. Human SERVE staff organized and often cochaired meetings, defined agendas, wrote affidavits, recruited plaintiffs for law suits, compiled and distributed statistical evidence suggesting how barriers kept registration down, and provided expert testimony. Typically, letters, memos, and leaflets gave Human SERVE's telephone numbers as the place to call for further information.

Meanwhile, the National Emergency Mobilization on the Right
to Vote changed its name to the Campaign for Full Political Participation. It continued to be an amalgam of hands-on groups (Midwest
Voter Registration Project, National Coalition on Black Voter Participation, the Churches' Committee for Voter Registration, and Jesse
Jackson's Citizenship Education Fund), and of legal defense organizations (the NAACP Legal Defense and Education Fund, Mexican
American Legal Defense and Education Fund, Lawyers Committee
for Civil Rights under Law, and the League of Women Voters Education Fund, which included the legal division). The campaign sponsored a series of meetings during the mid-1980s to plot out the fight
against barriers. The most important was a three-day "Conference on
Voting Rights" on October 22–24, 1987, in San Antonio. The opening
plenary on "Executive Orders and Agency-Based Registration Initiatives" was chaired by Human SERVE's Linda Davidoff, and featured
Iowa Secretary of State Elaine Baxter (a vigorous supporter of motor
voter), and Walter Martinez of the San Antonio City Council (which
had ordered voter registration in city agencies). Some of the panels
dealt with legal strategies: problems of proving racial discrimination
in voting rights cases under Section 2 of the Voting Rights Act, rebut-
tals of defense arguments, handling lay witnesses, and the like. Others
dealt with remedies, including agency-based registration. The closing
plenary featured Senator Cranston (who had begun shaping a reform
bill) and Henry Cisneros, then mayor of San Antonio, who had successfully lobbied the City Council to pass legislation mandating registration in various municipal agencies.

The growing emphasis on national legislation resulted partly from
disappointment in the results of litigation. Most suits failed. Public
officials did not give way easily, and the courts were generally reluctant
to intervene in local registration arrangements on either constitutional or Voting Rights Act grounds. An exception was a suit taken
against Mississippi's restrictive practices (no deputy registrars, for example) by the NAACP Legal Defense Fund and the Lawyers Committee for Civil Rights under Law, represented by Frank Parker, who had
litigated civil rights issues in that state for a decade. (When Parker
walked into the federal courtroom in Oxford, the judge, a conserva-

tive Reagan appointee, announced that he was "honored" by Parker's presence.) At trial's end, the court found that

> the existing statutory procedures for voter registration in the State of Mississippi violate the compliance provisions of the Voting Rights Act inasmuch as the statutes have a disparate impact on plaintiffs and all similarly situated blacks in Mississippi, which results in an abridgement of their right to vote.

A few such victories notwithstanding, it was clear by the late 1980s, as Cynthia Williams (one of Human SERVE's first staff members) observed, that "the struggle to prevail in the courts over the election clerks and the local political regimes that support them could go on endlessly."[6]

Nevertheless, the litigation movement succeeded in beginning to make the courts proponents of government agency registration. Human SERVE emphasized that attorneys should not be satisfied just to demand a few more deputy registrars or satellite centers but should seek remedies that would wipe out historic disparities. The way to do it, we argued, was to demand that voter registration be made available in agencies serving poorer and minority people.

ACORN initiated such a suit during the barrage of suits against election authorities in 1984, in this case against Arkansas Governor William Jefferson Clinton. Representation was provided by Lani Guinier and the NAACP Legal Defense Fund. ACORN v. Clinton resulted three years later, in December 1987, in a Consent Decree. County clerks were ordered to appoint as many deputy registrars as necessary "to register as many unregistered eligible residents as possible." In addition, one employee, suitably deputized, "shall be available during regular office hours to register or update the registration of all eligible citizens who have business" in county offices of the Department of Human Services. "Clearly visible signs" must be posted stating that eligible citizens may register to vote and directing them to the Deputy Voter Registrar. In addition, "all employees in each such state office shall, as a regular duty of employment, direct interested persons to the Deputy Voter Registrar." (As it happened, however, this program never got off the ground because the Department of Human Services dragged its feet, and some county clerks refused to deputize social agency personnel.) But now voting rights litigators were beginning to call for social agency registration.

A case in California in 1986 also illustrates this point. The Election Code already stated that:

> It is the intent of the Legislature that voter registration be maintained at the highest possible level. . . . County clerks shall deputize as registrars qualified citizens in such a way as to reach most effectively every resident of the county. In furtherance of this purpose, the governing board of any county, city, city and county, or other public agency, may authorize and assign any of its citizens or employees to become deputy registrars of voters and to register qualified citizens on any premises and facilities owned or controlled by such public agencies during the regular working hours of such officers or employees.

Since this provision had never been implemented, Human SERVE's California organizer, Barbara Facher, arranged for one of the two Democrats of the five-member Los Angeles Board of Supervisors to submit a motion to instruct county election officials "to work with all departments whose employees have daily contact with the public . . . to develop a voter registration program." This motion was rejected by a 3–2 vote of the Board, thus laying the basis for a lawsuit prepared by Mark Rosenbaum of the ACLU of Southern California. Human SERVE recruited the plaintiffs: chapters of Common Cause and the Southern Christian Leadership Conference, as well as the Southwest Voter Education Project. We also provided expert testimony. The League of Women Voters filed an amicus brief.

In July 1986, the Los Angeles Superior Court issued a preliminary injunction ordering the county to instruct 20,000 health and welfare workers to begin soliciting voter registration, and suggested that they engage in the following "brief dialogue with their clients":

(i) "Are you registered to vote?"
(ii) "If you would like to register, I can provide you with a voter registration card."
(iii) "Please fill out and sign the card, and I will forward it to the County Registrar, or you can mail it in yourself."
(iv) "The decision to register or not to register is yours. It will not affect your receipt of County services in any way."

The three Republican supervisors voted to appeal the decision (one of them called agency registration "socialism"). The three-judge panel of the Court of Appeals unanimously upheld the lower court in June 1987 and affirmed the obligation under law of county election officials to reach out to unregistered voters, including by deputizing county workers. The Appeals Court declared that the lower court had acted properly because "the use of county employees as deputy registrars will significantly increase the number of registered voters who are poor and non-white, in accord with the intent of the legislature." However, the three Republican supervisors appealed to California's highest court and won in August 1989. The reason they won was that Republican George Deukmejian had recently taken the governorship, and he replaced Rose Bird, the liberal head of the court, as well as two others who had been appointed by outgoing Governor Jerry Brown.

LOBBYING. Senator Cranston's announcement in the spring of 1987 that he was going to sponsor a registration reform bill galvanized the voting rights community. Since Cranston was the majority whip, there might be a new readiness in the Congress to enact reform. Cranston's staffperson, Candy Nelson, began fashioning a bill with day-of-election and mail registration at its core.

We doubted that day-of-election registration had any chance of passage or that mail registration would do any good without a requirement to distribute the forms widely. Integrating voter registration as part of the delivery of services by a range of government agencies would solve that problem. Human SERVE thought it might be possible to persuade Cranston's staff, and other key Democrats, to include provisions requiring the states to establish motor voter and social agency registration. To try to develop a supporting coalition, we hired Jeri Rasmussen in March 1987, and Deborah Karpatkin, Human SERVE's legal director, provided assistance in drafting legislative proposals.

Other groups saw Cranston's bill as a major opportunity, and devoted staff time to shaping it. Ira Glasser, national director of the ACLU, had supported government agency registration from the time Human SERVE first proposed it. Once congressional legislation seemed possible, Judy Crockett in the ACLU Washington office worked with congressional staff and kept coalition members informed about the dozens of proposed amendments to the pending legislation by cataloging and analyzing them. Martha Jimenez of the Mexican American Legal Defense Fund helped with legislative drafting.

People for the American Way was a constant source of support. The board president, John Buchanan, who had been a Republican congressman from Alabama between 1965 and 1981, roamed the halls of Congress importuning his former Republican colleagues to support registration reform, and Marsha Adler, senior lobbyist, made sure their public relations department was promoting voter registration reform in the press, partly to make Democrats sit up and listen. Ned McCulloch of ACORN kept lists of the roughly 150 endorsing organizations current. Some leaders in the disability community—attracted by the prospect that voter registration in vocational rehabilitation agencies would augment the electoral power of the disabled—also supported agency registration, including Durward K. McDaniel, chair of the Affiliated Leadership League of and for the Blind (an early Human SERVE board member), and Phil Calkins, the director of Disabled but Able to Vote. For all practical purposes, Jeri Rasmussen staffed this early coalition, and she got considerable advice and help from Gene Karpinski of USPIRG, who saw motor voter as a way of registering his college student constituency. (When Rasmussen left Human SERVE in August 1988, responsibility for our work at the federal level was assigned to Jo-Anne Chasnow.)

The effort succeeded. Cranston's staff was persuaded to include language drafted by Human SERVE:

> Notwithstanding any other provision of law, all Federal agencies and all State, county, municipal and non-profit agencies receiving grant-in-aid monies and serving the public directly shall, during the entire year, offer non-partisan voter registration services, including distributing voter registration forms, answering questions and assisting in completing forms, and ... forwarding completed registration forms to the proper local election officials.

At the end of 1987, Senator Cranston and Representative Conyers introduced companion bills with provisions for registration by mail, in government agencies, and on election day at the polls.

At the same time, Human SERVE and several other members of the coalition began working with Al Swift (D-WA), chair of the House Subcommittee on Elections of the Committee on House Administration, to fashion a government agency registration bill which featured motor voter and included social agencies. Swift held a series of hearings in 1988 at which many members of the voting rights coalition testified. At one such hearing in May, Ralph Munro, Republican secretary of state in Swift's own state (with whom we had worked beginning in 1984 when he initiated a government agency registration bill in his state legislature) waved his driver's license around exclaiming, "Why can't this be your voter registration card?" Swift would later say that this was when he "first heard about linking registration to drivers' licenses."[7] Rasmussen reported to Human SERVE's national office that Swift was "enormously excited" by the idea. Munro subsequently lobbied assiduously among Congressional Republicans. His authority as a champion of motor voter was enhanced when he was elected president of NASS in 1990–91. Human SERVE had a close relationship with him, as well as with Gary McIntosh, his state election director. (When we later asked Munro why he had become so vigorous an advocate, he replied that he hoped that broadening the electorate would help stem the rise of the Christian Right and the Republican party's rightward drift in his state.)

On September 14, 1988, Swift distributed copies of proposed legislation (drafted by Subcommittee Counsel Karl Sandstrom) mandating voter registration in both DMVs and public assistance agencies, and mandating mail-in in all states for federal elections. The traditional practice by election officials of purging people for not voting every two or four years was prohibited. Swift submitted his first bill (HR 15) in January 1989, which went through markup in March, and was reintroduced as HR 2190 in May by majority leader Tom Foley (also from Washington State) just weeks before he was elected speaker of the house.

This was the beginning of a conflict in the coalition over the preferred method of reform. The lines were drawn at a March 1989 hearing of Swift's committee. Ralph Neas of the Leadership Conference on Civil Rights testified that the bill was flawed because it excluded registration at the polls, and expressed support for the legislation sponsored by Representative Conyers. By contrast, Nancy Neuman, president of the national League of Women Voters, testified in favor of the Swift bill. Since the LWV was a member of the Leadership Conference, which had a tradition of operating on the basis of consensus among its diverse members, the defection caused hard feeling. No legislation was possible without the support of both organizations.

Human SERVE encouraged and supported the LWV breakaway. Government agency registration needed an influential champion. At this juncture, the LWV's Lloyd Leonard assumed leadership of the coalition members which supported the bill, including importantly the ACLU, the USPIRG, and influential disability groups, especially Disabled American Veterans, represented by Bruce Burgess. Looking back, it is clear that this split, however acrimonious, nevertheless led to the beginning of a gradual shift in the civil rights community away from advocating registration on election day and toward a reform that was already spreading among the states.

Motor Voter as Racially Biased

Unfortunately, the split in the coalition was exacerbated by fears that motor voter programs were racially biased. As we have said, we thought the same thing at first, but changed our minds because rapidly rising license rates in the 1980s were reducing racial differences. But some civil rights groups were not persuaded. On December 4, 1989, two letters were issued to "Interested Persons," one from Julius Chambers, director-counsel of the NAACP Legal Defense and Education Fund, and the other from Elaine Jones, deputy director-counsel, who headed the Washington office. Chambers said "The bill contains several weaknesses and may severely undermine current voter registration efforts." Jones said "The motor voter bill contained many weaknesses that might undermine existing gains in black registration and voting." Some months later, by arrangement with LDF, Benjamin F. Chavis, Jr., executive director of the United Church of Christ Commission for Racial Justice (who would shortly become the director of the NAACP), took up the issue in a press release entitled "Voting Rights Emergency." He urged the civil rights community to "Stop the motor voter bill before it is too late. Ensure voting rights not for some, but for all."[8] These actions were widely interpreted as an effort to prevent the Leadership Conference on Civil Rights from endorsing government agency registration.

According to Chavis, Human SERVE's claim that 90 percent of the eligible electorate drove or held photo IDs "misstated the truth." He charged that "the bill would disproportionately register white, middle, and higher income individuals" because poorer and minority families were less likely to own vehicles, and cited an LDF memorandum which claimed that "31 percent of African American households" in Louisiana had no motor vehicles. Writing in the *Yale Law & Policy Review,* Dayna L. Cunningham, an LDF staff attorney, noted that "42 percent of African-Americans, compared with 9 percent of whites, do not have access to vehicles in Eastern Arkansas," and she warned against a "motor-vehicle based" voter registration bill.[9]

This charge was wrong. Despite the word "motor," it was drivers who would be registered, whether or not they owned vehicles. Human SERVE circulated Department of Transportation (DOT) data showing that even in the 13 percent of American households without vehicles, 92.5 percent had one or more drivers,[10] and others had photo IDs.

If our estimate that 90 percent of the electorate had licenses or IDs was correct, there was little room left for variance by race. The remaining 10 percent included substantial numbers of disabled persons, many of whom cannot drive. To the extent that racial variations in license rates remained, the question was whether the rates among blacks were higher or lower than their voter registration rates. If license rates were higher, motor voter would reduce registration disparities by race; if lower, it would increase them.

Statistics distinguishing between blacks and whites with licenses were available from only four states (all border or southern). In 1990, 87 percent of white voting age persons in Louisiana had licenses versus 69 percent of blacks, a difference of 18 percentage points; in Alabama, the figures were 90 percent and 74 percent, a difference of 16 points; the figures were 95 percent and 83 percent in North Carolina, or 12 points; and 91 percent and 80 percent in Maryland, or 11 points. Overall, the range was 11 to 18 points, favoring whites. The black license rates appeared, on average, to be about 75 percent.

However, black registration rates were much lower than license rates, and they had been falling even as license rates rose. Sixty-four percent of blacks told Census interviewers in 1964 that they were registered; only 58 percent did in 1996. Normally one would adjust these figures downward by 10 percent to correct for overreporting. Moreover, it has long been known from studies published in the academic journals that blacks are much more likely than whites to overreport registration and voting, so the figure should be adjusted downward by more than 10 percent. Katosh and Traugott, for example, checked with election officials and found that 24 percent of blacks overreported being registered in 1976, and 26 percent in 1978, twice the white rate.

Hispanics had the lowest registration level—40 percent in 1984, according to the Census. Thomas Cavanaugh estimated that one-third were noncitizens. Adjusting for this, he concluded that 59 percent of eligible Hispanics were registered that year (53 percent if corrected for overreporting).[11] By contrast, the DOT reported in 1990 that 80 percent of Hispanics claimed to have licenses.

Finally, Human SERVE collaborated with Emmett Fremaux, executive director of the Board of Elections and Ethics, District of Columbia, to study the District's drivers' license voter registration program during the first four months after it was inaugurated in May 1989. Two conclusions emerged. More than 70 percent of all new voter registrations were transacted in the drivers' license bureau. Second, the impact was greater in the poor and black wards than in the rich and white ones: the registration rate in the richest ward rose by 2.0 percentage points, and in the poorest ward by 3.3 percentage points.

Minority women, especially in big cities, were the most likely to be left out by a motor voter program (unless they applied for photo IDs). Several sources of data confirmed that conclusion. To obtain more demographic information on drivers (income, race, etc.) than was available from state statistics, the DOT conducted two telephone surveys of national samples of more than 20,000 households, one in 1983 and the other in 1990. The 1990 survey showed that only 73 percent of black and Hispanic women had licenses. In addition, Human SERVE requested that New York City welfare officials conduct a drivers' license survey in two high-volume waiting rooms. In a center in Brooklyn that saw 600 recipients daily, 500 were questioned and only 12 had licenses. About 700 were questioned in a Manhattan center and eight had licenses. Nationally, there were approximately four million adults on AFDC in the early 1990s. There were more millions of poorer people on Medicaid and food stamps (in the 1990 recession, 10 percent of the population was on food stamps), and a significant fraction of them no doubt lacked licenses. Without agency-based registration to supplement motor voter, they would be missed.

In sum, we concluded that motor voter programs would substantially lessen disparities in registration rates by race, but not eliminate them. Still, some of the civil rights groups, LDF especially, remained unconvinced and continued to press for registration on election day at the polls. Greg Moore, who ran Jesse Jackson's national voter registration program, said this to us at the time: "The civil rights groups trust Human SERVE on agency-based registration; it's what you say about motor voter that they don't trust."

The Democratic leadership settled the issue. They were adamantly opposed to election-day registration. So were the election officials in their states, including secretaries of state. In 1988, the International Association of Clerks, Recorders, Election Officials, and Treasurers passed a resolution strongly opposing registration at polling places. Election officials claimed that registration at the polls would produce fraud and cause chaos on election day.

When the Cranston bill was referred to the Senate Committee on Rules and Administration, which had jurisdiction over the administration of federal elections, the chair, Wendell Ford of Kentucky, held hearings in November 1988 at which he arranged for the Kentucky secretary of state, Bremer Ehrler, to testify that election day registration would encourage and facilitate fraud. But Ford was not against reform. When he was governor of Kentucky, he discovered that the registration rolls exceeded 100 percent of the VAP, so he threw them out and opened the schools and other facilities nights and weekends for people to sign up again. It was a matter of good government, and Ford viewed motor voter registration in the same way. Ford's first proposed legislation, introduced in May 1989 (S 874), included registration by mail, at DMVs and at other agencies, and prohibited nonvoting purges, but omitted day-of-election registration.

In the House, Swift made it plain that he was prepared to move forward on a government agency registration bill, but only if the civil rights organizations dropped the demand for election-day registration. Writing in the *National Journal,* James A. Barnes wrote that election-day registration had received "an unenthusiastic reception in Congress."[12] And so by the late 1980s, it had become clear that there was going to be a government agency registration bill, or none at all.

Motor Voter Ineffective?

In 1988, just as a consensus favoring government agency legislation was beginning to grow, Curtis Gans released a report to the press claiming that motor voter would add only 5.8 million to the registration rolls.[13] That the Ford Foundation had funded this research added to its legitimacy, and it was reported in the press. Two years later, in 1990, the Congressional Research Service (CRS) dealt the cause of motor voter reform a near knockout blow. The House Subcommittee on Elections was at the time considering a motor voter bill and requested that CRS provide a report on registration levels in motor voter states, as of the 1988 presidential election. On the basis of a sample of ten motor voter states, CRS concluded that if Michigan's longstanding program were excluded, there was no average registration increase in the remaining nine, and no increase in turnout.[14] In short, motor voter didn't work.

As the research arm of the Library of Congress, the CRS is highly respected. During the several years leading up to final passage of the motor voter bill in the spring of 1993, the CRS report (and the Gans report) were cited dozens of times by Republicans to justify voting against the bill. Thus Mitch McConnell (R-KY) wrote an op-ed in the *Christian Science Monitor* summarizing the CRS report and concluding that the motor voter bill is "a solution in search of a problem."[15] This theme was sounded time and again in debates, and reported in the press, with the result that Human SERVE was flooded with letters and phone calls from funders, advocates, politicians, and elections officials questioning why they should proceed with a reform that failed to raise registration and turnout. Advocates of motor voter in the Congress were especially embarrassed. Swift had been sending out memos and letters based on Human SERVE's statistics: "Current estimates are that 87 percent of eligible voters have drivers' licenses, and if you add in those non-drivers who obtain identification cards issued by motor vehicle departments, you can see that we will reach perhaps 90 percent of the eligible voters with this approach."

It was immediately evident to us why these reports were wrong. Neither Gans nor CRS had conducted field investigations to see whether the state programs were actually up and running. For example, of the nine states (excluding Michigan) in the CRS sample,

1. Three states had motor voter programs on the law books that weren't yet operating.
2. Two states had started up motor voter programs only in 1988, the year of the CRS evaluation.
3. One state, North Carolina, began a motor voter system in 1984, but virtually suspended it when a Republican won the governorship the next year, and resurrected it only after a Democrat regained the statehouse in 1989 (one year *after* the 1988 election which CRS used as its benchmark), with these corresponding year-by-year variations in motor voter registration totals:

1984	60,000
1985	6,500
1986	6,200
1987	3,200
1988	3,300
1989	36,800
1990	84,000

4. Two states registered only new applicants, and not the much larger pool of those renewing their licenses.
5. Some states merely placed registration forms on tables in waiting rooms rather than using combined forms.

An adequate evaluation of the impact of motor voter reform would have limited the states to those with combined forms that were *operational* over a *four-year cycle,* and that, in addition to new applicants, registered both *in-person and mail renewals.* Considering that Michigan was the only state that more or less met these criteria, CRS ought to have informed Congress that an evaluation of motor voter programs was not yet possible.

But getting CRS to admit to some defects in its methodology was not enough to repair the public relations damage caused by its report. We needed some larger statement about the potential reach of motor voter. Consequently, Human SERVE prepared a letter to CRS, which the House Subcommittee on Elections forwarded, asking for an opinion on the proportion of the population holding drivers' licenses. CRS replied that:

> In our opinion, about 87 percent of the voting age population have drivers' licenses, to which one would add an unknown percentage of persons of voting age who held State personal identification cards issued in lieu of drivers' licenses.[16]

Confirmation by CRS of the high levels of drivers' licenses restored the credibility of motor voter programs as the core of a strategy toward universal voter registration. Gans also changed his mind. He reported in 1993 that motor voter programs could potentially "increase the present registration level from . . . 65 percent to 91 percent."[17] With the gradual acceptance of that conclusion, support for election-day registration faded, and both the voting rights coalition and supporters in the Congress began focusing on winning the best government agency registration bill possible.

It should also be said that there were moderating influences in the coalition which helped this shift to occur. One was the circulation of voting rights organization staff. Gracia Hillman, who oversaw Operation Big Vote, the national black hands-on coordinating group, became director of the League of Women Voters in 1990. Wade Henderson had been associate director of the Washington office of ACLU, which was strongly supportive of government agency registration. (Morton Halperin, the head of ACLU's Washington office, played a very important behind-the-scenes role moderating conflict over the pending legislation.) In 1991, Henderson then became the director of the Washington bureau of the NAACP, replacing Althea Simmons, a revered figure in the voting rights struggle who, until her death in 1990, was an adamant opponent of the bill. In his new position, Henderson played a critical role in persuading the civil rights community to support the legislation. So did Greg Moore, who worked for Jesse Jackson, who supported the bill. Several years before, Moore had been a leader in the United States Student Association; he knew from experience that setting up tables in student unions was futile, and saw motor voter as a way to sign up the student constituency. Sonia Jarvis, an important figure in the black voter registration community who held several different organizational positions during the period leading up to passage of the bill, consistently tried to keep lines of communication open.

There were also signs that Representative John Conyers, the leading advocate in Congress of election-day registration, was willing to compromise. On August 15, 1988, Davidoff reported to the Human SERVE staff that a critical meeting had taken place:

> Swift, Conyers, and Robert Borosage of the Institute for Policy Studies, who represented Jesse Jackson, met on August 10 in Washington, and apparently Borosage and Conyers thought it would be okay for Swift to continue developing his own version of the Universal Registration bill with heavy reliance on motor voter and mail-in, but without election day registration. However, they urged that the agency-based provisions be strengthened.

Improving the Legislation

Early government agency legislative proposals had been framed without much reference to the Voting Rights Act (VRA). The NAACP Legal Defense and Education Fund, guardian of the VRA, was troubled that features of the NVRA bill could be used to weaken it. For example, the VRA specified that both "individuals" and "persons" (i.e., organizations) had standing to sue; NVRA mentioned only individuals. That omission was remedied. LDF was also concerned that language in the voter registration bills could be interpreted as conflicting with the VRA. The final legislation contains this language: no "provision of this Act shall supersede, restrict, or limit the application of the Voting Rights Act," and "nothing in the Act authorizes or requires conduct that is prohibited by the Voting Rights Act."

What social agencies would be included was also a contested issue. The coalition wanted human service agencies to be required to conduct voter registration. The Republicans wanted the matter left to the discretion of state officials. But if specific state agencies were to be mandated, then the Republicans wanted some agencies that served their constituents, such as tax bureaus, and Mom and Pop stores that issue hunting and fishing licenses. The more the list grew, the more election officials objected that the system would be unmanageable. The Republicans then argued that the list should be restricted to DMVs and agencies serving the disabled. But Jim Dickson, who is blind and who represented the disability groups in the coalition, and who had once been a welfare rights organizer, urged the disability groups to press to have agencies serving other groups included.

When all was said and done, the final legislation required that voter registration be conducted in DMVs, public assistance agencies (AFDC, Food Stamps, Medicaid, and WIC), agencies serving the disabled, and military recruitment offices. Unemployment agencies, originally mandatory, were made optional, a concession to the Republicans in the bargaining process. State officials were also required to designate several other agencies, at their discretion, in which registration would be available, such as libraries, public schools, and unemployment offices.

There was a related struggle over whether voter registration procedures would be as routinized and automatic in human service agencies as in DMVs. Motor voter programs in the states were evolving toward the use of combined forms, a trend that Human SERVE had promoted, and that the final federal legislation encouraged by requiring that a voter registration application be made "part of an application" for a driver's license. When human service registration first began to appear in federal bills, the language was much looser. There was no outright requirement; instead agencies were to establish voter registration "to the greatest extent practicable." There was a continuing and partially successful struggle to strengthen the language. The final bill required that human service agencies "must provide to each applicant who does not decline to register to vote the same degree of assistance with regard to the completion of the registration application forms as is provided by the office with regard to the completion of its own forms, unless the applicant refuses assistance." Senator Paul Wellstone of Minnesota, another former welfare rights organizer, campaigned constantly among his colleagues for this provision (and presided over the Senate on the day in 1993 when the National Voter Registration Act was enacted).

Civil rights groups, the LDF especially, were deeply suspicious of purging practices, which had been used traditionally to help keep minority voting low, and to their minds the U.S. Postal Service was an unwitting accomplice because of its poor service in the ghettos. The final bill prohibited the customary practice of purging people for not voting. Election officials had to use some other criterion (such as the

Postal Service National Change of Address System) and then send address verification notices to voters who they believed had moved. If the notices were not returned, the voters could not be purged but instead were to be placed on an "inactive list" until they either returned notices or failed to vote in the next two federal elections. This is now the national system, and it is hard to see how people can any longer be mistakenly or deliberated purged.

Finally, LDF insisted on a "fail-safe" provision that when people move within the jurisdiction of the same registrar in the same congressional district, these voters may go to either the old or new polling place on election day to update their registration and vote. Many people thought this provision was revolutionary; it was day-of-election reregistration.

It took roughly four years for this consensus to emerge. Some members of the coalition would probably have compromised earlier, and settled for less. Human SERVE would have. At various times along the way, we would have been satisfied with a one-sentence bill saying that states were free to use matching and social service block grant funds to conduct nonpartisan voter registration in welfare, unemployment, and anti-poverty agencies, including community action agencies, Head Start, and legal services, as well as nonprofit social service organizations which received federal money. Our hope was that industrial-state Democratic governors would then act. (That strategy would have failed because Republicans had captured many of the key northern industrial-state governorships by the 1990s). In early October 1989, after hearings and negotiations led to some strengthening amendments to HR 2190, the Washington office of the ACLU distributed a memo to "Interested Persons": "We believe that improvements have produced legislation whose gains outweigh any disadvantages and should be supported."[18] A week later, Jesse Jackson, as president and founder of the National Rainbow Coalition, wrote William H. Gray III, a highly respected black House member who was at the time Democratic Majority Whip:

> We have reached another critical juncture in our efforts to pass a comprehensive voter reform bill. After many months of negotiation it is clear that we have made considerable progress, but apparently not enough to satisfy some members of the civil rights community. I applaud the work of the House

Leadership, the civil rights and voting rights groups that have worked end-lessly to reach common ground. But we must now move quickly if we are to have any chance of seizing this historical opportunity to expand the right to vote. I am proposing that we convene an emergency meeting of the civil rights groups through the House Majority Whip's Office at the earliest possible op-portunity.

Gray intervened with the civil rights groups, as did his staff per-son, Steve Champlain. And then Eddie Williams, executive director of the Joint Center for Political Studies (the black think tank) sent a let-ter to Dorothy Height, president of the National Council of Negro Women; to John Jacobs, executive director of the National Urban League; and to Julius Chambers of LDF: "Subject: Urgent Need to Move on Voter Registration Bill." Williams made a plea for compro-mise:

> Based on everything I know, the House bill, as amended up to now, should be supported and passed, and we should continue efforts to strengthen the legis-lation in the Senate and in the conference committee. The House bill has many positive features that our forces have been fighting for years to get [such as mail-in]. It would be a pity to lose them.

But the NAACP Legal Defense and Education Fund persevered. Herbert Stone, as senior staff member of Swift's House Elections Sub-committee, described discussions between his staff and LDF's Elaine Jones and her staff, particularly Penda Hair, as akin to a labor negotia-tion. "They wanted as much as they could get, and held out to the end. They were responsible for major improvements in the bill." We share that view.

In April 1991, Human SERVE received a letter from LDF's Julius Chambers: "I understand that we have reached an agreement with the Coalition and have clearly indicated our support for the Act, as amended."[19] This letter followed a "summit" meeting in March that had been called by LWV, NAACP, ACLU, and LDF, and the meeting was packed with forty or fifty people. ACLU's Judy Crockett had chaired some of the earlier meetings, and then began cochairing the revived coalition meetings with Mary Brooks, Leonard's deputy. In 1992, after Crockett left the Washington office of ACLU, Edward A. Hailes Jr., Henderson's deputy at the NAACP, joined Brooks as cochair. The symbolism was significant. With the ACLU, the League of Women Voters, and the civil rights groups acting in concert, there was a good chance legislation would result. By this time, the active membership of the coalition included senior lobbyists from the National Education Association, the United Auto Workers, the AFL-CIO, the American Federation of State, County and Municipal Employees, the American Association of Retired Persons, the American Bar Association, and a broad spectrum of religious and other national organizations.

One favorable and unexpected sign was the absence of concerted opposition from election clerks, who would lose power over deputization and power over times and places of registration as a result of the NVRA. In an interview with us, William Kimberling, deputy director of the FEC's Office of Election Administration, who has the reputation of being more familiar with local registration officials and practices than anyone in the country explained why:

> Election officials are a quiescent lot. They are slow to organize and react. They don't appreciate their potential power. They complain about things, say things are terrible, but don't raise up an army. This is particularly true of federal legislation. They don't think their voices carry that high, although they can be quite influential at the state level.

That the NVRA had the support of a majority of the secretaries of state was probably also a factor. In 1989, NASS had passed a lukewarm resolution endorsing motor voter, but they passed a strong one in 1991. Local election officials had to take that into account, given that the secretaries were the chief state election officers in most states.

Republican Opposition to Reform

Republicans had championed voting rights after the Civil War in order to build a base in the South with black voters. But when they again championed voting rights in the 1950s and 1960s, it was to build a base in the South by fanning the white racism that was eroding the Democratic party's southern base. In the 1950s, Republican strategists saw in the fragmenting of the Democratic southern wing the beginnings of a regional (and even national) realignment which, by the late 1960s, they could claim was actually taking place. Consequently, northern Republicans in the Congress broke ranks with their conservative southern Democratic coalition partners and seized the initiative on voting rights. Their reasoning was clear: If blacks were enfranchised, southern white Democrats could be expected to defect to the Republicans, as indeed many did. The Civil Rights Act of 1957 was enacted largely because of unanimous support among Senate Republicans who also gave the same unanimous support to the Civil Rights Act in 1960. At the height of the voting rights conflict in the South, twenty-seven of the thirty-one Senate Republicans voted to override a filibuster by southern Democrats that stood in the way of the Civil Rights Act of 1964. And again in 1965, all Senate Republicans supported the Voting Rights Act with the exception of J. Strom Thurmond of South Carolina. Thurmond was a leader in the Senate of southern Democratic opposition to civil rights who had run as the States Rights party presidential candidate in the 1948 southern breakaway from the Democratic party. He changed parties again in 1964, this time to campaign successfully as South Carolina's Republican Senate candidate, a sure sign that the South was realigning racially.

By the 1970s, with as many as 70 percent of southern whites voting Republican in presidential contests, and blacks voting overwhelmingly Democratic, Republicans abandoned support for voting rights. A two-part national strategy developed, with the goal of weakening Democrats by limiting minority voting. One part of the strategy involved a revival of tactics of intimidation:

- In 1981, the New Jersey Republican party established a "Ballot Security Task Force," which hired off-duty police officers to intimidate minority voters as they came to the polls.
- In 1982, Texas Republicans posted election-day signs at the polls in minority neighborhoods that began, "You can be imprisoned if . . ."
- In 1986, Louisiana Republicans mailed thousands of nonforwardable postcards to minority persons, and election officials cooperated by purging the names on the returned cards from the registration rolls.
- In 1990, the North Carolina Republican State Committee sent 150,000 postcards mainly to black persons warning that "If you

haven't lived where you now live for 30 days you can't vote"—
although the law in fact allowed recent movers to vote at their
previous places of residence.

- In 1992, Wisconsin Republican governor Tommy Thompson
sent out a fundraising appeal that would finance a "ballot security program," which led Democrats to charge that this was
a tactic to scare voters at the polls.

- In 1994, Republicans in Baltimore proposed to pay for security
guards at balloting locations throughout the city. Mayor Kurt
Schmoke accused the Republicans of "an attempt to intimidate black people." Wade Henderson of the NAACP said that
"attempts to intimidate and suppress minority voters have become common over the past 13 years. These tactics are most
often used in close races where black and Hispanic turnout is
likely to be a key factor."[20]

The second part of the Republican strategy was to obstruct registration reform. That strategy had been clearly visible beginning in the
1970s. Groarke points out that 69 percent of House Republicans voted
for the extension of the Voting Rights Act in 1975 because it served
their interests in the South, but only 9 percent voted for a postcard
registration bill in that same year because it was thought that Democrats would benefit.[21] And then there was Republican opposition to
gubernatorial executive orders, and to state motor voter legislation.
Republicans in the Congress were near-unanimous in opposition to
liberalizing registration procedures, which were regarded as ways to
increase minority—and Democratic—turnout.

However, for a brief period in 1989–90, there was significant Republican support for the motor voter bill in the House. Representative
Bill Thomas (R-CA), vice-chair of the Committee on House Administration and ranking minority member of Swift's subcommittee, saw
registration reform as a way to remove deadwood from registration
lists. Many Republicans were obsessed with the prospect that Hispanic noncitizens would vote, and they thought that purging deadwood would reduce that possibility. Republicans apparently also used
registration lists for mailings much more than Democrats did, and
letters to deadwood registrants wasted money. Herbert Stone re-

ported, "As staff of the subcommittee, we were told repeatedly that the purging section was the key to any bipartisan support. Thomas was interested in the purge provisions almost to the exclusion of the registration section" and said he would support the bill if it provided that addresses be verified every four years; he also promised to enlist the support of Republican Minority Whip Newt Gingrich. Swift also favored periodic purging, and he was pleased that his bill had won bipartisan support.

As for Gingrich, he was impressed by several surveys after the 1984 and 1988 elections showing that Republicans would have won by larger margins if the unregistered had voted. "That's an extraordinary change from 15 years ago," he told the *New York Times*.[22] This was the result of the changing partisan tilt of young people, whose traditional preference for the Democrats was reversed during the Reagan years. Reagan had won 43 percent of the under-29 age group in 1980, but 59 percent in 1984, and Bush won 52 percent in 1988. After the 1988 election, the *New York Times*-CBS postelection poll found that

> Mr. Bush would have been helped by a bigger turnout because a vast majority of those who did not vote were young. Of voters, 24 percent were under 30 years of age; 42 percent of nonvoters were. These young nonvoters would have chosen Mr. Bush by a much bigger margin than the rest of the population and were more pro-Bush than the young people who actually voted.

In other words, some Republicans saw the possibility of an age-based realignment, and when Foley introduced HR 2190 in May 1989, Thomas and Gingrich signed on as cosponsors. A *New York Times* editorial concluded that "the Republican Party now senses an opportunity to build support among highly mobile young professionals, who, polls suggest, tend to be increasingly Republican."[23]

When HR 2190 came up for consideration in the 1990 congressional session, Gingrich and Thomas sent out a "Dear Republican Colleagues" letter[24] giving three reasons why Republicans should support it, two of them in capital letters:

1. Expands opportunity for citizens to register. POLLS SHOW THAT MORE UNREGISTERED CITIZENS ARE REPUBLICANS THAN DEMOCRATS. This bill helps our new GOP majority to register.

2. Requires states to confirm voter addresses at least every four years. CLEAN VOTER ROLLS HAVE BEEN A MAJOR REPUBLI-CAN GOAL FOR YEARS.

3. Strengthens federal authority to prosecute voter fraud and requires an oath affirming citizenship on voter registration forms.

The bill passed handily on February 6, 1990, and sixty-one Republicans voted with the majority.

Of course, the 1992 election dashed Republican hopes for the youth vote. Clinton won with 43 percent of those under 30 who voted (Bush 34 percent, Perot 22 percent), and he won with 53 percent of the youth vote in 1996 against both Dole and Perot, giving Republicans reason to oppose reform and Democrats reason to support it. But even before this youth shift back to the Democrats was known, traditional "rainy day" Republicans mobilized to make opposition to reform a straight party matter. The conventional wisdom was that Republicans do best when there is low turnout. In August 1980, Paul Weyrich, director of the Committee for the Survival of a Free Congress, told more than two hundred business and conservative religious leaders who had gathered at a fundraiser for Reagan, "I don't want everyone to vote; our leverage in the election quite candidly goes up as the voting populace goes down. It's important to turn out those who are with us." As debate over the motor voter bill began in 1990, House Republican leader Robert Michel of Illinois said he heard strong objections to the motor voter bill from Governor James Thompson and other Illinois Republicans on just this ground.[25] The House and Senate Republican leadership therefore insisted on opposition to reform. In the House, this meant that Gingrich and Thomas switched sides; in the Senate it meant filibusters.

Still, the matter of the youth vote did not go away. In October 1990, Steve Barr, chief organizer for an outfit called Rock the Vote, appeared in our offices. He had been staging voter registration activities at rock concerts, with modest success. Then he heard that young people might be registered by the millions in DMVs, and Rock the Vote became a champion of motor voter.

Rock the Vote had formed when the Florida police jailed several performers in the rock group 2 Live Crew on obscenity charges in 1990. Some twenty states were considering legislation to censor lyrics with too much sex and violence. The record industry decided to try to frighten politicians by mobilizing millions of young people to defeat the censorship drive by registering and voting. Jeff Ayerhof, coordinator of Virgin Records, established Rock the Vote, and the record industry helped with contributions. Most important, MTV, with an audience of twenty million, joined the campaign at the urging of vice presidents Judy McGrath and Sara Levinson, who wanted to raise political awareness among youth. Rock the Vote and MTV tried to mobilize their constituency, as the Christian Right did, with television appeals. A staff writer for the *New York Times* made much of this:

> If MTV succeeds in this voter-education-and-registration campaign, the electorate it helps deliver could well affect the outcome of the 1992 presidential race. The figures are formidable. MTV has about 20 million viewers, two-thirds of whom are between the ages of 18 and 34. Of this group, only 44 percent voted in the last Presidential election.
>
> But this year could be different. According to an MTV survey late last month, 76 percent of viewers said that in this election they were "very likely" to vote, with 61 percent reporting that they were "almost certain" to do so. This could be bad news for George Bush. MTV's own recent polls show that its viewers favor Clinton by 25 points.[26]

With Rock the Vote's prodding, dozens of top rockers and rappers made public service announcements condemning censorship, exhorting young people to register and vote, and praising motor voter. MTV aired them constantly. The most celebrated featured Madonna in a red bra and combat boots, her lower half wrapped in the American flag, with the punch line, "If you don't vote, you're going to get a spankie." The press paid attention; the *New York Times* devoted a full column to Madonna's skit. The Congress also knew that Rock the Vote organizers were out there, because they lobbied for motor voter.

The recording-industry press subsequently revealed that half the stars had not voted in the last election. Iggy Pop, age forty-three, had never registered, but his manager explained that he had "begun the process to register. It just came too quickly for him." Rock the Vote staffer Beverly Lund reacted to these revelations with good humor:

"It's kind of like if you're an environmental spokesman and someone finds Styrofoam cups in your garbage."

MTV had never before reported news. But they started a brief news spot to keep younger people abreast of every move in Congress on motor voter as well as on issues of the environment and reproductive rights. The result was a decidedly partisan newscast, since Republicans were always the villians. And as the 1992 New Hampshire Democratic presidential primary approached, Rock the Vote made a big push, registering 10,000 college students, who were clearly pro-Clinton. Megadeth's lead singer, Dave Mustaine, and rap artist MC Lyte served as special correspondents for MTV during the Democratic convention, and heavy metal rockers Ted Nugent and Treach, from the popular rap group Naughty by Nature, covered the Republicans.

After Clinton won the nomination, we thought it would be important to get him and Gore publicly committed to motor voter. Barr worked with MTV to schedule their appearances, and they were asked bluntly before an audience of millions whether they supported motor voter; both said they did. Bush declined to appear. Ethan Zindler, the twenty-three-year-old youth outreach coordinator for Clinton, defined this as "a turning point for the election. MTV and Rock the Vote have tremendous power in defining youth culture. If they define voting as something that is cool, the waves definitely go out to young people."

In the event, Clinton won the youth vote, and Democratic National Committee chairman Ron Brown served as cochair of the MTV inaugural ball in Washington. Nor did Clinton forget youth at the NVRA signing ceremony some months later. Who is to say that Rock the Vote and MTV didn't deserve some of the credit for electing a Democratic President who would sign a motor voter bill?

Democratic Support for Reform

The Democrats regained the Senate in 1986 and held it until the 1994 presidential election. When the crucial votes on registration reform came up between 1990 and 1993, there were 57 Democrats in the Senate, three short of the number needed to shut off Republican filibusters. To win, the Democrats had to vote unanimously and pick up three Republican votes.

The racial realignment in the South had done much to heal the Democratic party's regional division over voting rights. Unity became possible because the Voting Rights Act (and subsequent amendments) raised southern black registration rates; given the loss of white votes, this made Democratic politicians dependent on black votes. In effect, the Democratic and Republican parties had changed places in the historic struggle over voting rights. By the 1990s, it was Republicans who filibustered in order to suppress black political participation, and it was southern Democrats who joined their northern wing to cut off debate.

Strident partisan conflict contributed to Democratic unity. In the Senate, there was intense rivalry between Wendell Ford and Republican Mitch McConnell, both from Kentucky. When Ford became the champion of government agency reform, McConnell decided to lead the fight against it, making Ford all the more determined to win. Party rivalry in the Congress intensified after the 1992 presidential election. George Mitchell, as majority leader, was determined to pass Clinton's legislative program, and numbered family leave S 1 and motor voter S 2. Mitchell, it should be added, had shown no great enthusiasm for registration reform. In the 1990–1992 period, coalition members had to nag him to call cloture votes. But now he was defending the president's program. At the same time, the Republicans, with only 43 votes, were determined not to be trampled on, and minority leader Bob Dole made it plain in public statements that they would use the filibuster to defend themselves. This fractious spirit encouraged Democrats to vote as a bloc, including those from white working-class districts—such as Chicago's Dan Rostenskowki, patriarch of the powerful House Committee on Ways and Means—who would otherwise have opposed the bill.

The three Republican defectors in the Senate were liberals. Mark Hatfield (OR) had a record of supporting liberal causes. He enjoyed a close collegial relationship with Ford, who very much wanted a bill with bipartisan support. Hatfield also represented a state with a model motor voter system, which began in 1991. For advice, Hatfield enlisted Vicki Ervin, the nonpartisan director of elections in Multnomah

County, and Republican Al Davidson, director in Marion County and president of the Oregon Association of County Clerks in 1991; both of them encouraged Hatfield to sponsor the legislation with small changes, and Ervin worked with Hatfield's staff person, Sue Hildick, on technical amendments.

Jim Jeffords (VT) had a long history of support for civil rights and women's rights, and his Republican secretary of state, Jim Douglas, supported motor voter. Dave Durenberger of Minnesota came from a state with the most liberal voter registration procedures in the country, including both motor voter and election-day registration. Disability groups in Minnesota, mobilized by James Dickson, were also crucial in securing his vote.

However, to appease his colleagues, Durenberger extracted a concession dealing with Republican concerns that agency-based registration would be coercive. According to Thomas E. Zoeller, counsel to Ford's committee, Republicans portrayed the recipients of benefits as "weak-minded and susceptible to intimidation" and argued that public assistance agency workers would coerce recipients to register as a condition of getting benefits because they were "survivors of the New Deal who were trying to put socialism in this country."[27] Durenberger's amendment required that every recipient who chose to register be shown a special form which included these statements:

> Applying to register or declining to register to vote will not affect the amount of assistance that you will be provided by this agency.
>
> If you believe that someone has interfered with your right to register or to decline to register to vote, your right to privacy in deciding whether to register or in applying to register to vote, or your right to choose your own political party or other political preference, you may file a complaint with _____ (the blank being filled by the name, address and phone number of the appropriate officials to whom such a complaint should be addressed).

On September 26, 1990, 55 senators voted to bring the bill to the floor with a rule limiting debate, just five votes short of the 60 needed. All but two Democrats, Heflin (AL) and Baucus (MT), voted in favor; two Republicans, Hatfield and Packwood, voted yes, and Durenberger was absent.

There were two votes on July 18, 1991. In the morning, there were 57 yes votes, 41 no and 2 not voting. All Democrats voted yes; all but two Republicans (Hatfield and Durenberger) voted no; and two Democrats were absent: Dixon (IL) and Pryor (AR) who was ill. In the evening there were 59 yes votes and 40 no votes. Hatfield, Durenberger, and Jeffords voted yes. Had Pryor been present, the filibuster would have been broken. However, 57 Democrats and these same three Republicans voted for cloture on May 7, 1992. The bill went to President Bush, who vetoed it on the eve of Independence Day.

The 1992 presidential election put a Democrat in the White House who had named the government agency bill his second priority. On February 4, 1993, with the 103rd Congress in session, the House passed HR 2 by a vote of 259 to 160. The Democrats voted 237–14 in favor, the Republicans 21–146 opposed, and there was one independent vote in favor. In the Senate, S 2 was filibustered for eleven days. Social agency registration was especially assailed in both chambers. In the House, Spencer Bachus (R-AL) warned that the NVRA would register "millions of welfare recipients, illegal aliens, and taxpayer-funded entitlement recipients." Phil Gramm (R-TX) constantly asked in Senate floor debates, "Why are you helping the people in the wagon, and not the people pulling the wagon?"

A cloture vote (including the votes of Hatfield, Durenberger, and Jeffords) finally succeeded on May 11, 1993. President Clinton signed the bill on May 20. Speakers at the signing ceremony tended to emphasize different themes. Representative Swift, Senator Hatfield, and Becky Cain (president of the League of Women Voters) emphasized democratic principles. Representative Conyers, Benjamin Chavis (the newly appointed director of the NAACP), and Cloward and Piven talked mainly about the prospect that this Act could diminish historical class and racial inequalities. Senator Ford mentioned all themes, and noted how attached his grandchildren were to MTV. Joel Shulkin, a college student from New Hampshire representing Rock the Vote, spoke about youth enfranchisement. The president and vice-president struck all themes, and Clinton held up a Rock the Vote tee-shirt with the band playing the civil rights hymn "We Shall Overcome."

The Politics of Implementation

The states were required to implement the NVRA system by 1995, roughly eighteen months from the signing. During this interval, they had to pass enabling legislation and devise procedural changes in a range of state agencies.

It is virtually a theorem in political science that the politics of legislation and the politics of implementation are distinct, and each deserves attention for its effects on policy. The groups that win legislation may fade or lose interest, or the political alignments that made them influential may change. New groups focused on implementation come to the fore, taking advantage of new political conditions or of the relative obscurity, if not secrecy, of the implementation process.

If political science had not alerted us to the distance between legislation and implementation, our experience in the states certainly would have. We were particularly concerned that social agency registration would get short shrift. And our concerns were heightened because the politics of implementation was played out in the midst of the Republican surge in the Congress and in the state capitols in the election of 1994. Moreover, the election had resounded with the battle cry for devolution of federal power—and that could be ominous for the NVRA.

When Human SERVE was formed in 1983, there were 16 Republican governors, but only three of them in big industrial states: California, Illinois, and Pennsylvania. By the time the NVRA passed in 1993, there were 29 Republican governors, including the additional big industrial states of Massachusetts, Michigan, New Jersey, New York, Ohio, and Texas. A similar trend was at work in the state legislatures. In 1983, Democrats controlled both houses in 29 states. A decade later, they controlled 19, and 13 of these were either southern states (including Florida and Texas) or border states. Massachusetts was the one major holdout. With the Congress and the industrial states under Republican control by 1994, the split-level realignment beginning with Nixon's election in 1968 had developed depth. Moreover, congressional Republicans would not have been enthusiasts for devolution if the states had remained Democratic. And absent the call for devolution, the Republican governors would probably not have been as belligerent as they turned out to be about the implementation of NVRA.

Their resistance was foreshadowed by the recurrence of the themes of states' rights and unfunded mandates in the congressional debate over the NVRA. Aside from accusations that government agency registration would lead to fraud and coercion and that empowering the dependent poor was bad public policy, Republicans also inveighed against federal usurpation of the traditional right of the states to control the mechanics of the electoral system. As our history shows, this had always been a crucial source of power, as state and local parties competed to manipulate electoral arrangements for partisan purposes. And the Republican governors who had come to power in the North surely did not want to be compelled to register welfare, food stamp, and Medicaid recipients.

The Republican governors were also emboldened to drag their feet by a series of bills that were quickly introduced after the 1994 election to repeal the NVRA or to make it voluntary or contingent on federal funding. As it turned out, nothing came of these initiatives, but they probably stiffened the resolve of Republican governors to delay and obstruct implementation, not least by raising the Constitutional challenges that states' rights were being trampled. In a word, the old southern Bourbons had reappeared as northern Republicans.

IMPLEMENTATION MANUAL. At Human SERVE, we were alert to the pitfalls of implementation. As soon as Clinton took office in January 1993, with registration reform high on his agenda, it seemed a good bet that the bill would pass. We therefore turned to preparing a detailed implementation manual so that state officials could not stall by pleading ignorance of the Act or claiming that it was too complicated or too costly to implement. The manual summarized the provisions of the bill and provided model language for state enabling legislation, and full descriptions of how motor voter programs were being run in different states, together with copies of forms already in use. Human SERVE staff visited local welfare agencies in a half-dozen states to observe how applicants were processed for benefits. In some states, applicants filled out forms. In others, the eligibility workers asked questions and entered answers on the forms. And in still other states, the eligibility worker entered the answers directly into a computer. The manual contained detailed recommendations on how to adapt voter registration to each of these systems. By the time the president signed the bill in May, the manual was ready, and secretaries of state and state election officials were startled to find copies in their mail a month later. The manual was a great success; in addition to the several hundred mailed to state officials, we filled more than eight hundred requests for copies, including requests from advocacy groups. There was one outraged objection from Betty Carter, supervisor of elections in Orange County, Florida, who was an active opponent of NVRA. She wrote Human SERVE:

> I cannot believe that you would be a party to writing an implementation manual before the Federal Election Commission writes theirs. And if we don't do it according to Human SERVE's instructions, you will probably sue us.[28]

The trouble was that the FEC manual would not be ready for six months, although when it did appear, it was a masterful job.

CONSTITUTIONAL CHALLENGES. We expected the Republican governors to mount states' rights challenges in the courts. On the one hand, Article 1, Section 4 of the Constitution grants Congress the explicit power to "make or alter" regulations governing the "time, places, and manner" of federal elections. On the other hand, the Tenth Amendment directs "that powers not delegated to the United States by the Constitution, nor prohibited by it to the States, are reserved to the States respectively, or to the people." We discussed the impending conflict with Juan Cartagena, Human SERVE's board president at the time, and also general counsel to the Community Service Society of New York (CSS). The decision was that CSS would host a two-day conference of voting rights organizations and advocates, with Human SERVE and the Puerto Rican Legal Defense and Education Fund, represented by Arthur Baer, as cosponsors. Human SERVE and CSS did much of the staff work on what we called "The NVRA Implementation Conference: A Response from the Voting Rights Community," held in October 1994. We prepared several volumes for attendees on legal theories to support congressional supremacy over the Tenth Amendment, theories on the linkage between the NVRA and the Voting Rights Act, copies of pertinent court decisions, pages of supporting statistics, and model briefs. Some one hundred voting rights experts, litigators, and advocates attended to plan the legal defense of the NVRA, their expenses paid by a Ford Foundation grant. Five representatives of the Civil Rights Division of the Department of Justice were also there. It was a spirited meeting because everyone felt that the governors could be bested (which they were).

In 1994 and 1995, two states filed Constitutional challenges, *Wilson v. United States* in California, and *Virginia v. United States*. Four others simply refused to implement the Act—Pennsylvania, Illinois, Michigan, and South Carolina—which provoked advocates to file suits against them. Usually, it was conference attendees who were the plaintiffs and plaintiff attorneys. The Southern California chapter of ACLU took up Governor Wilson's challenge, with the California Voting Rights Coalition as plantiff. ACORN was lead plaintiff in the main cases in Pennsylvania, Illinois, and Michigan. The LWV and the League of United Latin American Citizens filed separate suits in Illinois. The same was true of the LWV and the Richmond Crusade for Voters in Virginia. Cartagena and the CSS assumed the role of information clearing house, distributing periodic bulletins on the progress of cases.

Members of the voting rights coalition also lobbied the Department of Justice, which filed suit against all six recalcitrant states. It was Cartagena's opinion that DOJ "had rarely been that aggressive on voting rights issues, and early courtroom battles would not have gone so smoothly without DOJ's intervention,"[29] although there were other litigators who were less sanguine. Human SERVE played what had by now become its usual role of staff assistance. For example, we prepared memoranda to be used at trial with descriptions of the successful implementation of government agency registration in various states and its low cost.

All of the state challenges to the NVRA lost in the U.S. District Courts. Those that reached the U.S. Court of Appeals, in several different circuits, were also lost. The 9th Circuit unanimously rejected Governor Wilson's challenge with these words: "Congress may conscript state agencies to carry out voter registration for federal elections. The exercise of that power by Congress is by its terms intended to be borne by the states without compensation." When Illinois Governor Jim Edgar lost his appeal to the 7th Circuit, the *Washington Post* editorialized that

> the handful of states that are continuing to challenge the "motor voter" law passed by Congress could usefully consult the opinion on the matter handed down this week in the 7th Circuit of the Court of Appeals. Since almost all objections to this law seem to be coming from Republicans, it is of interest that the ruling declaring it constitutional comes not from judges famed for "liberal activism." Rather, it is a unanimous decision by a three-judge court, two of whose members—Chief Justice Richard Posner and Circuit Judge Frank Easterbrook—are respected by conservatives as two of the most thoughtful jurists in the country. We hope it persuades Republican governors to drop their suits and obey the law.[30]

And in January 1996, the U.S. Supreme Court refused to hear California's appeal by denying *certiorari*. In less than two years, the challenges to the NVRA had been put down. Still, with the 1996 presidential election looming, the court actions gained key Republican states up to a year's delay in implementing the Act.

PRECLEARANCE UNDER THE VOTING RIGHTS ACT. Section 5 of the Voting Rights Act, initially covering seven states, had come to cover sixteen. These states were required to obtain approval in advance of all proposed changes in registration and voting arrangments, either from the U.S. District Court in the District of Columbia or from the DOJ, although in practice it was the Voting Section of the Civil Rights Division of DOJ that carried out the preclearance function. From Human SERVE's perspective, preclearance was an obvious opportunity to influence state enabling legislation and administrative procedures to ensure that agency-based registration got a fair shake. The civil rights groups did not object to our playing this role. Consequently, the Voting Section of DOJ regularly forwarded preclearance materials from the states to Rebekah Evenson of our staff, and she replied with detailed objections and recommendations, usually dealing with questions of whether the registration process in public assistance agencies was integrated with the application process, and whether the same degree of assistance was provided in filling out both forms. We also alerted advocates in the states to the pitfalls of implementation by sending them these preclearance materials, and encouraging them to communicate with DOJ in support of our objections and recommendations.

The Voting Section accepted most of our recommendations, but not all. Enabling legislation had to designate several agencies other than DMVs and public assistance offices, and libraries were a popular choice. We wanted DOJ to press for the inclusion of unemployment agencies, but they thought that would be overreaching. And we also wanted DOJ to press for combined forms, but they took a wait-and-see attitude on whether using combined rather than separate forms made any substantial difference in the number registered. Still, without DOJ looking over their shoulders, covered states might have neglected social agencies. As it was, they developed some of the best programs.

ACTIVATING FEDERAL AGENCIES. Human SERVE staff worked strenuously to persuade the heads of relevant federal departments to issue memoranda to state and local agencies describing their obligations under the NVRA—especially Health and Human Services (welfare agencies) and Agriculture (food stamps). We also tried to persuade the Labor Department to encourage states to establish registration in unemployment agencies, and Housing and Urban Development to do the same for public housing (HUD prepared and distributed a manual to local housing officials). Millions of Medicaid applications are processed by public hospitals, community health centers, and other health facilities, and we encouraged the Health Care Financing Administration to use its influence to promote voter registration in these agencies. At the request of the White House, we also worked with the President's Management Council, consisting mainly of deputy secretaries of the various departments. Although Human SERVE staff participated in countless meetings and exchanged countless memos, the departments did not do much to prod state agencies to implement voter registration. After the 1994 Republican congressional sweep, with its emphasis on devolution and unfunded mandates, our effort to get the federal departments to exert pressure on the states seemed hopeless.

LOBBYING. We also worked with state officials with whom we had developed relationships, including legislators, in an effort to get model state enabling legislation adopted, and we had some success. However, litigation sometimes was required. The Indiana General Assembly adjourned for the year in March 1994 without passing legislation, and the AFL-CIO of Indiana filed the first NVRA lawsuit in the country in July 1994. In December, the parties signed a consent decree calling for implementation, and enabling legislation was passed in March 1995. In Kansas, where enabling legislation did not pass in either the 1994 or 1995 session, a lawsuit was filed in August by a local attorney and by the Southern Regional Office of the ACLU on behalf of the LWV of Kansas, the Kansas AFL-CIO, and several individual plaintiffs. The Court issued a preliminary injunction requiring the state to comply with the provisions of the NVRA, and enabling legislation was finally passed in April 1996, more than a year after the start-up date.

MONITORING. The FEC would not issue a report on implementation until after two years, so Human SERVE staff called all states much earlier to obtain statistics, and issued periodic reports so as to give advocates some idea of progress, and whether litigation needed to be started in particular states. The gross figures were encouraging: 1.8 million transactions during the first quarter (January–March 1995); 5 million after six months; 7.3 million after nine months; 12 million by the end of the first year. We held a well-attended press conference in Washington, D.C., jointly with the League of Women Voters, to announce that there had been 20 million transactions during the first 18 months. When the FEC issued its report for the first two years, they showed that there had been 41 million transactions.

But we could not get good figures on what was happening in public assistance agencies; these agencies needed to be monitored on the ground. To spur interest in monitoring by the local affiliates of the national organizations, we prepared and circulated regular reports describing progress and problems in implementation by the states. And we pleaded with the national organizations, such as the NAACP and the LWV, to urge their state and local chapters to monitor local agencies. It could have been done easily. We also tried to mobilize legal service attorneys who were in and out of welfare centers daily. ACORN did in fact undertake monitoring in a half dozen states, and we tried to persuade other grassroots networks to do the same. We made and distributed thousands of forms on which observers could report back to Human SERVE what they saw, so that we could recommend litigation where needed. Overall, however, the monitoring project was a bust. Once the national organizations got the bill through the Congress and then through the courts, they lost interest.

Fortunately, the Federal Election Commission is required under the NVRA to make a biennial report to Congress on implementation, together with recommendations for changes in the law. To compile reports, the FEC distributes a questionnaire to state officials which they are required to complete. The first report appeared in 1997, covering the 1995–96 period, and the second in 1999, covering the next two years. These reports contain information on the tens of millions of voter registration transactions that now take place in DMVs, public assistance agencies, and in other designated agencies. We turn to an assessment of these findings on voter registration in the next chapter, and to the impact on turnout.

CHAPTER TWELVE

Remobilization?

*T*he NVRA reforms produced an unprecedented increase in voter registration. Turnout, however, did not rise.

Voter Registration

The Federal Election Commission (FEC), in its two biennial reports to Congress evaluating the NVRA system, concluded that voter registration rose by 3.72 percentage points, from 67.83 percent in 1994 to 71.55 in 1998, in the forty-three covered states and the District of Columbia.[1] That was more than the 3.2 percentage point increase that resulted from the 1983–84 voter registration war. Still, we think that the methodology used by the FEC substantially underestimated the impact of the NVRA upon registration rates.

To see why, we note that state election officials reported a far larger rise in registration rates to the FEC—up from 68.63 to 79.58 percent between 1994 and 1998, an extraordinary increase of eleven percentage points. To put that figure in perspective, state statistics showed that the rate was 70.6 percent in 1976, and it eroded by only 2 percentage points to 68.6 percent in 1994. Moreover, the rate varied by little more than 3 percentage points from one federal election to the next. An 11-point increase was unparalleled.

The explanation of the difference is that the FEC treated 14.6 million people who had been placed on NVRA-prescribed "inactive lists" as if they would otherwise have been purged by the end of 1998. This represented the equivalent of 12 percent of the 126 million on the rolls in 1994. By contrast, state statistics included the inactives because they were in fact still on the rolls, and could not be purged until they had failed to respond to an address confirmation notice and failed to vote in the next two federal elections (2000 or 2002). It's not that either method is wrong. It's that the FEC did not call attention to the fact that 14.6 million additional people had to register to make up for the 14.6 million who were subtracted because they were on the inactive list.

Millions of additional people also had to register to make up for the way that the NVRA enhanced the efficiency of regular purging practices. Election officials reported to the FEC that they had actually purged 17.8 million individuals from their lists during the first four years of the NVRA system: 8.7 million during 1995–96, and 9.1 million more during 1997–98.[2] This represented the equivalent of 14 percent of the 126 million on the rolls in 1994.

Under the NVRA system, states are still permitted to purge people who died or committed disqualifying criminal offenses or became mentally incapacitated. And they are still, as in the past, permitted to remove people who have moved, but with an important constraint. In the past, election officials assumed that people who failed to vote in two or four years had probably moved, and were free to strike them from the rolls. Under the NVRA system, purging nonvoters is no longer permissible unless the nonvoters themselves notify election officials that they have moved—for example, by filing a change of address in DMVs that is transmitted to election offices. Otherwise, they go on inactive lists.

The NVRA system made it easy for millions of people to notify elections officials about address changes. Between 1995 and 1998, public agencies reported 36 million voter registration transactions to election officials: motor vehicle offices reported 29 million; 4 million were reported by public assistance offices; and 3.4 million in other offices, including 525,000 by disability and military recruitment offices. According to the FEC, only about 6 percent of this information duplicated what was already in election office files.[3] So election officials were inundated with 34 million items of new information. Indeed, the major change forced on local election offices by the new system is that they had to reorganize their procedures, typically by computerizing, in order to cope with the year-round torrent of information from DMVs, public assistance, and other state agencies.

Some of this information was about people registering for the first time. Some of it was about people reregistering after having been purged at an earlier time. There were also name changes, and changes of party affiliation. But the largest proportion of this information was about millions of people who took advantage of the new system to keep their voter registration status current by updating their addresses. In other words, the NVRA system provided election officials with information about movers as never before, permitting them to purge movers as never before (while also, of course, permitting them to reregister movers as never before).

Purging also increased because of the NVRA requirement that states purge regularly. Before NVRA, purging was much more haphazard, often depending on the availability of funds for staff and postage. The FEC reports show that nine states did not purge in 1994, the year before the NVRA start-up; several states hadn't purged for three or four years. Registration in Mississippi and Maine exceeded their VAPs. During the first two years of NVRA, the registration rate in Maine jumped five percentage points, from 101 percent in 1994 to 106 percent in 1996; then, during the next two years, Maine also began to comply with NVRA purging procedures, and the rate dropped to 92 percent in 1998. The FEC reported, "Numerous states indicated that they had made adjustments to their procedures in order to better their list maintenance programs."[4] The FEC's William Kimberling told us that purging had become "considerably more" efficient under NVRA.

In sum, an extraordinary 32 million people (14.6 million "inactives" and 17.8 million actually purged) were deleted from the rolls during the first four years and they represented the equivalent of 26 percent of the 126 million on the rolls in 1994. If these 32 million had not been replaced by an equivalent number of additional registrants, there would have been a net decrease at the end of the first four years. Pundits would have had a field day: the easier it is to register, the fewer people who do, and so on. As it was, the 32 million were not only replaced, but the rolls rose an additional 3.72 percentage points, or by 7.1 million more. By counting inactives as purged, and by not noting how NVRA facilitated purging, the FEC made it appear that the NVRA system registered far fewer millions than it did when in fact it registered far more millions than ever before.

Our central interest has been public assistance agencies. According to the FEC, approximately 4.1 million recipients engaged in voter registration transactions between 1994 and 1998—2.6 million in the first two years, and another 1.5 million during the second period. The numbers would have been higher except that public assistance registration programs got started late in many states. We also have no evidence on how effectively these programs are being administered. As we said earlier, despite Human SERVE's strenuous efforts to persuade the affiliates of various national organizations to monitor state compliance, none save ACORN showed any interest. We were not reassured by our experiences in New York City. Human SERVE assigned a staff member to hang around a central office where tens of thousands of recertifications for Medicaid took place, and discovered that many workers were throwing the voter registration forms away. We complained to Stanley Hill, director of DC-37 AFSCME, and he agreed to bring the matter up with stewards in the local of eligibility workers. Nothing happened.

Monitoring was especially needed after federal welfare reform legislation went into effect in 1996. What happened to voter registration as a result of the transition from Aid to Families with Dependent Children (AFDC) to Temporary Assistance to Needy Families (TANF) is unclear, and we also do not know how the cutbacks in other welfare-related programs affected the availability of voter registration.

Implementation in disability agencies was a disaster. The FEC reports that 430,000 transactions took place during the first four years, although polls show that only one-third of the disabled are registered. Disability activists worked hard for the passage of the NVRA. But the agency administrators did virtually nothing to implement it, and such national organizations as those for disabled and handicapped veterans did little to press them. However, in October 1999 the National Council on Disability released a survey report on state compliance with the NVRA in vocational rehabilitation agencies with the conclusion that implementation "is inconsistent and uncoordinated." Douglas Kruse, at Rutgers University, estimated that if the disabled registered and voted at the same rate as the rest of the population, there would have been five million more voters in 1998.[5] Separately, Jim Dickson estimated from polling data that the disabled were 70 percent Democratic, as might be expected given their stake in the social programs. Republicans might not want to see the disabled registered, but Democrats showed no interest either.

Turnout

Registration rose but turnout did not. Four years into the NVRA system, turnout had fallen another 2.8 percentage points, from 38.8 percent in 1994 to 36 percent in 1998. Moreover, "Southern turnout dropped 3.6 points to 30.5 percent, a larger drop than the rest of the nation."[6] Florida and Kentucky reported that as few as 20 percent of those registered in public assistance agencies went to the polls. In sum, more accessible registration procedures did not increase voting rates.

Why? A formidable body of evidence and opinion predicted that what Arend Lijphart calls "voter-friendly" registration rules lead to higher turnout levels. In fact, we think the procedures of the National Voter Registration Act (NVRA) should over time bring us close to the automatic voter registration procedures that characterize European polities, which Powell concluded could boost turnout by 14 percentage points.[7] More recently, in 1992, Ruy Teixiera conducted an exhaustive review of the American data and reported that, while voter registration barriers could not explain the recent declines in turnout, they nevertheless remained the most costly feature of the voting act in the United States. He concluded that the reduction of these costs was the single most credible reform that would increase turnout, by 8 to 15 percentage points.[8] Comparisons of turnout in states with the least restrictive registration arrangements and in other states yield similar estimates of a potential increase of from 9 to 15 percentage points.[9] So why have the expectations implicit in these arguments so far been disappointed? Why the continuing fall in turnout, rising registration rates notwithstanding?

Most studies of voter turnout attempt to disaggregate the effects of registration barriers and an array of other influences. If registration barriers are less significant in depressing turnout, then other factors must be more significant. Consistent with the traditional emphasis on social-psychological explanations, the usual approach has been to scrutinize changes in the capacities and attitudes of individual voters in the search for the factors contributing to the demobilization of the electorate. All else being equal, some changes in the characteristics of voters are expected to raise turnout while other factors depress turnout. Thus the growing numbers of young people in the electorate, who have traditionally voted less, at least in the United States, should depress turnout.[10] But rising educational levels should increase turnout, at least in the United States. All this is familiar.[11] The new variable proposed by recent analyses is that lower turnout seems to be associated with the fact that Americans are less embedded in social networks that encourage participation. Teixiera, for example, emphasizes "a substantial decline in social connectedness" through family and church.[12]

The perspective on the causes of low turnout delineated in chapter 2 reveals the limits of attempts to disaggregate the impact of particular variables on voter turnout. The effects of legal and procedural barriers are closely intertwined with the political factors that draw people to the ballot box, and especially with the strategies the political parties employ to attract or pull voters to the polls. Moreover, the barriers and political appeals and strategies together go far to determine which individual-level variables are related to turnout. When issue and cultural appeals resonate with the electorate, contests are tight, and the parties work to get the vote out, then legal and procedural barriers matter much less—as in the big cities in the years immediately after the introduction of voter registration barriers at the beginning of the century. And under these conditions, the relationship between turnout and education and income evaporates. To put the matter clearly, hotly contested elections about intensely felt issues still draw voters, and when they do, the impact of barriers dwindles, and so do differentials in turnout that can be ascribed to individual-level social and psychological traits. Rosenstone and Hansen point to the mayoral election in Chicago in 1983 when the nomination of Harold Washington raised black turnout by 17 percentage points, despite a restrictive voter registration system, because the keenly felt issue in the election was racial ascendance in the city's political regime.

But when political appeals lose their salience and party efforts to bring people to the polls slacken, as they did in the wake of progressive-era party reforms, voter registration barriers loom much larger, class-related disparities in voting widen, and so should the impact of such individual traits as education, income, or social connectedness. Moreover, the pattern of nonparticipation that is initially constructed by the interplay of barriers and party indifference tends to reproduce itself over time. Party operatives assume, even naturalize, low participation rates, and hence tend to take the absence of the marginalized for granted in fashioning appeals and mobilizing strategies.[13] In time the attitudes of the marginalized come to reflect their disaffection with a party system that pays them little heed.

Thus, the most provocative data reported in recent studies purporting to account for declining turnout describe dramatic changes in attitudes toward politics over the past three decades. "Americans," say Rosenstone and Hansen, "have lost their confidence in the effectiveness of their actions."[14] They have also lost their attachment to electoral politics: Americans are less satisfied with the electoral choices offered them and, indeed, had less good to say even about the parties and candidates they favored than they had in the 1960s.[15] Abramson, Aldrich, and Rohde also emphasize the erosion of party loyalties and a declining belief in the responsiveness of politicians to voter influence.[16] And Teixiera reports consistent findings.

Changes in political attitudes are of course changes in individual-level traits, but since the traits at issue are attitudes toward politics, and since they have changed so rapidly, it seems reasonable to suspect that the broader political system is implicated. If turnout is falling be cause of declining party loyalties or lowered feelings of political efficacy, something is probably going on in the larger environment of American politics.[17]

In chapter 2, we argued that the correlation of such individual-level attributes as education with turnout was misleading, that it did not reflect the direct impact of education on participation but the tilt of party appeals and strategies away from the less educated and worse-off, and toward the more educated and better-off. The decline in political efficacy and increase in political alienation, and the impact of these attitudes on turnout, suggests a further elaboration of the relationship between individual-level attributes and politics. The political system not only selectively mobilizes people according to their class-related attributes, but it also creates the attributes that depress turnout. On both these counts, the statistical evidence on the bearing of individual attributes on turnout points the finger of blame at the performance of the American political parties.[18]

This closing chapter is not the place to begin an examination of the features of recent American electoral politics that are increasing various measures of political alienation. The much discussed and debated decline of party organization (at least in the Democratic party), the flood of special interest money pouring into the campaigns, the growing presence of the K Street lobbyists, the gap between the issues Americans say are important and the national legislative agenda, the increasing complexity of policy initatives riddled with pork barrel giveaways—all of these probably contribute to growing public cynicism. Perhaps the rise of neoliberalism as the current ideological orthodoxy also turns people away from electoral politics, if only because it argues the futility of government intervention in a world dominated by markets, especially international markets. In short, the political parties and their interest-group allies are constructing a political environment that is demobilizing the American electorate, lowered barriers notwithstanding.

The very success of this development may even help to explain why the business opposition to government agency registration we initially anticipated never materialized. In the late nineteenth century, at least some business interests treated the shape and scale of electoral participation as a potential threat to their influence and worked to reduce participation by the lower strata. But on the eve of the twenty-first century, the big automobile companies readily conceded Election Day as a paid holiday to unionized auto workers. Predictably, Republican party leaders railed at the contract concession, as they had railed at the NVRA. But General Motors, Ford, and Daimler Chrysler, the world's three largest auto companies, were unfazed. Perhaps electoral politics has evolved to the stage where money, advertising, and special-interest lobbies, together with the dampening effect on democratic aspirations of neoliberal ideology, have combined to neutralize the age-old class threat posed by an enfranchised population.

It followed from our perspective on the closely interbraided causes of low turnout that we did not think voter registration would have its most important effects on turnout directly. True, accessible voter registration procedures would lower the costs, in rational-choice terms, of the voting act, and Human SERVE's public relations material emphasized that if registration barriers were eliminated, millions of new voters could flock to the polls. But we personally did not believe that the mere fact of lower costs was likely to draw people to the polls in large numbers. Rather, as we said in chapter 9, our hope was that once rates of registration rose among low income and minority citizens, this pool of newly available voters would attract at least some entrepreneurial politicians who would then begin to raise the issues and organize the get-out-the-vote efforts that would bring new voters to the polls.

That has yet to happen. In fact, however logical such recruitment efforts might seem from a narrow focus on electoral incentives, the century-long reliance of the American parties on electoral demobilization recounted in chapters 3 and 4 suggests that it may never happen. So does our own very limited success in trying to make allies, even of politicians who were likely to benefit at the polls. Some Democratic governors issued executive orders to be sure, but then declined to implement them. Even when state legislatures controlled by Democrats mandated motor voter, they refused to include social agencies as registration sites. Our successes at initiating registration in some municipal agencies were typically short-lived; when we stopped prodding, registration flagged or ceased. Similarly, earlier agency-based legislation had simply been ignored in California. On the federal level, Democrats were at best reluctant allies. Mondale had turned down staff recommendations that the 1984 campaign concentrate on recruiting new voters. To be sure, the Democratic National Committee ostensibly allocated funds to the state parties for registration, but most of it was spent as "street money," a kind of patronage to local groups, and usually not groups that were doing effective registration.

The Democratic leadership in the Senate didn't use any bargaining chips to promote voter registration legislation, but relied on the coalition to do its work. Even when Senator Mitchell ostensibly made it a sort of priority in 1993, it was scheduled to fill in the dead time between other legislative priorities. And once the bill was passed, neither the White House nor the federal agencies did much to promote implementation.

Our experience in New York in the late 1980s and early 1990s is illustrative of the reluctance of the Democrats to recruit new voters. It also suggests some of the reasons why. At first glance it would seem that Democratic stakes in the mobilization of new voters were high in New York, with both Governor Mario Cuomo and Mayor David N. Dinkins of New York City facing tough reelection contests. Surely they would want to register voters, especially the likely Democrats who used social agency services. It should have been easy, too. The New York City Charter that was approved by referendum in 1988 included a provision to establish a Voter Assistance Commission (VAC), for which Human SERVE and others had lobbied hard. VAC was assigned the explicit obligation to establish voter registration in city agencies, including the public assistance agencies which the mayor controlled. The VAC's first-year budget in 1989 was $750,000. A year later, Dinkins was elected, the first black mayor of New York City. He appointed Charles Hughes as president of VAC. Hughes also headed AFSCME Local 372 of DC 37, a union of low-paid Board of Education employees, such as cafeteria workers. In the city's decentralized school system, power over hiring, budgets, and contracts was largely determined by the outcome of community school board elections. Hardly anyone voted in these elections, so the union could virtually determine the outcome, and the last thing Charles Hughes wanted was to change that. VAC's budget under Hughes was $644,000 in 1990 and $523,000 in 1991, and he subsequently reported that 15,000 to 25,000 people were registered, mainly at parades and other public events. That worked out to be a cost of $50 per registrant. However, no one was registered in the public assistance and health agencies where Dinkins' natural constituency was concentrated. Louise Altman, Human SERVE's associate director, blew the whistle in early 1991 by giving VAC a grade of D in an evaluation published in the New York City

PIRG newsletter. In 1993, Dinkins lost his reelection bid to Republican Rudolph Giuliani by 53,000 votes. A year later Cuomo lost as well, by 174,000 votes statewide.

The moral seems to us clear. The scale and shape of the active electorate can determine electoral outcomes. But left to themselves, the parties are unlikely to work to expand participation. Perhaps part of the reason is simply that politicians have come to absorb the conventional wisdom that ascribes nonparticipation to the individual traits of voters. More likely, they mouth such explanations for comfort. Indeed, party competition is more likely to take the form of strategies to demobilize sectors of the electorate, than of strategies to expand it. Shefter suggests why, with an explanation that makes sense of what would otherwise be Mayor Dinkins's inexplicable behavior: "Bringing a new group into the political system has the potential of disrupting established patterns of political precedence and public policy."[19]

How, then, have the tendencies toward electoral demobilization sometimes been reversed? We think history suggests that political movements sometimes do the work of mobilizing outsiders that the major parties avoid.[20] The pattern of electoral turnout over the last century suggests a correlation between the rise of major political movements and the surge of new voters into the electorate. The pattern is complicated because movements develop in close interaction with state leaders, who respond to early signs of insurgency by making promises to appeal to newly at-risk voters. These promises simultaneously signal new political possibilities to the insurgents, thus encouraging the movement and setting in motion a process in which rising insurgency spurs rhetorical and programmatic concessions that draw new voters to the polls.

Thus, complications notwithstanding, the rise of the Populists and their alliance with the Democratic party resulted in a spurt of rising turnout in the years between 1896 and 1900, and this on a base of already high turnout.[21] Turnout rose again in the 1930s, as the rise of protest movements forced a reform agenda on the newly reigning Democratic party, as we explained in chapter 5. "It was not the depression and attendant perceptions of economic plight that stimulated increased participation; it was the New Deal, Roosevelt's political response, that mobilized the economically discontented," says Paul Kleppner.[22] And as we explain in chapter 6, turnout rose again in the 1960s as the civil rights movement forced the Democratic party to take the decisive step of enfranchising southern blacks, even at the cost of alienating its southern wing. And then the urban black protests that followed close on the heels of the civil rights movement prodded the Democrats to reach out to newly urban blacks with a new inclusive rhetoric and new social programs, with the consequence that black turnout levels outside the South also surged at least briefly.[23]

In sum, we think it possible that the NVRA and the pool of potential voters it is creating might yet matter in American politics. If it does, it is not likely to be because the dynamic of electoral competition itself prods the major parties to reach out to new voters. It is more likely to be because a new surge of protest, perhaps accompanied by the rise of minor parties and the electoral cleavages that both movements and minor parties threaten, forces political leaders to make the programmatic and cultural appeals, and undertake the voter recruitment, that will reach out to the tens of millions of Americans who now remain beyond the pale of electoral politics.

Notes

1. Does Voting Matter?

1. Key (1955:3).
2. See Chapter 9, table 9–1.
3. Demographic data are provided later in this chapter.
4. This phrase is taken from the title of an article by Eulau (1956). Gary Orren (1985:52, n. 2) quotes a *Boston Globe* columnist writing in the same vein: "Low voter turnout is . . . a symptom of political, economic, and social health. . . . If you'd rather watch "All My Children" or "Family Feud" than nip over to the firehouse to vote, then you can't be feeling terribly hostile toward the system." Will (1983:96) also defines nonvoting as a "form of passive consent." See Jackman's (1987:418) review of this perspective.
5. See, for example, Almond and Verba (1963:343–65, 402–69, 472–505); Eckstein (1966); Dahl (1961); and Huntington (1974).
6. This perspective is set out in Crozier et al. (1975); Huntington (1975); Brittan (1975); and Bell (1978).
7. Lipset (1960). Prothro and Grigg (1960) are also pertinent. But see Rogin (1967) for a rebuttal.
8. Will (1983:96). For another study that draws the lesson of the dangers of high participation from the fall of Weimar, see Brown (1987).
9. Cited in McGerr (1986:47). Petrocik (1987a:244) contains a discussion of the literature that claims that new or irregular voters are more volatile.

10. The exception to this assertion is France, where universal manhood suffrage was won during the Revolution, albeit only briefly.

11. The vote was the core demand of the Chartists, for example. Ernest Jones explained at a Chartist Council meeting in January of 1848 that "there are some gentlemen who tell the people that they must grow rich and then they will be free. . . . No, my friends, above all we need the vote. . . . Go in person and knock at the doors of St. Stephen's, knock till your privileged debtors give you back, trembling, what they have owed you for centuries! Go knock, and go on knocking until justice has been done." Quoted in Sheila Rowbotham, "The Tale That Never Ends," *Socialist Register*, 1999.

12. The warning was issued by the historian J. A. Froude in an address to the Liberty and Property Defence League in London in the aftermath of the passage of the Third Reform Bill in England. See Brittan (1975:146).

13. Chapter 3 of *The New Class War* (Piven and Cloward 1985) contains an extended discussion of the distinctive political arrangements—including constitutionalism, a complex but flexible federal system, fragmented and bureaucratized government authorities, and clientelism—that contributed to the vigor of laissez-faire in the nineteenth-century United States, both by obscuring government activities in the interests of business and by creating a realm of government and politics within which politics did indeed seem to be separate from the larger economy.

14. The argument that broad and pervasive government interventions in the twentieth century generated new political forces is developed in *The New Class War* (Piven and Cloward 1985).

15. For recent discussions of the correlation of low levels of electoral turnout and a class bias in party politics and public policy, see Arend Lijphart (1997:1–14); and Rosenstone and Hansen (1993:234–35). For an analysis that goes part of the way toward explaining why attitudinal survey data is not a good measure of the potential impact of higher turnout from the bottom on politics, see Verba et al. (1993:303–18).

16. DuBois (1989:704) makes this point strongly, attributing the weak labor movement in the United States to the intransigence of the South.

17. On the impact of voting on public policy in the South, see Bensel and Sanders (1986:52–70).

18. We discuss these multiple influences as they shaped American welfare state policies in *Regulating the Poor* (1993: chapter 12).

19. On the role of political parties in shaping class consciousness, see Przeworski (1977). We do not do justice here to the diverse arguments in the literature on "American exceptionalism." More recent work fastens on the distinctiveness of American working-class ideology in the antebellum period, and particularly on the vigor of working-class "republicanism."

See for example Dawley (1976); Faler (1981); Montgomery (1981); Wilentz (1984); and Steffen (1984).

20. The sources on the business mobilization are numerous. See for example Edsall (1984); Ferguson and Rogers (1986); Vogel (1989); Plotke (1996); Martin (1994); Phillips (1994).

21. On the coordination of business contributions and the increasing scale of those contributions, see Edsall (1984); Vogel (1989); and Clawson et al. (1998).

22. In any case, the meaning of "big government" was unclear. Republican politicians used it as a euphemism for New Deal interventions. But its meaning to survey respondents was ambiguous. See Nie et al (1976); and Petrocik (1987a).

23. Using data from the 1980 National Election Study surveys, Markus (1982) finds no evidence for the contention that the election was a referendum on Reagan's policy positions. The data indicate instead that voters shifted because of dissatisfaction with Carter's economic performance. Burnham's (1981A) analysis of exit poll data from the 1980 election concludes that the paramount issue among voters who swung to Reagan was unemployment. See also Miller and Wattenberg (1985); and Kelly (1986).

24. The argument that incumbents are judged by performance was originally put forward by Key (1966), and is authoritatively examined by Fiorina (1981). The significance of the state of the economy in assessing performance and determining the reelection chances of incumbents is stressed by Tufte (1978). The pattern appears to be common to democratic and industrialized nations. See for example Hibbs (1977 and 1982), who showed the critical importance of the economic performance of government in British elections during the same period we are discussing here. The importance of high unemployment levels in recent European elections that displaced conservative governments would seem to confirm this point.

25. Tufte (1978).

26. In fact, surveys indicated that opposition to the Reagan program intensified as time went on. See for example Lipset (1985 and 1986); Navarro (1985); and Ferguson and Rogers (1986: chapter 1).

27. Petrocik (1987a:240–253) maintains that both the 1980 and 1985 elections broke with a pattern in which irregular voters or nonvoters who are "without settled habits and, therefore, sensitive to short-term tides" surge in the direction of the majority. He goes on to show that while there was a smaller discrepancy between voters and nonvoters in 1984, "again nonvoters were less supportive of the winner than voters were."

28. Lefkowitz (1999:42).

29. Piven and Cloward (1979:15).

30. Charles Tilly (1984:310–11).
31. The phrase is the title of an early article by Burnham (1965).

2. Why Nonvoting?

1. The main proponents of the party emphasis are Schattschneider, Burnham, and Kleppner; legal barriers are emphasized by Campbell, Converse, Miller, Stokes, Kelley, Kousser, Rusk, and Stucker. Specific works by these authors are discussed and cited in this and subsequent chapters.
2. Schattschneider (1960:100–101 and 105).
3. Ibid. (80).
4. For a summary, see Kleppner (1981a). See also Jensen (1971). While both Kleppner and Jensen have clearly been influenced by Burnham, their work concentrates on the enthnoreligious bases of nineteenth-century politics.
5. The term "legal-institutional" is taken from Rusk's characterization of his own work. See Rusk and Stucker (1978:199).
6. Campbell et al. (1960: chapter 11). These authors also consider individual social characteristics, namely education and motivation, to be important determinants of turnout.
7. Campbell and Miller (1957).
8. Miller (1963).
9. The best expositions of the contending positions in this debate are to be found in a series of articles published together in the *American Political Science Review* (September 1974); see Burnham, "Theory and Voting Research," together with the comments by Converse and Rusk, and Burnham's rejoinder.
10. See Argersinger (1985–86:684–85). Argersinger observes cogently that there is a wide tendency to underestimate voter fraud, simply because a good deal of academic work hangs on the validity of nineteenth-century electoral data, but concludes nevertheless that fraud was common. For a discussion of the problem of evidence, see Allen and Allen (1981:153–93).
11. Rusk (1974:1028–45).
12. Converse (1972:286).
13. Ibid. (297).
14. Converse (1974:1040).
15. Kleppner and Baker (1980:205–26).
16. See Burnham (1965:7–28).
17. Burnham (1970:90).
18. Burnham (1974b:1012).
19. Schattschneider (1960:72).
20. Ibid. (48).

21. Ibid. (72).

22. This thesis about the historical interaction between procedural barriers and party behavior finds support in the contemporary period as well. The University of Michigan's National Election Study found in 1980 that two-thirds of those who were not registered received neither mail from party campaigns, nor visits from precinct workers; by contrast, only one-third of those who were registered were similarly ignored (Squire, Glass, and Wolfinger, 1984:9). See also Rosenstone and Hansen (1993: chapter 6).

23. To establish the preeminence of politics over rules, Burnham repeatedly returns to data showing that turnout also dropped in counties which had no personal voter registration (Burnham, 1974b:1005 and 1007). Converse's response is to postulate that the heightened political controversy over vote fraud during the 1890s and 1900s could have led to curtailment of the more blatant forms of vote corruption, and hence to lower turnouts, even where registration was not imposed (Converse, 1974:1024–25). This sort of county-by-county comparison, varieties of which are also employed by Kleppner and Carlson, grossly simplifies the dynamics through which party and rule changes combined to affect turnout levels.

24. Burnham asks this question as well when he says that "the most compelling reason for rejecting the legal-structural change theory . . . is that, from beginning to end, Professors Rusk and Converse have treated this intervention as though it were an uncaused cause, a kind of external intervention into the history of men" (Burnham, 1974c:1054). What Burnham means is that he rejects Converse's cause, that well-meaning reformers were merely acting on their ideals.

25. 1942:47.

26. 1942:48.

27. 1942:49.

28. Shefter, 1984:140–48. Lowi proposes that the failure of competitive parties to "function appropriately" may be that they are too competitive, neither wishing to risk new ideas or new commitments. See Lowi (1963:570–83).

29. 1984:142.

30. Finegold and Swift observe that parties seek advantage by trying to "influence [both] the system and the electorate to their advantage" and that these efforts include voter mobilization and demobilization. See Finegold and Swift (1996).

31. Burnham (1974b:1004).

32. Burnham (1974a:688).

33. Converse (1972:286).

34. McCormick (1956:149).
35. Ibid. (149–50). See also the discussion of the history of voter registration laws in Harris (1929: chapter 3).
36. McCormick (1953:215–17).
37. Some of these legislative battles are described in Harris (1929: chapter 2).
38. McCormick (1953) makes this point. While changes in election machinery were motivated by efforts to affect the electorate, the reforms in New Jersey actually had slight effect during the period from 1870 to 1900. We think the answer to this apparent puzzle is that new and obstructive procedures took their toll on electoral participation only very gradually, and only in the context of changes in party organization and the pattern of party competition.
39. Kleppner (1982:28 and 33). Kleppner points out that strong parties succeeded in sustaining high participation despite such lingering barriers to the suffrage as residency requirements, poll or registry taxes, and inconvenient polling places.
40. For example, Formisano (1969:688) points to the large impact of party organization in driving up turnout in the 1830s and 1840s: "Historians sometimes get confused about whether organization caused voter participation or vice versa, missing the point that both are dependent as well as independent variables." Chambers and Davis (1978:188–89) try to estimate the relative impact of competition and party "organizational inception" on turnout during approximately the same period.
41. Shefter (1978b:263–66).
42. See Shefter (1986:268) for a description of the "naturalization frauds" of 1868 in which hundreds of immigrants at a time were naturalized by Tammany judges.
43. Harris (1929:76).
44. Burnham (1974b:1006).
45. See Burnham (1979:138, fn. 31).
46. Harris (1929:83–84).
47. Kleppner (1982:74). See also Harris (1929:179–268), and Jensen (1971:238–68).
48. "[E]very rational man decides to vote just as he makes all other decisions: if the returns outweigh the costs, he votes; if not, he abstains." Downs (1957:260).
49. Burnham made this argument with particular boldness in 1965 and 1970. In subsequent work, however, he also makes what would seem to be the inconsistent argument that most Americans agreed with the political directions of the system of 1896.
50. Schaffer (1981).

51. Almond and Verba (1963: esp. chapters 11 and 12), and Verba and Nie (1972:125–37).

52. Campbell et al. (1954 and 1960).

53. Wolfinger and Rosenstone (1980).

54. Abramson and Aldrich (1982) emphasize both partisanship and political efficacy as determinants of turnout.

55. Aldrich and Simon (1986:293).

56. Lazarsfeld, Berelson, and Gaudet (1948:47).

57. Aldrich and Simon (1986:271–301).

58. Verba and Nie (1972:126–27) call this the "baseline" model: "Individuals of higher social status develop such civic orientations as concern for politics, information, and feelings of efficacy, and these orientations in turn lead to participation."

59. The economic model of the decision whether or not to vote is associated with the rational-choice school, particularly with Anthony Downs's (1957) economic model of political choice. There is, however, a major dispute as to whether the preferences which govern the voting decision have to do with the outcome of the election, or with the process of voting itself. Or, in other words, whether the motivation is instrumental or expressive, whether voting is an investment to realize an end, or valuable in its own right. See also Riker and Ordeshook (1968) for an early development of the expressive view of voting. And see also Shienbaum (1984). However, something like this view was advanced as early as 1924 by Schlesinger and Erikson (1924). See also Lipset (1960:205) for a similar explanation of nonvoting.

60. Wolfinger and Rosenstone (1980:88). Campbell et al. (1960:476) also think low educational levels deter participation because the less educated cannot deal with the overflow of political information. Other demographic factors, such as residential mobility, have also been put forward as explanations of nonvoting. See Alford and Scoble (1968); Verba and Nie (1972, chapter 13); Cavanaugh (1981).

61. Berelson, Lazarsfeld, and McPhee (1954:32).

62. Australia, Belgium, and Italy require citizens to vote by law, and nonvoters are subject to mild penalties, such as small fines, although these sanctions are rarely invoked. However, the legal requirement to vote does not explain the broad differences that also exist between the United States and other democracies, such as Britain, France, West Germany, Canada, and the Netherlands. See Powell (1986) for an analysis of the comparative data. Jackman (1987:414) discusses the uniqueness of the American system.

63. We are hardly the first to make this observation. Schlesinger and Eriksson

pointed out more than seventy-five years ago (1924:164) that educational levels had skyrocketed since 1890, while turnout had plummeted. See also the comments of Orren and Verba in the Harvard/ABC Symposium (1984:14).

64. See Kim, Petrocik, and Enokson (1975:107–31) for an effort to disentangle the effects of rules, party competition, and socioeconomic characteristics in comparing contemporary turnout among the states. Their comments (1975:110, and fn. 22) on the methodological problems of attempting to model these relations so as to permit the discovery of interaction effects between contextual variables and individual characteristics are especially interesting.

65. Phillips (1975:38–39) makes this point.

66. Verba and Nie (1972:340).

67. Teixiera (1987).

68. Rosenstone and Hansen (1993:242).

69. Chambers and Davis (1978:177–78). See also Kleppner (1982:34–36) for an historical commentary which gives qualified weight to such individual characteristics in the nineteenth century.

70. Verba and Nie (1972:126–27); and Verba, Nie, and Kim, (1978: esp. chapters 5, 6, and 7).

71. Kleppner (1982:34–36). We should note, however, that Kleppner (1982:149) nevertheless holds a hybrid position. Gienapp (1982:61) makes a similar though less categorical point, asserting "sound reasons to reject the assumption that education played as important a role in past politics as it does today."

72. See Burnham (1979:114).

73. See Burnham (1982:169, and table 5).

74. Verba, Nie, and Kim (1978).

75. Powell (1986:29). The standardized beta coefficient was 0.33 in the United States, but only 0.05 in the ten other nations.

76. Kleppner and Baker (1980:218–19) provide data suggesting that the system of 1896 involved "the development of a different set of age-cohort-with-turnout linkages, and that this difference was especially marked among the young of immigrant parentage."

77. Ibid. (17–19).

78. The general suggestion that independent demographic variables ought to be reconstructed as dependent social and economic variables to understand the behavior of voters and parties is made by Hays (1981:265).

79. Burnham (1974b:1019).

80. Powell's (1986 and 1982) comparative data speak only to aggregate national attitude measures, and do not contradict other studies which show

that nonvoting is correlated with attitudinal measures of political alienation within the United States.

81. Kleppner (1982:66–68) provides data on turnout changes in the Metropole between the late nineteenth and early twentieth centuries which shows that the impact of registration procedures on turnout depended on per capita wealth.

82. Carlson's (1976) otherwise excellent study of the impact of registration requirements early in the century is a regrettable example of this widespread modeling error. He establishes that turnout was significantly lower in counties with personal voter registration requirements than in counties with no registration or with nonpersonal registration in the presidential elections between 1912 and 1924. But when he then controls this finding by demographic, party competition, and urbanization variables, it disappears! As a result of this "nonfinding," the contribution his research makes to the literature has not been recognized.

3. The Mobilization and Demobilization of the Nineteenth-Century Electorate

1. Tocqueville (1969:242–43).
2. Hays (1981:244).
3. Gienapp (1982:38).
4. For a state-by-state review of suffrage restrictions and their impact in the post-Revolutionary period, see Williamson (1960); Campbell (1979: chapter 1); Flanigan and Zingale (1979); Crotty (1977). See also Becker (1968) for a study in detail of the politics which led to the relaxation of suffrage restrictions in New York during the Revolutionary period. And see Burns (1982:362–66) for a more general discussion of the political dynamics through which suffrage restrictions were removed in the early nineteenth century. On voter turnout by state from 1808 to 1828, see McCormick (1960:194, table 2).
5. To Tocqueville, this was a remarkable development, because nearly universal white male suffrage was won so early in the United States, by the 1830s. It was several decades ahead of France, a half century ahead of England, and almost a full century ahead of Italy, Germany, Russia, and Scandinavia. Chambers (1967:11) points out that even after the Reform Bill of 1832, the British electorate numbered only about 650,000 in a population of about 16 million. By contrast, in the United States, a population of 17 million in 1840 generated an electorate of 2,409,474.
6. See Formisano (1974:482); McCormick (1967:95–96). This volatility from election to election notwithstanding, turnout in gubernatorial elections was almost as high as in presidential elections. McCormick (1967:108) re-

ports turnouts of 81.9 percent in Delaware in 1804; 80.8 percent in New
Hampshire in 1814; 80 percent in Tennessee in 1817; 79.9 percent in Vermont in 1812; 79.8 percent in Mississippi in 1823; and (an unlikely) 96.7
percent in Alabama's first gubernatorial contest in 1819.

7. McCormick (1960:295).

8. Gienapp (1982:20). See Chambers and Davis (1978) for turnout by state in
the elections of 1824–44. They argue that turnout variations by state in
this period are strongly related to the level of competition and strength of
party organizations. McCormick (1960) makes the same argument. See
also Formisano (1974:688–89) for a detailed analysis of voter participation in Michigan during this period.

9. McCormick (1967:108). For a book-length discussion which applauds the
spectacular politics of the nineteenth century and mourns its passing,
see McGerr (1986). See also Gienapp (1982); McCormick (1979:282). The
spectacular aspect of American politics also impressed foreign observers,
although it did not always excite their admiration. Ostrogorski (1964:165)
deals with this matter; Rusk (1974) makes some contemporary observations in a similarly sober vein.

10. Alford (1963:1) makes the point that a democratic polity requires that
voters be available for competitive party appeals, which means they are
not "tightly integrated into enclaves of traditionalism which reinforces
ancestral political loyalties."

11. Cited in Hammond (1983:208).

12. Gienapp (1982:36–37). The literature that stresses the ethnoreligious
bases of partisan identification and cleavage in the nineteenth century is
extensive. See Benson (1961); Kleppner (1970:93–100, 1979, and 1981:114,
139–40); Hays (1967:158–59, and 1981:246); McCormick (1979:282).

13. Gienapp (1982:46–47). See for example the descriptions of political gangs
in New York City in Buckley (1987); Bridges (1987); and Asbury (1928).

14. Tilly, Tilly, and Tilly (1977).

15. Bridges (1987:106).

16. Wilentz (1982:50). See also Johnson (1978).

17. Bensel (1984:5).

18. As in the contemporary world, tribalism did not yield either a simple or
a neatly ordered politics. For the emerging industrial working class in the
North after the Civil War, ethnic and religious identities often strained
against what might otherwise be their sectional loyalties, keeping them
divided from the dominant northern Republicanism and huddled in
what Goodwyn (1978:4) calls urban Democratic "lifeboats" in a sea of
Republicanism.

19. Bensel (1984:4) says that "although expressed in cultural or religious
terms at times, the historical alignment of sectional competition in

America is primarily a product of the relationship of the separate regional economies to the national political economy and the world system." In this same vein, Shefter (1986:250) points out that the claims by Republican party politicians that industrial workers shared the interests of their employers on the tariff question was "substantially correct."

20. Burnham (1981c:151).

21. Converse (1972:287) also draws a parallel between high turnout in the United States in the nineteenth century and in some Third World contemporary countries, such as Turkey and the Philippines, a parallel he attributes to social intimidation and large-scale corruption. Burnham (1974b:1018–20) takes issue with this argument, but only by attributing rather improbable virtues of political literacy, seriousness, and attentiveness to nineteenth-century voters.

22. The now familiar characterization of the U.S. political system in the nineteenth century as a "state of courts and parties" is Skowronek's (1982).

23. Bridges (1987:95) emphasises the importance of early widespread suffrage in accounting for the spread of machine politics in the United States during the antebellum period. See also Bridges (1984). There are numerous suggestive parallels from our own time, including the reliance on clientelism by the Christian Democratic party in the economically more backward *mezzogiorno* region in Italy, by the New Society Movement in the Philippines, by the ruling PRI in Mexico, or the Israeli Likud bloc in its organization of newly arrived Jews from Northern Africa and the Middle East.

24. See Lemarchand (1981), and Mouzelis (1987). See also Key (1984: chapter 4) for a more general argument about the crucial role of organization in making the votes of the "lower brackets" effective. Eisenstadt and Roniger (1981) make a similar argument about the conditions which encourage clientelism. They go on to point out, however, that these are not simple relations of domination. The very introduction of clientelist arrangements signals that clients have political resources which patrons need to suppress or circumvent. In personal correspondence to us, Shefter makes the strong point that nineteenth-century property owners bore the costs of patronage reluctantly. "Patronage can thus be regarded as a concession to the working class extracted from the middle and upper classes, and the machine can be seen as embodying a class compromise. Thus the impact of mass participation on politics may have been limited in the antebellum period, but it was not completely insignificant."

25. On clientelism, see also Scott (1969). Huntington (1968:59–64) also relates clientelism to economic development, making the different but consistent argument that the new sources of wealth and power generated

by development provide the resources that can be used to establish a clientelist basis for assimilating new groups into the polity.

26. Formisano (1974:486).
27. Gienapp (1982:43).
28. Polakoff (1981:244). See also Keller (1977:256–57 and 310–12) for a discussion of the uses of federal patronage, particularly the patronage generated by the postal service, in party building.
29. Goodwyn (1978:5). Veterans' pensions were granted by special acts of Congress, which in the late nineteenth century constituted a substantial portion of the business of the Congress. By 1900, 753,000 veterans and 241,000 of their dependents were receiving pensions, the Pension Office had some 6,000 employees, and the pension program had also generated "an extensive infrastructure of pension and claim agents, pension attorneys (an estimated 60,000 by 1898), medical boards, and 4,000 examining surgeons" (Keller, 1977:311). Bensel (1984:60) draws a close link between Civil War pensions, the tariff, and the broad path of American development: "Because pension recipients allied themselves with the core industrial elite and thus formed a coalition large enough to successfully defend a high tariff as part of the national political economy, the redistribution of this tariff revenue through the Civil War pension system became a major element in the political strategy of development."
30. Scholarly scrutiny of clientelism in the United States has mainly been directed to the political machines which developed in most big cities after the Civil War. See, for example, Katznelson (1981); Banfield and Wilson (1963); Ostrogorski (1964); Bryce (1924); Miller (1968); Gosnell (1957); Bean (1952); Riordan (1963); and Reynolds (1936). For an exhaustive review of the literature, see DiGaetano (1985). The urban political machines of nineteenth-century America have become the prototype for the study of clientelism everywhere in the world.
31. Clientelism implies, according to Mouzelis (1985:343), that the local patron has a certain amount of autonomy vis-à-vis the national organization and leadership.
32. Bridges (1987:109–10). On the symbiotic relationship between decentralization and clientelism in the United States, see Piven and Cloward (1985:93–95). On the significance of state and local issues in antebellum politics generally, see Gienapp (1982:49–51). See also Benson (1961:292) passim. Gienapp points out that control of the states and state patronage was critical even to national political leaders.
33. Chambers (1967:14).
34. The stories abound of voter fraud by methods ranging from bribing voters, to stuffing ballot boxes, to importing outsiders, to voting the names on cemetery stones, to straightforward thuggery at the polling places.

Still, for all of the stories, there is not much reliable information on the extent of voter fraud by the machines.

35. Myers (1971:217).

36. Burnham (1979:124).

37. This is also Rusk's (1974) point, and we consider it his most incisive criticism of Burnham.

38. Polakoff (1981:245) reports that despite the enormous expansion of economic activity, the currency supply per capita actually declined from $30.30 in 1865 to $27.06 in 1890.

39. *Wabash* vs. *Illinois*.

40. Fully half of the farmers in the South, including the overwhelming majority of black farmers, had become tenants or sharecroppers. They, along with poor farmers who still owned their land, were preyed upon by local merchants who extended credit in exchange for liens on the farmers' crops or on their land.

41. In 1890, three-quarters of manufacturing was located in the northeastern and north-central states, according to Burnham (1974a:672–73, and table 6).

42. Gutman (1976:33).

43. See David Montgomery (1980); Raybeck (1966); Shefter (1986); Brecher (1974:1–23); Taft and Ross (1969:290–99).

44. Brecher (1974:1–23).

45. Walsh (1937:20).

46. Rosenstone et al. (1984:63). The vigor of these third-party movements among western farmers might well have been owed to the fact that nineteenth-century parties were weaker in the West and thus less able to suppress electoral challenges. Shefter suggested this point to us in a personal communication.

47. Ibid. (65).

48. Polakoff (1981:251). For a breakdown of the regional basis of Greenback support, see Burnham (1981:155–56, and table 5.1), and Kleppner (1981b:126–29).

49. Polakoff (1981:248).

50. See Shefter (1986:270–71).

51. Goodwyn (1978:114).

52. Hofstadter (1955:61).

53. Rosenstone et al. (1984:70).

54. Ibid. As it turned out, however, the new party had little leverage over its erstwhile candidates once they were elected. See Sundquist (1973:121) and Woodward (1951:241).

55. See for example the discussion in Kousser (1974:37).

56. Goodwyn (1978:142); Woodward (1951: chapters 9 and 10).

57. Kousser (1974:38).
58. Cited in Polakoff (1981:260).
59. Goodwyn (1978:168).
60. Shefter (198:257).
61. Galabos (1975:112).
62. See Polakoff (1981:263).
63. McGerr (1986:140–41). As McGerr goes on to say, this amount does not take account of the funds spent by other Republican operations. The Chicago Literary Bureau, for example, spent $500,000, and "poured out" more than a hundred million documents.
64. The Republican campaign is described in McGerr (1986:137–45), and Goodwyn (1978:279–83).
65. Sundquist (1973:132) reports that during 1893 alone, "one-sixth of the nation's railroads, more than six hundred banks and other financial institutions, and some thirty-two iron and steel companies failed."
66. For this analysis, see Jensen (1971: chapter 10).
67. The margin of Republican victory was wide only by comparison to the narrow margins by which presidential contests had been decided in earlier elections during the intensely competitive post-Civil War period. In fact, 1896 was the first in a series of elections in which the presidency was decided by comparatively large majorities.
68. Burnham (1981c:182).
69. See Goodwyn (1978, and 1976: chapters 16 and 17). See also Jensen (1971: chapter 10).
70. Schattschneider (1960).
71. Turnout levels in the nineteenth century are very probably inflated by the undercounting of the voting age population, owing to the crude counting techniques employed by the Census Bureau. Using various retroactive estimations, Shortridge judges that the consequent rate of inflation of turnout might have been 10 percent. When this adjustment is made, the "sharp differences in turnout between the nineteenth century and the twentieth century tend to diminish" (1981:47). The issue is not simply a technical one, since different estimates of nineteenth-century turnout support different explanations of turnout decline. See Rusk (1974:1041) and Converse (1972:290) in their debate with Burnham, whose argument hinges on high turnout in the nineteenth century. In fact, Burnham (1974b:1004) also acknowledges the enumeration problem. We think that Shortridge's proposed qualification is sensible. Underenumeration does not, however, explain the sharp downward trend in turnout from 79 percent in the election of 1896 to an average of 60 percent in the elections of 1912 and 1916, unless one makes the improbable assumption that census procedures were so radically improved in this period as to expand the

enumerated voting age population by fully one-third. It therefore seems reasonable to conclude that while turnout in the nineteenth century may be overestimated, the relative magnitude of the drop in turnout that began in the early twentieth century is not.

72. See Kleppner and Baker (1980:218–19).
73. One explanation of granting of female suffrage is that politicians were confident that mainly middle- and upper-class women would make use of it, thus further diluting the working-class vote.
74. Kleppner (1982:69–70).
75. By 1904, for example, a thousand railroad lines had been consolidated into six great combinations, each allied with either the Morgan or Rockefeller empires (Zinn, 1980:316).
76. Zinn reports that while there had been a thousand strikes a year in the 1890s, there were four thousand strikes each year by 1904. See also Montgomery (1979).
77. Zinn (1980:331). The downturns of 1903 and 1907 were relatively minor, and the more serious depression of 1913–14 was overcome quickly as European war-production orders revived the economy.
78. For a concise discussion of the electoral successes of this generation of farmer insurgents, see Sundquist (1973:168–71).
79. The Socialist candidate for mayor of New York City, Morris Hillquit, won 22 percent of the vote, and ten Socialists were sent to the New York state legislature. In Chicago, the Socialists won 34.7 percent of the vote, and in Buffalo, 30.2 percent (Zinn, 1980:356). See also Weinstein (1969).
80. Polakoff (1981:287–88).
81. Sundquist (1973:162).
82. Ibid. (163).
83. Polakoff (1981:290–91).
84. Ibid.
85. Hofstadter (1948:222).
86. Hofstadter (1948: chapter 9). See also Zinn (1980:342–43).
87. Hofstadter recounts Wilson's rebuff of the bankers' demand for outright control of the Federal Reserve Board. But he makes clear that this was pretty much a matter of allowing Wilson to feel himself independent (1948:258–59).
88. Kolko (1977). See also Weinstein (1968).
89. On repression during the World War I period, including a proposal to round up radicals and detain them in camps in the central Pacific, see Burns (1985:499–507); Zinn (1980: chapter 14); and Goldstein (1978).
90. Zinn (1980:372).
91. On political hysteria in the United States, see Levin (1971).
92. Polakoff (1981:303).

93. The Emergency Tariff of 1921 actually applied mainly to agricultural products, which made little sense since the United States was primarily an exporter of agricultural goods. A year later, the Fordney-McCumber Tariff of 1922 partially restored the high tariffs that had been enacted after the election of 1896, but had been lowered in 1909 under the Taft administration (Polakoff, 1981:305).
94. Ibid. (306).
95. Zinn (1980:375).
96. Polakoff (1981:315–16).

4. How Demobilization Was Accomplished

1. Converse (1972:301) warns that "[i]n most instances where the division of the vote swerves dramatically in a particular election, the worst prediction for the next election is an extrapolation of the trend."
2. See Kleppner (1981b:124–25 and table 4.3) for a regional breakdown of party strength in the 1876–1892 period.
3. Burnham (1981c:180). Burnham (183) goes on to say: "[T]he proportion of geographical areas in which there was relatively close two-party competition showed a strong tendency to decline across the 1896–1930 era. In particular, the near Midwest became much more solidly Republican at most levels of election after World War I than it had been before. By 1924 close Republican–Democratic competition at the presidential level had come to be confined almost exclusively to the Border states and counties immediately adjacent to them, the Appalachian uplands of the South, and the two southernmost Mountain states, Arizona and New Mexico." See also Kleppner (1982:26 and table 2.6) for longitudinal measures of declining competition. Schattschneider (1960:82–83) presents tables showing the singular impact of the election of 1896 itself on sectional party strength. And Carlson (1976:134 and table 4.1) contains a state-by-state accounting of partisan shifts between 1896 and 1930.
4. Burnham (1974c:672, table 6).
5. Schattschneider (1960:79).
6. Ferguson's (1983) effort to recast the concept of critical elections as resulting not from electoral realignments but from investor realignments is perhaps especially illuminating of this period of party development. See Ferguson (1984) for a further discussion.
7. Burnham (1981c:192).
8. Schattschneider (1960:85)
9. Ibid. (1960:80), emphasis in the original. Schattschneider's view assumes the absence of effectively contested primaries with a mass electorate. In fact, even after direct primaries were introduced early in the twentieth

century, they tended toward a factional politics centered on individuals, with very narrow participation. See Key (1956:169–96).

10. Thus Kleppner's (1982:148–49) description of the major parties in the decade after the debacle of 1896 does not much distinguish the pre- and post-1896 periods, and in any case it seems a more apt characterization of the party system as it had evolved by the 1920s: "Class-based discontent percolated at the grassroots, but it could not be aggregated by the newly emergent party system. . . . [T]he capitalist consensus limited the scope of partisan disagreement. . . . Since neither major party self-consciously and explicitly represented the economic discontents of the lower strata of society, those group interests remained unpoliticized and unmobilized."

11. Burnham (1965) in particular stresses the alienation of voters which resulted from the "takeover" of 1896, at least in his earlier work. For a strident attack on this thesis, see Rusk (1974).

12. Burnham (1981c:190). For another discussion of this relationship pointing out some of the ambiguous findings, see Kelley (1967:365–66).

13. Kleppner, who is a qualified advocate of the party competition or behavioral explanation of falling turnout, also makes this point about the inadequacy of the thesis (1982:73).

14. Other rule changes which made third-party challenges more difficult may also have inhibited electoral participation, especially in the West. See Argersinger (1980).

15. On this point, see McCormick (1981:248); Weibe (1967); and Weinstein (1968: chapter 4).

16. The several waves of government reform in the late nineteenth and early twentieth century, and the animus of the reformers toward party organizations, and especially toward big-city machines, have been extensively examined. See Wiebe (1967), Hays (1958 and 1964), Haber (1964), and Weinstein (1968). Shefter (1978a) distinguishes between the Mugwumps who advocated a posture of independence toward the parties, and the later Progressive movement which tried to destroy the parties as an instrument of governance. See also Bridges (1984). There is a debate among historians about whether businessmen or a disgruntled middle class made up the leading edge of these reform campaigns. Hays (1964) and Weinstein (1968) stress the role of business.

17. McGerr (1986: chapter 4) devotes extensive attention to these extraparty organizations. See his discussion of "educational politics."

18. Shefter (1984:145) suggests a parallel with civil service reform in England. After having been roundly defeated in 1854, reform was rapidly passed on the heels of the extension of the suffrage in 1867, presumably to ensure that the aristocracy and the upper-middle class would not be displaced

by the politicians who arose on the basis of newly enfranchised working-class and lower-middle-class voters.

19. Some three hundred smaller cities were reorganized under a commission form of government between 1900 and 1913, and one hundred were changed to city manager types by 1919, according to Polakoff (1981:277).

20. Alford and Lee (1968) concluded that "cities without the council-manager form and with partisan elections have higher voting turnout." The difference was large. Median turnout in partisan elections was 50 percent, for example, and only 30 percent in cities with nonpartisan elections. This is consistent with findings reported by Lee (1960). See also Lineberry and Fowler (1967), who concluded that under reformed governments, public policy is less responsive to demands arising out of social conflicts.

21. Rusk (1974:1941).

22. Banfield and Wilson (1963:116).

23. The definitive study of the Australian or office block ballot is by Rusk (1970).

24. Gosnell (1937).

25. Bridges (1987:111 and 1984: chapter 7).

26. In the mid-nineteenth century, the major parties had been internally divided on the tariff, but in the elections of 1880 and 1884, the Democratic party gradually adopted a low-tariff position so that the cleavage that divided business interests became a partisan issue. See McGerr (1986:78).

27. Shefter (1983:467). In personal correspondence to the authors, Shefter makes the additional point that businessmen who supported the national party that was the minority locally—whether Republican or Democratic—were readier to join reform coalitions. For a general discussion of the interrelationship between tariff policy and other key issues of the era, including military pensions, imperialism, and federal intervention in the southern electoral system, see Bensel (1984: Chapter 3).

28. Burnham (1981c:166) and Key (1956:169–96). See also Key (1949) for a discussion of the role of the direct primary in the South in promoting a politics of faction.

29. Burnham (1981c:166).

30. McCormick (1981:271).

31. Ibid.

32. Kleppner (1982:71). Similarly, Ranney and Kendall (1956) maintain that "a community . . . needs *some* agency or agencies (a) to define the alternatives open to it, [and] to make clear to the voters what is involved in the choice among those alternatives."

33. See Burnham (1981c:170–75).

34. Shefter (1984:143).

35. McCormick (1979:295).
36. For an overview, see Woodward (1966). The techniques pioneered during reconstruction to obstruct black voting have been described by John Hope Franklin (1969: esp. chapter 18). The definitive work on the use of force in deterring blacks from voting is V. O. Key (1984: chapters 25–28).
37. Kousser (1974:17–18, 28, and 78).
38. Ibid. (46–47).
39. Bensel (1984:76 and 81). For a description of the heated congressional battles over legislative proposals for federal intervention in southern elections before 1896, see Bensel (1984:73–88). The last effort to impose federal supervision, known as the "Force Bill," did not die in the Congress until Cleveland's reelection in 1892.
40. Kousser (1974:263) thinks that southern elites also preferred legal methods of preventing blacks from voting. However, Rusk and Stucker (1978:207) disagree with Kousser on this, speculating that had informal methods of disfranchisement been sufficiently successful, the southern states would have avoided legal changes that were susceptible to constitutional challenge.
41. Kousser (1974:39).
42. Rusk and Stucker (1978:211).
43. Kousser (1974:67 and table 3.2).
44. Dunning (1901:443). Dunning also reports a remarkable instance of gerrymandering. "In Mississippi appeared the 'shoestring district,' three hundred miles long and about twenty wide, including within its boundaries nearly all of the densest black communities of the state." See Kousser (1974:50) as well.
45. Harris (1929:157); Kousser (1974:48–49).
46. See Phillips (1975:8).
47. Kousser (1974:41 and table 1.5).
48. McDonald (undated:112–13).
49. A witness cited by Pendleton (1927:459) offered this description of how poor whites reacted: "It was painful and pitiful to see the horror and dread visible on the faces of the illiterate poor white men who were waiting to take their turn before the inquisition. . . . This was horrible to behold, but it was still more horrible to see the marks of humiliation and despair that were stamped on the faces of honest but poor white men who had been refused registration and who had been robbed of their citizenship without cause. We saw them as they came from the presence of the registrars with bowed heads and agonized faces; and when they spoke, in many instances, there was a tear in the voice of the humiliated citizen." Of course, this was only one of the ways in which poor southern whites were victimized by their own racism.

50. Kousser (1974:236).
51. Phillips (1975:8).
52. Kousser (1974:103).
53. Burnham (1974c:1054).
54. Cited in McGerr (1986:46).
55. Kleppner (1982:8); Williamson (1960); Riker (1965:38).
56. McGerr (1986:49–50).
57. "Durational residency requirements of a year or more were a feature of most state codes since the 1780s when," according to Riker (1965:57–58), "they were invented precisely because universal suffrage seemed imminent, to substitute for land ownership as proof of an 'interest' in the election of local officials." These restrictions persisted until the Voting Rights Act amendments in 1970, which reduced the residence requirement for presidential elections to thirty days, with the practical effect that thirty days became the requirement for all elections.
58. Kleppner (1982:57–58 and 60). Between 1848 and 1890, eighteen states adopted these alien-with-intent laws (Rusk and Stucker, 1978).
59. McGerr (1986:47); Kleppner (1982:59).
60. Kleppner (1982:10).
61. Riker (1953:59–60).
62. Ibid.
63. Carlson (1976:105).
64. Phillips and Blackman (1975:8).
65. There exists no adequate political history of voter registration. Harris (1929) is a fairly thorough compilation of the main legislative developments. The review which follows also draws on a paper by Hayduk (1986).
66. Cited in Harris (1929:70).
67. Ibid. (69–70).
68. Cited in ibid. (1929:68).
69. Carlson (1976:155, table 4.11) compares turnout in counties with nonpersonal and personal voter registration systems in early twentieth-century elections, and shows that turnout was consistently lower in counties with personal registration systems.
70. See Kelley et al. (1967:367) on the impact of closing dates on rates of registration. See also Gosnell (1927:104).
71. Harris (1929:186).
72. Cited in McGerr (1986:48).
73. Even so staunch an advocate of registration as Harris (1929:80–81) was confounded by the system that had developed in Philadelphia by 1929 as a result of the accumulation of restrictive procedures: "No one may register who has not paid a poll tax, occupation tax, or some other form of state taxation within a period of two years, and to pay the poll tax, one

must be listed by the assessor. In Philadelphia it is notorious that the assessors' lists are grossly inaccurate and inflated, and serve no useful purpose. The poll tax required in Philadelphia is only fifty cents, and payment serves to qualify one for two years, but many persons are omitted by the assessor and find themselves unable to register."

74. Carlson (1976:107).
75. McCormick (1953:149–53).
76. Harris (1929:89).
77. Kleppner (1982:60).
78. Carlson (1976:105).
79. Harris (1929:76).
80. Carlson (1976:110).
81. Harris (1929:89).
82. Burnham's (1981c:167) suggestion that the reliance on personal voter registration systems in the United States owed something to the weakness of state bureaucratic capacities in this country is inconsistent with the historical evidence, which shows that increasingly elaborate bureaucratic machinery did in fact exist, although it was used to impede voting. Thus he says that "elsewhere in the West (including neighboring Canada), it was early accepted that it was the state's task to compile and update electoral registers" because of the existence of state bureaucracies capable of carrying out such a task or a "consensus that such a bureaucracy should be created." But American registration systems were also initially based on the presumption that registering people was a state responsibility; only later were they changed to shift the obligation to the citizen of getting one's name on the register.
83. Campbell et al. (1960:152) make this point about Southern systems; it is informal barriers, rather than legislative restrictions, that account for variations in turnout among Southern blacks.
84. Kleppner (1982:61–62). His conclusion is based on a comparison of turnout rates in areas covered by personal registration requirements, and areas in which there was either no registration or a nonpersonal registration system. It should be noted that Kleppner concludes that the impact of personal voter registration was substantially weaker in the Metropole than in the Periphery, especially after 1900. See also Kleppner and Baker (1980).
85. Burnham (1974b:1011, and see also 1970: chapter 4, and 1979).
86. Burnham (1981c:191) is also pertinent; he rephrases his estimate of the turnout decline due to voter registration "as much less than one half." Carlson (1976: chapter 4) contains a systematic comparison of turnout in counties and states with personal registration, nonpersonal registration, and no registration in the presidential elections from 1912 to 1924.

5. *The New Deal Party System: Partial Remobilization*

1. See Mollenkopf (1983) for a similar analysis of the Democratic party's electoral problems, although not applied to levels of participation.

2. Key's (1955) classic article on critical elections locates the beginnings of the New Deal realignment in 1928.

3. Sundquist (1973:177).

4. Polakoff (1981:317).

5. However, the data do not support the thesis, advanced by Kleppner, Jensen, and others, that the primary ethnocultural division in 1928 was between pietists and liturgicals. This was a straightforward conflict between Protestants and Democrats. See Lichtman (1979) for an exhaustive study of the voting data. The surge was actually larger among Republican voters than among Democrats, which also suggests a reaction by Protestants against Catholics. Of course, the religious basis of electoral division also marks the difference from the realigning elections of the 1930s. See Burnham (1982:177).

6. There were some small signs in the farm belt, however, that severely depressed agricultural conditions in the 1920s were moving voters into Democratic columns. Smith carried 45 counties in Illinois, Iowa, Minnesota, and North Dakota. See Sundquist (1973:174–76).

7. Bernstein (1970:255–56) reports that by January 1930, 30 to 40 percent of the male labor force in Toledo was out of work. By the end of 1930, half the textile workers in New England were unemployed; and the Metropolitan Life Insurance Company discovered that one-quarter of its policy holders in forty-six cities were jobless.

8. Kleppner (1982:85).

9. Ibid. (98).

10. The literature on this point is immense, but V. O. Key (1966) is definitive.

11. The interaction of protest movements with the electoral context is the main theme of the analysis of twentieth-century movements in Piven and Cloward (1977).

12. See Piven and Cloward (1977: chapters 2 and 3), as well as Bernstein (1970) and Schlesinger (1957). See also Goldfield (1985) for a judicious review of the diverse political forces accounting for New Deal labor legislation, which nevertheless emphasizes the importance of mass protest. Ferguson (1984) describes the divisions between business and the New Deal.

13. White and White (1937:84).

14. Kleppner (1982:100). See also Leuchtenberg (1963:53, 120–32, and 157–58).

15. Jensen (1981:205–6). The reorganization of federal agencies to facilitate the institutionalization of linkages to a new constituency during the New

Deal is discussed in Shefter (1978a:39–41) and Mollenkopf (1983: chapter 2).

16. See Mann (1965).
17. Jensen (1981:210).
18. For a close study of the Chicago machine during the depression, see Gosnell (1937). On FDR and the machines, see also Dorsett (1977).
19. See Pelling (1962:166). See also Schlesinger (1960:594); and Greenstone (1969:49).
20. Schattschneider (1960:49) reports on polls taken at the time that showed CIO members voting 79 percent and 78 percent Democratic in the elections of 1940 and 1944. And Bernstein (1971:720) reviews an analysis of election results in 1940 in sixty-three counties and fourteen cities that showed the strength of the Roosevelt vote paralleled the concentration of CIO members.
21. Kleppner (1982:89).
22. Jensen (1981:212).
23. *Ibid.* (103).
24. These data are reprinted in Sundquist (1973:202).
25. Kleppner (1982:105) claims that in 1936 the difference in turnout between the top income group and the lowest had narrowed to 7 percentage points. However, Jensen (1981:211, and table 6.5) reports data for 1940 and 1942 (from the American Institute of Public Opinion Poll no. 294, April 1943) which shows a wider gap of 18 percentage points in 1940, and as has become typical, an even wider gap in the off-year election of 1942.
26. There is a debate about whether the New Deal Democratic majority was constructed from the entry of previous nonvoters, or the conversion of former Republicans. Anderson's (1982:9) position is that the New Deal realignment resulted from the mobilization of previous nonvoters in the big cities: "[T]he Democratic party, beginning in 1928, changed its bases of support largely by appealing to the hitherto politically uninvolved groups such as women, young people, and the foreign stock urban working class." For the view that it resulted from converting Republicans, see Erikson and Kent (1981) and Sundquist (1973: chapter 10). Among others, Burnham (1982a:179) challenges Anderson, concluding on the basis of a detailed analysis of California data that a little more than half of the Democratic gains in 1932, and about a third of the increment in the 1936–1940 period, came from new registrants rather than former Republicans. This does not quite justify Burnham's (1982b:181) conclusion that "[n]o such thing as a huge implicit or potential Democratic majority existed among the 'party of nonvoters' until *the Great Depression and the New Deal created one*" (emphasis in original).

27. In 1900, only 30 percent of the counties outside of the South had registration requirements, although of course these were more likely to be urban and populous counties. By 1930, 52.5 percent of the counties required voter registration, and by 1940, 59.2 percent (Kleppner, 1982:86).

28. Ibid. (86–87). Kleppner (1982:155) himself seems somewhat undecided about the significance of this obstruction, arguing that the "more powerful constraint . . . was the reigning ideological consensus on the central principle of political economy—the preservation of a capitalist mode of production." The New Deal, in other words, mobilized fewer nonvoters than it might have because it was constrained by the ideologically ambivalent and "morselized" character of majority opinion. However, as we have been at pains to argue, the legal obstructions which had contracted the electoral universe, and delinked the parties from "discordant elements," also meant that the dominant ideological consensus went unchallenged.

29. Bensel (1984:151–52).

30. Ibid. (233).

6. The Decline of the New Deal Party System

1. Bensel (1984:181–82).

2. On the changing class structure in the South, see Wright (1986). The dispersal of branch plants to the South was said to have brought with it northern executives and technicians who were Republicans. See Converse (1972:313–14) and Campbell et al. (1965: chapter 12) for data on the impact of the migration of better-off whites into the South on patterns of partisanship among white southerners. However, Petrocik (1987b:45) disagreed, asserting that the Republican shift occurred entirely among native southerners. In either case, the long-term dilution of Democratic partisanship as a result of changes in the southern class structure should be distinguished from defections by southern whites over the race question, particularly in presidential contests.

3. The fact that Truman was fending off Henry Wallace's third-party challenge from the left in a close election may have forced the civil rights issue into national politics rather earlier than would otherwise have been the case. Clark Clifford, Truman's chief campaign strategist, warned that unless Truman acted the Republicans would offer a legislative program to appeal to blacks, including a Fair Employment Practices Commission, an anti-poll-tax bill, and an antilynching bill. See Yarnell (1974:35–69); Bernstein (1970); Berman (1970); and Vaughan (1972).

4. Ladd (1985:5).

5. Bartley (1969); and Tindall (1972).

6. Evans and Novak (1966:481).

7. Kleppner (1982:116).
8. Converse (1972:6).
9. Kleppner (1982:120–21).
10. Bensel (1984:76).
11. Ladd (1985:5).
12. Sundquist (1985:10–11).
13. Except Florida where the black population is relatively small.
14. Petrocik (1987b:52).
15. Ibid. (49).
16. Lichtman (1987). We should note that Lichtman uses uncorrected Census data on white registration levels, so the racial discrepancy he reports is overstated.
17. Ladd concludes that the "racial background of voters, the region in which they live, and the extent of their religious participation have become in the postindustrial-party system especially powerful factors." By contrast, "neither race nor religiosity had been key variables in the New Deal years; and though region was central then as now, today's regional alignment is virtually a mirror image of the preceding eras." See Dougherty et al. (1997:15).
18. See Pomper (1977:34).
19. Norpoth and Rusk (1982).
20. Jensen (1981:220–21).
21. For several views, see Miller and Miller (1977); Converse (1976); and Nie, Verba, and Petrocik (1976).
22. Burnham (1974a:678–79, 720; 1981b; and 1981c).
23. Those reforms, which Burnham thought led to the "partial dissolution of the traditional linkages between elite and public, mediated by the party system" included the spread of direct primaries, the rise of political action committees, and the growth of "campaign technology," including polling, focus groups, targeting, advertising, and so on. See Burnham (1995:188).
24. Pomper (1977:21–41 and 1975:163) also thought there was a "countervailing trend": while state parties were losing strength and coherence, the national parties were gaining. Nevertheless, he thought the decline of partisanship that he documented pointed to "a nonpartisan electoral future."
25. Jensen (1981:219). As late as 1968, only 40 percent of the delegates to the nominating convention were chosen by primary elections.
26. Norpoth and Rusk (1972:526). The emergence of an issue-oriented (and ideologically consistent) electorate was documented comprehensively in Verba, Nie, and Petrocik (1976). See also Nie and Andersen (1974, especially 573–78 and 581–85). Most studies used survey data from the 1950s as their base line.

27. Converse (1972:329–30). See Teixiera (1992) for the argument that these chaotic events drove turnout down more among groups in the population who were less likely to vote in the first place.

28. There are of course other ways of assessing party weakness or strength. See Aldrich (1995:14–18) for a discussion.

29. For the point that the decline of partisanship and the rise of issue orientations were no longer independent of each other, see Rusk (1974:1047). However, Pomper (1975 and 1977) saw the rise of issue politics as a by-product of the decline of partisan allegiance. Thus for him the declining party command over key resources ultimately caused electoral fragmentation.

30. Galston (1985:23).

31. Schneider (1987:45–46).

32. For a rather overworked interpretation of this sort, see Shefter (1978a:245). See also Ginsberg and Shefter (1985:11–12). Kleppner (1982:157) also more or less adopts this interpretation.

33. George McGovern chaired the Commission on Party Structure and Delegate Selection that set the rules for the 1972 Democratic convention.

34. See Edsall (984:159 and chapter 1), and Huntington (1985:63–78).

35. It was by no means clear that this alienation was permanent. Opinion polls in the 1980s showed there was in fact wide public support for the causes associated with the New Politics, including disarmament, environmental regulation, minority and women's rights, and expanded social programs. For comprehensive reviews of the survey data on these issues see Navarro (1985) and Lipset (1985).

36. Lipset (1986:223) made the point that while privileged, this educated stratum was less conservative than elites had been in the past. For a very different outlook, in which the New Politics activists were defined as reformers who temporarily opened the Democratic party to popular influences, see Karp (1984).

37. The apparatus that made possible the fantastic expansion of the U.S. economy and its penetration of the world economy is familiar. It included the Marshall Plan, which revived the European economies and made them major markets for American goods, at least for a time; the Bretton Woods agreement, which fixed and stabilized international exchange rates and established the dollar as the currency of international trade; the International Monetary Fund and the World Bank, which regulated credit; and the General Agreement on Tariffs and Trade, devoted to lowering tariff barriers. See Ferguson and Rogers (1986: 49–50).

38. For discussions of the business-labor accord see Gold (1977); Wolfe (1981); Bowles and Gintis (1982); Bowles, Gintis, and Weisskokopf (1984); and Cohen and Rogers (1983).

39. For a critique of the economic indicators that support the widespread view that growth had been slowing and investment declining in the United States, see Block (1987).

40. This trend continued. The Bureau of Labor Statistics reported in May 1986, for example, that 30.5 percent of the jobs added since January 1980 were in retail trade, and nearly 60 percent were in miscellaneous services. According to Morehouse and Dembo (1986:14, emphasis added), annual wages in retailing averaged $9,036, or about $2,000 less than the poverty level for a family of four, and only 44 percent of average earnings in manufacturing, *down from 63 percent of manufacturing wages in 1962.*

41. Edsall (1984:107 and chapter 3.) See also Ferguson and Rogers (1986: chapter 3) who provide an account of the shift, and of the role of different business sectors in it.

42. Edsall (1984:108). On the corporate political mobilization, see also Vogel (1983). Vogel thinks American business was reacting to the successes of the public interest movement in the decade from 1965 to 1975, and particularly to administrative and financial costs of government regulation. Accordingly, American corporate leaders themselves became political activists, investing themselves in "public affairs," mobilizing stockholders to make campaign contributions, engaging in political advertising, and vastly expanding their Washington-based lobbying operations.

43. In Edsall's (1984:156) view, the unstinting efforts of big business to defeat this measure, which was a high priority for labor, signaled to union leaders more than anything else that the accord had broken down. He quotes A. H. Raskin on the matter: "What galled labor beyond measure, oddly enough, was not the treason of politicians who had taken labor's shilling at election time. It was the defection to the anti-union camp of a raft of chief executives from the Fortune 500—men whom the unions had come to think of almost as allies. As many labor leaders see it, that crucial battle marked the end of a thirty-year *entente cordiale.*"

44. The National Council on Employment Policy reported that in 1984 about 8 million workers received wages at or below the minimum wage of $3.35 an hour, and according to Sar Levitan, another 6 million received wages just above the minimum (*New York Times*, June 8, 1986).

45. See Kelley (1986) for strong evidence that New Deal issues remained as salient as ever to the voters in 1980 and 1984, but confidence in the Democratic party's ability to deliver on these "bread-and-butter" issues had dropped sharply.

46. Cavanaugh (1981); Wolfinger and Rosenstone (1980:58); Boyd (1981). However, even low rates of voting among the young should not be taken for granted. We remind the reader of our critique of such social-psychological explanations in chapter 4.

47. For a brief period, the combination of rising protest and national Democratic response did increase turnout among blacks in the North, although the increase was modest compared to that among southern blacks. Between the 1952–60 and the 1964–80 periods, black voter turnout outside the South rose by 8 percentage points. See Kleppner (1982:22).

48. Burnham (1979:114–15).

49. Ibid. (114 and 137, fn 11).

50. The national registration level is shown in table 6.6 as having fallen to 66.9 percent in 1980, but the actual figure was about 60–62 percent when overreporting is taken into account.

51. Galston (1985:17). Edsall (1984:189–90) made a geographic variant of this mobility argument, namely that the population had increased in the more conservative southern, southwestern, and western regions of the country.

52. Ferguson and Rogers (1986:47–48) made the point that a small but powerful sector of the business community in fact supported the New Deal during the 1930s. These were the firms that were capital intensive—and so not especially averse to the prolabor policies of the New Deal—internationalist, and imbued with the norms of scientific advance. They cite General Electric, IBM, Pan Am, and R. J. Reynolds; oil companies such as Standard Oil of New Jersey, Standard Oil of California, Cities Service, and Shell; and major commercial and investment banks, including Bank of America, Chase National Bank, Brown Brothers Harriman, Goldman Sachs, Lehman Brothers, and Dillon Read. See also Ferguson (1983 and 1984).

53. On this point, see Davis (1986:75); and Ginsberg and Shefter (1985:2). See also Waddell for an exhaustive study of the impact of the war on the New Deal.

54. See Millis and Brown (1950).

55. Of the 219 Democratic congressmen who voted for Smith-Connally, 191 had been supported by the CIO's Political Action Committee. Moreover, Taft-Hartley was passed over Truman's veto by margins of 331 to 83 in the House and 68 to 25 in the Senate. In any case, Truman's largely symbolic gesture of the veto freed him to use the legislation against strikes twelve times in the first year after its passage. See Green (1975:34); Yarnell (1974:22–25); Sitkoff (1974:92–97); Hartmann (1971:86–91); Martin (1976:540, 643, 660, 691).

56. Davis (1986:84, 98n). See also Lens (1959:298).

57. Ferguson and Rogers (1986:84). Freeman provides similar indicators (1986:14–16).

58. Edsall (1984:153).

59. Ferguson and Rogers (1986:85).

60. The same overall problem afflicted a number of the West European working-class parties based primarily on unionized workers in heavy industries, including the Social Democrats in West Germany, the Communists in Italy, and the Socialists in France. England was a dramatic case. The Labor party's poor showing partly reflected the fact that since 1979 and the late 1980s, union membership had fallen from 12 million to 9 million, and the unionized share of the workforce had fallen from 51 percent to 37 percent.

61. Discussions of the bureaucratization of city politics can be found in Lowi (1968); Piven (1974a and 1984); and Shefter (1977).

62. An analysis of this competitive process and its bearing on the evolution of the urban fiscal crisis that developed in the late 1960s can be found in Piven (1974a).

63. On urban renewal and the Democratic party, see Friedland (1983) and Mollenkopf (1983).

64. Moon (1957:221).

65. Ibid. (228). Overall, turnout in the 1956 election was down from 72.1 percent in 1952 to 69.8 percent in 1956, according to Burnham (1981a:100, table 1).

66. Fuller (1962:113).

67. For a fuller analysis of the Great Society programs as political strategy, and the effort to change the relationships between levels of government in the federal system that the strategy entailed, see Piven (1974b and 1974c).

68. For example, these programs were the crucial stimulant to the formation of the welfare rights protests in the late 1960s. For a history and analysis of the Great Society origins of the National Welfare Rights Organization, see Piven and Cloward (1977: chapter 5).

69. The percentage of Americans working for political parties continued to decline. Rosenstone and Hansen (1993:90) report a decline from 5.9 percent in the early 1970s to 3.1 percent in the late 1980s.

7. The Welfare State and Voter Registration Mobilization

1. See letter of February 16, 1983, from Wattleton to affiliates.

2. Rossi (1992).

3. Manza and Brooks (1998:1235–66) present data showing that changing rates of labor force participation explain the gender gap. They make the additional argument that attitudes toward welfare state spending mediate the relationship of labor force participation and vote choice.

4. *Congressional Quarterly* (1983:1503).

5. Ibid.

6. *New York Times,* January 4, 1984.

7. Phillips (1983:103).
8. See, for example, Leibman (1983b).
9. Harris Poll press release, November 4, 1980.
10. For a general summary of these actions, see Smith (1985).
11. September 28, 1984.
12. *Congressional Quarterly* (1983:1504, 1507).
13. Marable (1986).
14. *Newsweek,* Election Extra, November/December 1984, p. 81.
15. *Congressional Quarterly* (1983:1503).
16. Edsall and Johnson (July 7, 1984).
17. Salmans (July 6, 1984).
18. Thomas B. Edsall and Haynes Johnson, *Washington Post,* May 6, 1984.
19. See Salmore and Salmore (1985:188) for a further description of the Republican computer strategy.
20. *Newark Star Ledger,* September 3, 1984.
21. April 22, 1984.
22. January 2, 1983.
23. Howard Phillips, *Conservative Digest,* January 1984, p. 41.
24. Letter, July 8, 1983.
25. Letter, November 14, 1983.
26. March 14, 1984.
27. Vol. 14, no. 1, Monday, May 9, 1983.
28. Letter from Larry P. Weinberg to Josiah Beeman, August 11, 1982.
29. Memo to presidents of AFSCME Hospital and Human Service Locals, August 31, 1984.
30. *New York Times,* July 2, 1999.
31. Letter to the Field Foundation dated February 28, 1985.
32. Cain and McCue (1985:17).

8. Party Competition and Electoral Mobilization

1. Booklet published by the Office of the Secretary of State, Michigan, entitled "A New Approach to Voter Registration," no date.
2. Monday, December 5, 1983.
3. December 17, 1983.
4. Letter dated April 3, 1984.
5. September 7, 1983.
6. From the files of People for the American Way, Washington, D.C.
7. January 4, 1984.
8. January 10, 1984.
9. April 30, 1984.
10. Press release, April 18, 1985.

11. August 18, 1985.
12. September 3, 1985.

9. Barriers or Mobilization? The Debate over Nonvoting

1. *Washington Post,* September 30, 1984.
2. "Voting and Registration Highlights From the Current Population Survey: 1964 to 1980," U.S. Department of Commerce, Bureau of the Census, Series P-23, No. 131, February 1984.
3. Jerry T. Jennings, "The Current Population Survey of Voting and Registration: Summary and History," Bureau of the Census, undated.
4. Harvard/ABC News Symposium. (1984:27).
5. Glass, Squire, and Wolfinger (1984:52).
6. June 16, 1984.
7. For our part, we had seen it all before. In the 1960s, many agency administrators barred welfare rights organizers from waiting rooms. In response, the National Welfare Rights Organization, aided by antipoverty legal services staff and by the American Civil Liberties Union chapters, initiated suits arguing that waiting rooms are public places, and won.
8. June 24, 1984, p. 3.
9. Source: reports issued by Curtis Gans and the Committee for the Study of the American Electorate.
10. November 11, 1984.
11. David Osborne, "Getting Out the Vote," *The Atlantic,* May 1985.
12. Burnham (1985).
13. INTERFACE (July 10, 1985:16).
14. Cain and McCue (June 1984).
15. March 1987.
16. Burnham, May 9, 1988.
17. Letter from Walter Dean Burnham, November 17, 1988.
18. Report by the Committee for the Study of the American Electorate, 1998, p. 3.
19. See esp. chapter 4.
20. Press release, Committee for the Study of the American Electorate, September 27, 1998, p. 7.
21. Burnham, May 9, 1988.

10. The States as Laboratories of Democracy

1. Executive Summary, Commission on National Elections, 1986.
2. Citizens' Commission on Civil Rights, *Barriers to Registration and Voting: An Agenda for Reform,* published by the National Center for Policy Alternatives, Washington, D.C., April 1988.

3. Letter from Allen J. Beermann, Secretary of State of Nebraska, and Chairman NASS Committee on Awards, July 7, 1994.

4. National Association of Secretaries of State (Undated:4).

5. Letter dated July 30, 1986: "When I spoke to Cindy Williams of Human SERVE at the conference, she suggested that there might be a need for a broader review of the sorts of voter registration obstacles to which Dr. Fleming alluded in his remarks. I think a study of any such obstacles might be very helpful, and Cindy thought you might be interested in chairing a committee."

6. The remaining members of the bipartisan taskforce were: Elaine Baxter (D-IA), Dick Molpus (D-MS), Allen J. Beermann (R-NE), Natalie Meyer (R-CO).

7. The figure for 1969 is taken from *Personal Travel in the U.S.*, Volume 1. *A Report on Findings from the 1983–1984 Nationwide Personal Transportation Study*. Federal Highway Administration, August 1986, Table 4–1. The figure for 1988 is taken from U.S. Department of Transportation, *Highway Statistics, 1988*, Table DL-20, p. 32. We have adjusted this figure upward by two percentage points because it includes drivers younger than 18 years of age who are only half as likely to drive as persons of voting age, thus making it appear that fewer voting age adults drive than actually do.

8. *Personal Travel in the U.S. A Report on Findings from the 1990 Nationwide Personal Transportation Study,* based on a nationwide sample of 22,000 households and conducted by the U.S. Department of Transportation. The data reported for 1983 are from a similar national survey, released in 1986.

9. Karen Woodrow, "Undocumented Immigrants Living in the United States." U.S. Census: November 1989.

11. Federal Reform

1. See Groarke (2000) for a detailed analysis of the voter registration legislation in the 1970s.

2. Ibid.

3. Personal communication.

4. Wolfinger and Rosenstone (1980:109).

5. Cohen and Ganz (Undated:13–14).

6. Human SERVE memo, April 4, 1987.

7. *Christian Science Monitor*, March 30, 1993.

8. September 9, 1990.

9. (1991:389, fn 117).

10. Source: U.S. Department of Transportation, *Highway Statistics, 1988*, Table DL-20, p. 32.

11. (1985:9).

12. February 25, 1989.

13. See press release of the Committee for the Study of the American Electorate, "More Than Six Million Eligible Americans May Be Blocked from Voting by Registration Barriers," Washington, D.C., January 22, 1988.

14. Crocker (1990:15).

15. March 30, 1993.

16. Memorandum from Royce Crocker, Congressional Research Service, to the House Subcommittee on Elections, May 28, 1981.

17. Press Release, Committee for the Study of the American Electorate, "Study of the Impact of Motor Voter Laws in 1992 Election on Registration and Turnout," Washington, D.C., February 11, 1993.

18. Memo dated October 10, 1989.

19. Dated April 30, 1991.

20. These examples were taken from the files of People for the American Way, Washington, D.C.

21. Groarke (2000).

22. January 31, 1990.

23. May 17, 1989.

24. February 5, 1990.

25. *New York Times*, January 31, 1990.

26. October 12, 1990.

27. Personal communication.

28. Letter dated July 9, 1993.

29. Personal communication.

30. June 7, 1995.

12. Remobilization

1. Six states were exempt from NVRA because they had day-of-election registration (MN, WY, NH, ID, and WI) or no registration (ND); and one state failed to report to the FEC (NV). See the two Federal Election Commission reports to Congress on "The Impact of the National Voter Registration Act of 1993," one published in 1997 for the 1995–96 period, and the other published in 1999 for the 1997–98 period.

2. See table 5 in both the 1997 and 1999 FEC reports.

3. See table 2 in both the 1997 and 1999 FEC reports.

4. See 1999 FEC report, p. 2.

5. Letter to Jim Dickson dated January 12, 1999.

6. Committee for the Study of the American Electorate, report dated February 8, 1999, p. 2.

7. See G. Bingham Powell (1986:36).

8. Teixiera (1992: chapter 4).

9. See Wolfinger and Rosenstone (1980: chapter 4) and Abramson (1995).

10. Rosenstone and Hansen (1993:215). Warren Miller (1992:1–43) makes the further argument that young potential voters were exposed to a series of political experiences, including the Vietnam War and Watergate, which led to their disaffection from politics.

11. See for example Paul Kleppner (1982: chapter 6), a review of the causes of the turnout decline that began in the 1960s.

12. Teixeira, 57. Rosenstone and Hansen, however, see the bearing of social networks on turnout as mediated by party mobilization strategies.

13. We are here raising a question about the methodological approach of Rosenstone and Hansen, which attempts to disaggregate the effects of individual-level and political factors in determining turnout, although they are clearly aware of some interaction between voter characteristics and party mobilization strategies.

14. Rosenstone and Hansen (1993:145).

15. Rosenstone and Hansen (1993:216–17).

16. See Abramson, Aldrich, and Rohde (1999:79–86).

17. We should note that Teixeira (1992:57) does not draw this conclusion. Rather, he thinks that it is the decline in social connectedness that is responsible for "declining psychological involvement in politics and a declining belief in government responsiveness."

18. These political attitudes account for 20 percent of the decline in turnout, according to Rosenstone and Hansen (1993: table 7–1, 215).

19. Shefter (1990:199).

20. Shefter looks to political outsiders, "counterelites, insurgents, reformers," who have less to lose by mobilizing outsiders (1990:199).

21. See Paul Kleppner (1982).

22. Kleppner (1982:85).

23. Ibid., table 6.2, p. 117.

Cited References

Abramson, Paul R., and John H. Aldrich. 1982. "The Decline of Electoral Participation in America." *American Political Science Review* 76, 3 (September).

Abramson, Paul R., John W. Aldrich, and David W. Rohde. 1983. *Change and Continuity in the 1980 Elections.* Washington, D.C.: Congressional Quarterly Press.

———. 1986. *Change and Continuity in the 1984 Elections.* Washington, D.C.: Congressional Quarterly Press.

Paul R. Abramson, "Political Participation," In Seymour Martin Lipset, ed. *The Encyclopedia of Democracy.* Washington, D.C.: Congressional Quarterly, 1995.

Aldrich, John H., and Dennis M. Simon. 1986. "Turnout in American National Elections." In *Research in Micropolitics,* vol. 1. Greenwich, Conn.: JAI Press.

Alford, Robert R. 1963. *Party and Society: The Anglo-American Democracies.* Chicago: Rand McNally.

Alford, Robert R., and Eugene C. Lee. 1968. "Voting Turnout in American Cites." *American Political Science Review* 62, 3 (September).

Alford, Robert R., and Harry Scoble. 1968. "Sources of Local Political Involvement." *American Political Science Review* 62, 4 (December).

Allen, Howard W., and Kay Warren Allen. 1981. "Voter Fraud and Data Validity." In Jerome Clubb, William H. Flanigan, and Nancy Zingale, eds., *Analyzing Electoral History.* Beverly Hills, Calif.: Sage Publications.

Almond, Gabriel, and Sidney Verba. 1965. *The Civic Culture: Political Attitudes and Democracy in Five Nations.* Boston: Little, Brown.

Andersen, Kristi. 1982. *The Creation of a Democratic Majority, 1928–1936.* Chicago: University of Chicago Press.

Argersinger, Peter H. 1980. "A Place on the Ballot: Fusion Politics and Antifusion Law." *American Historical Review* 85 (April).

———. 1985–86. "New Perspectives on Election Fraud in the Gilded Age." *Political Science Quarterly* 100, 4 (Winter).

Asbury, Herbert. 1928. *The Gangs of New York.* New York: Alfred A. Knopf.

Banfield, Edward, and James Q. Wilson. 1963. *City Politics.* Cambridge: Harvard University Press.

Bartley, Neuman V. 1969. *The Rise of Massive Resistance.* Baton Rouge: Louisiana State University Press.

Bean, Walter. 1952. *Boss Ruef's San Francisco.* Berkeley: University of California Press.

Beck, Lewis. 1985. "Pocket Book Voting in U.S. Election Studies: Fact or Artifact." *American Journal of Political Science* 29, 2 (May).

Becker, Carl Lotus. 1968. *The History of Political Parties in the Province of New York.* Madison: University of Wisconsin Press.

Bell, Daniel. 1978. *Cultural Contradictions of Capitalism.* New York: Basic Books/ Harper Colophon Books.

Bendix, Reinhard. 1964. *Nation Building and Citizenship.* New York: John Wiley.

Bensel, Richard Franklin. 1984. *Sectionalism and American Political Development, 1880–1980.* Madison: University of Wisconsin Press.

Bensel, Richard Franklin, and Elizabeth Sanders. 1986. "The Impact of the Voting Rights Act on Southern Welfare Systems." In Benjamin Ginsberg and Allan Stone, eds., *Do Elections Matter?* New York: M. E. Sharpe.

Benson, Lee. 1961. *The Concept of Jacksonian Democracy: New York as Test Case.* Princeton, N.J.: Princeton University Press.

Berelson, Bernard, Paul F. Lazarsfeld, and William McPhee. 1954. *Voting.* Chicago: University of Chicago Press.

Berman, William. 1970. *The Politics of Civil Rights in the Truman Administration.* Columbus: Ohio State University Press.

Bernstein, Irving. 1970. *The Lean Years: A History of the American Worker, 1930–1933.* Baltimore: Penguin Books.

Block, Fred. 1987. "Rethinking the Political Economy of the Welfare State." In Fred Block, Richard A. Cloward, Barbara Ehrenreich, and Frances Fox Piven, *The Mean Season: The Attack on the Welfare State.* New York: Pantheon Books.

Bowles, Samuel, and Herbert Gintis. 1982. "The Crisis of Liberal Democratic Capitalism: The Case of the United States." *Politics and Society* 11, 1.

Bowles, Samuel, David M. Gordon, and Thomas E. Weisskopf. 1984. *Beyond the Wasteland: A Democratic Alternative to Economic Decline.* Garden City, N.Y.: Doubleday/Anchor Books.

Boyd, Richard W. 1981. "Decline of U.S. Voter Turnout: Structural Explanations." *American Politics Quarterly* 9 (April).

Brecher, Jeremy. 1974. *Strike!* Greenwich, Conn: Fawcett Publications.

Bridges, Amy. 1984. *A City in the Republic: Ante-Bellum New York and the Origins of Machine Politics.* New York: Cambridge University Press.

———. 1987. "Rethinking the Origins of the Political Machine." In John Mollenkopf, ed., *Power, Culture, and Place.* New York: Russell Sage.

Brittan, Samuel. 1975. "The Economic Contradictions of Democracy." *British Journal of Political Science* 5, 22 (April).

Brown, Courtney. 1987. "Voter Mobilization and Party Competition in a Volatile Electorate." *American Sociological Review* 52, 1 (February).

Bryce, James. 1924. *The American Commonweal.* New York: Macmillan.

Buckley, Peter G. 1987. "Culture, Class, and Place in Antebellum New York." In John Mollenkopf, ed., *Power, Culture, and Place.* New York: Russell Sage.

Burnham, Walter Dean. 1965. "The Changing Shape of the American Political Universe." *American Political Science Review* 65, 1 (March).

———. 1970. *Critical Elections and the Mainsprings of American Politics.* New York: W. W. Norton.

———. 1974a. "The United States: The Politics of Heterogeneity." In Richard Rose, ed., *Electoral Behavior: A Comparative Handbook.* New York: Free Press.

———. 1974b. "Theory and Voting Research: Some Comments on Converse's 'Change in the American Electorate.'" *American Political Science Review* 68, 3 (September).

———. 1974c. "Rejoinder to Comments by Philip Converse and Jerrold Rusk." *American Political Science Review* 68, 3 (September).

———. 1979. "The Appearance and Disappearance of the American Voter." In *The Disappearance of the American Voter.* Washington, D.C.: American Bar Association.

———. 1981a. "The 1980 Earthquake: Realignment, Reaction, or What?" In Thomas Ferguson and Joel Rogers, eds., *The Hidden Election: Politics and Economics in the 1980 Presidential Campaign.* New York: Pantheon Books.

———. 1981b. "Toward Confrontation." In Seymour Martin Lipset, ed., *Party Coalitions in the 1980s.* San Francisco: Institute for Contemporary Policy Studies.

———. 1981c. "The System of 1896: An Analysis." In Paul Kleppner, et al., eds., *The Evolution of American Electoral Systems.* Westport, Conn.: Greenwood Press.

———. 1982a. *The Current Crisis in American Politics.* New York: Oxford University Press.

———. 1982b. "The Eclipse of the Democratic Party." *Democracy: A Journal of Political Renewal and Radical Change* 2, 3 (July).

———. 1985. "The 1984 Election and the Future of American Politics." In Ellis

Sandoz and Cecil V. Crabb, Jr., eds., *Election 1984: Landslide Without a Mandate?* New York: New American Library/Mentor Books.

———. "The Class Gap," *The New Republic*, May 9, 1988.

Burns, James MacGregor. 1982. *The Vineyard of Liberty.* New York: Alfred A. Knopf.

———. 1985. *The Workshop of Democracy.* New York: Vintage Books.

Cain, Bruce E., and Ken McCue. June 1984. "The Efficacy of Voter Registration Drives." Social Science Working Paper 531, Division of the Humanities and Social Sciences, California Institute of Technology, Pasadena.

———. 1985. "Do Registration Drives Matter? The Realities of Partisan Dreams." Paper delivered at the 1985 Annual Meeting of the American Political Science Association, New Orleans, August 29–September 1.

Campbell, Angus, and Warren Miller. 1957. "The Motivational Basis of Straight and Split Ticket Voting." *American Political Science Review* 51, 2 (June).

Campbell, Angus, Philip E. Converse, Warren Miller, and Donald Stokes. 1960. *The American Voter.* New York: John Wiley.

———. 1965. *Elections and the Political Order.* New York: John Wiley.

Campbell, Bruce A. 1979. *The American Electorate: Attitudes and Action.* New York: Holt Rinehart & Winston.

Carlson, Richard John. 1976. *The Effect of Voter Registration Systems on Presidential Election Turnout in Non-Southern States: 1912–1924.* Ann Arbor, Mich.: University Microfilms International.

Cavanaugh, Thomas. 1981. "Changes in American Voter Turnout, 1964–76." *Political Science Quarterly* 96, 1 (Spring).

———. 1985. "Blacks, Hispanics, and Women in the 1984 Elections: Trends in Voter Registration and Turnout." Prepared for delivery at the League of Women Voters Education Fund Conference on Electoral Participation, Washington, D.C., July 18–19.

Center on Budget and Policy Priorities. Undated. *Economic Recovery Fails to Reduce Poverty Rate to Pre-recession Levels: Gaps Widen Further Between Rich and Poor.* Report no. 71:18. Washington, D.C.

Chambers, William N. 1967. "Party Development and the American Mainstream." In William Nisbet Chambers and Walter Dean Burnham, eds., *The American Party Systems: Stages of Political Development.* New York: Oxford University Press.

Chambers, William N., and Philip C. Davis. 1978. "Party Competition and Mass Participation: The Case of the Democratizing Party System, 1824–1852." In Joel Silbey, Allen G. Bogue, and William H. Flanigan, eds., *The History of American Electoral Behavior.* Princeton, N.J.: Princeton University Press.

Clauson, Aage. 1968. "Response Validity: Vote Report." *Public Opinion Quarterly* 32, 4 (Winter).

Clawson, Dan, Alan Neustadl, and Mark Weller. 1998. *Dollars and Votes*. Philadelphia, Pa.: Temple University Press.

Clubb, Jerome M., William H. Flanigan, and Nancy H. Zingale. 1980. *Partisan Realignment: Voters, Parties, and Government in American History*. Beverly Hills, Calif.: Sage Publications.

Cohen, Ellie M., and Marshall Ganz. Undated. "Analysis of a Community Organizing Approach: Increasing Citizen Participation in Disadvantaged Communities." The Organizing Institute, San Francisco.

Cohen, Joshua, and Joel Rogers. 1983. *On Democracy: Toward a Transformation of American Society*. New York: Penguin Books.

————. 1988. " 'Reaganism' After Reagan." *Socialist Register*.

Commission on National Elections. April 1986. *Final Report of the Commission on National Elections*. The Center for Strategic and International Studies, Georgetown University, Washington, D.C.

Committee for the Study of the American Electorate. Press release dated November 1, 1984. Washington, D.C.

————. Press release dated November 9, 1984. Washington, D.C.

————. Undated. *Voter Registration 1984: A Report and Evaluation*. Washington, D.C.

Congressional Quarterly. July 23, 1983. Editorial article entitled "Reagan's Legacy: 'Have-Not' Surge to Polls: Major Force in 1984 Election." Washington, D.C.

————. August 1, 1987. Editorial article entitled "Changing South Perils Conservative Coalition." Washington, D.C.

Converse, Philip E. 1972. "Change in the American Electorate." In Angus Campbell and Philip E. Converse, eds., *The Human Meaning of Social Change*. New York: Russell Sage Foundation.

————. 1974. "Comment on Burnham's 'Theory and Voting Research.' " *American Political Science Review* 68, 3 (September).

————. 1976. *The Dynamics of Party Support*. Beverly Hills, Calif.: Sage Publications.

Crocker, Royce. 1990. *Voter Registration and Turnout in States with Mail and Motor-Voter Registration Systems*. CRS Report for Congress, February 23.

Crotty, William J. 1977. *Political Reform and the American Experiment*. New York: Thomas Y. Crowell.

Crozier, Michael, Samuel P. Huntington, and Joji Watanuki. 1975. *The Crisis of Democracy: Report on the Ungovernability of Democracies to the Trilateral Commission*. New York: New York University Press.

Cunningham, Dayna L. 1991. "Who Are to Be the Electors? A Reflection on the History of Voter Registration in the United States." *Yale Law & Policy Review*, 9, 2, p. 389, fn. 117.

Cunningham, N. 1957. *The Jeffersonian Republicans: The Formation of Party Organization, 1789–1801*. Chapel Hill: University of North Carolina Press.

Dahl, Robert. 1961. *Who Governs?* New Haven, Conn.: Yale University Press.

Dalton, Russell J., Scott C. Flanagan, and Paul Allen Beck, eds. 1984. *Electoral Change in Advanced Industrial Democracies: Realignment or Dealignment?* Princeton, N.J.: Princeton University Press.

Davidson, Chandler, ed. 1984. *Minority Vote Dilution*. Washington, D.C.: Joint Center for Political Studies.

Davis, Mike. 1980. "Why the U.S. Working Class Is Different." *New Left Review* 123 (September/October).

———. 1986. *Prisoners of the American Dream: Politics and Economy in the History of the United States Working Class*. New York: New Left Books.

Dawley, Alan. 1976. *Class and Community: The Industrial Revolution in Lynn.* Cambridge: Harvard University Press.

DiGaetano, Alan. 1985. *Urban Political Machines: A Structural Approach*. Doctoral diss., Boston University.

Dohlbeare, Kenneth M. 1984. *Democracy at Risk: The Politics of Economic Renewal*. Chatham, N.J.: Chatham House Publishers.

Dorsett, Lyle W. 1977. *Franklin D. Roosevelt and the City Bosses*. Port Washington, N.Y.: Kennikat Press.

Downs, Anthony. 1957. *An Economic Theory of Democracy*. New York: Harper & Brothers.

Dreiser, Theodore. 1956 [1925]. *An American Tragedy*. New York: Modern Library.

———. 1981 [1917]. *Sister Carrie*. Philadelphia: University of Pennsylvania Press.

Dubois, W. E. B. 1989 [1903]. *Souls of Black Folk*. New York: Bantam Books.

Dunning, W. A. 1901. "The Undoing of Reconstruction." *Atlantic Monthly* 88.

Eckstein, Harry. 1966. *Division and Cohesion in Democracy: A Study of Norway.* Princeton, N.J.: Princeton University Press.

Edelman, Murray. 1971. *Politics as Symbolic Action*. New Haven, Conn.: Yale University Press.

Edsall, Thomas B. 1984. *The New Politics of Inequality*. New York: W. W. Norton.

Edsall, Thomas B., and Haynes Johnson. April 22, 1984. "High-Tech Impersonal Computer Net Is Snaring Prospective Republicans." *Washington Post*, A8.

———. July 7, 1984. "In Mississippi District, Race and Class Likely to Govern Turnout." *Washington Post*.

Eisenstadt, S. N., and Luis Roniger. 1981. "The Study of Patron-Client Relations and Recent Development in Sociological Theory." In S. N. Eisenstadt and René Lemarchand, eds., *Political Clientelism, Patronage and Development*. Beverly Hills, Calif.: Sage Publications.

Enelow, James M., and Melvin J. Hinich. 1982. "Ideology, Issues, and the Spatial Theory of Elections." *American Political Science Review* 76, 3 (September).

Epstein, Gerald. 1981. "Domestic Stagflation and Monetary Policy: The Federal

Reserve and the Hidden Election." In Thomas Ferguson and Joel Rogers, eds., *The Hidden Election: Politics and Economics in The 1980 Presidential Campaign*. New York: Pantheon Books.

Erikson, Robert S. 1981. "Why Do People Vote? Because They Are Registered." *American Political Science Review* 75, 2 (July).

Erikson, Robert S., and Kent L. Tedin. 1981. "The 1928–1936 Partisan Realignment: The Case for the Conversion Hypothesis." *American Political Science Review* 75, 4 (December).

Eulau, Hans. 1956. "The Politics of Happiness." *Antioch Review* 16.

Evans, Rowland, and Robert Novak. 1966. *Lyndon B. Johnson: The Exercise of Power*. New York: New American Library.

Faler, Paul. 1981. *Mechanics and Manufacturers in the Early Industrial Revolution: Lynn, Massachusetts, 1780–1860*. Albany, N.Y.: State University of New York Press.

Ferguson, Thomas. 1983. "Party Realignment and American Industrial Structure: The Investment Theory of Political Parties in Historical Perspective." *Research in Political Economy*, vol. 6. Greenwich, Conn.: JAI Press.

———. 1984. "From Normalcy to New Deal: Industrial Structure, Party Competition, and American Public Policy in the Great Depression." *International Organization* 38, 1 (Winter).

Ferguson, Thomas, and Joel Rogers. 1986. *Right Turn*. New York: Hill & Wang.

Finegold, Kenneth, and Elaine K. Swift. 1996. "Major Parties Out of Power and How They Respond: A Theory." Paper presented to the Annual Meeting of the American Political Science Association, San Francisco, August.

Fiorina, Morris. 1981. *Retrospective Voting in American Presidential Elections*. New Haven, Conn.: Yale University Press.

Flanigan, William H., and Nancy H. Zingale. 1979. *Political Behavior of the American Electorate*. Boston: Allyn and Bacon.

Formisano, Ronald. 1969. "Political Character, Antipartyism and the Second Party System." *American Quarterly* 21, 4 (Winter).

———. 1974. *Political Order in Changing Societies*. New Haven, Conn.: Yale University Press.

Franklin, John Hope. 1969. *From Slavery to Freedom. A History of Negro Americans*. 3d ed. New York: Vintage Books.

Freeman, Richard B. 1986. "Why Are Unions Faring Badly in NLRB Representation Elections?" Cambridge, Mass.: National Bureau of Economic Research.

Friedland, Roger. 1983. *Power and Crisis in the City: Corporations, Unions and Urban Policy*. New York: Schocken Books.

Galambos, Louis. 1975. *The Public Image of Big Business in America, 1880–1940*. Baltimore, Md.: John's Hopkins University Press.

Galston, William. 1985. "The Future of the Democratic Party." *The Brookings Review* (Winter).

Gienapp, William E. 1982. " 'Politics Seem to Enter into Everything': Political Culture in the North, 1840–1860." In Stephen E. Maizlish and John J. Kushman, eds., *Essays on Antebellum Politics, 1840–1860.* College Station: Texas A&M University Press.

Ginsberg, Benjamin, and Martin Shefter. 1985. "Critical Realignment? The New Politics, the Reconstituted Right, and the 1984 Election." In Michael Nelson, ed., *The Elections of 1984.* Washington, D.C.: Congressional Quarterly Press.

Glass, David, Peverill Squire, and Raymond Wolfinger. 1984. "Voter Turnout: An International Comparison." *Public Opinion* 6, 6 (December/January).

Gold, David. 1977. "The Rise and Decline of the Keynesian Coalition." *Kapitalistate* 6 (Fall).

Goldfield, Michael. 1985. "Labor's Subordination to the New Deal. Part One: The Influence of Labor on New Deal Labor Legislation." Paper delivered at 1985 meeting of the American Political Science Association, New Orleans.

Goldstein, Robert Justin. 1978. *Political Repression in Modern America from 1870 to the Present.* Boston: G. K. Hall.

Goodman, Paul. 1967. "The First American Party System." In William Nisbet Chambers and Walter Dean Burnham, eds., *The American Party Systems: Stages of Political Development.* New York: Oxford University Press.

Goodwyn, Lawrence. 1976. *Democratic Promise: The Populist Moment in America.* New York: Oxford University Press.

———. 1978. *The Populist Moment: A Short History of the Agrarian Revolt in America.* New York: Oxford University Press.

Gosnell, Harold G. 1927. *Getting Out the Vote.* Chicago: University of Chicago Press.

———. 1930. *Why Europe Votes.* Chicago: University of Chicago Press.

———. 1937. *Machine Politics: Chicago Model.* Chicago: University of Chicago Press.

Green, James. 1975. "Fighting on Two Fronts: Working Class Militancy in the 1940s." *Radical America* 9, 4–5.

Greenstone, J. David. 1969. *Labor in American Politics.* New York: Vintage Books.

Groarke, Margaret. 2000. *Expanding Access to the Vote: An Analysis of Voter Registration Reform in the United States, 1970–1998.* Ph.D. diss. Political Science, Graduate School and University Center, City University of New York.

Grob, Gerald N., and George Athan Billias, eds. 1987. *Interpretations of American History, vol. 2: Since 1877.* 5th ed. New York: Free Press.

Gurr, Ted Robert. 1968. "A Causal Model of Civil Strife: A Comparative Analysis Using New Indices." *American Political Science Review* 62, 4 (December).

Guth, James L. 1983. "Southern Baptist Clergy: Vanguard of the Christian Right?" In Robert C. Liebman and Robert Wuthnow, eds., *The New Christian Right: Mobilization and Legitimation.* New York: Aldine Publishing.

Gutman, Herbert G. 1976. *Work, Culture and Society in Industrializing America.* New York: Alfred A. Knopf.

Haber, Samuel. 1964. *Efficiency and Uplift: Scientific Management in the Progressive Era, 1890–1920.* Chicago: University of Chicago Press.

Hammond, Phillip E. 1983. "Another Great Awakening." In Robert C. Liebman and Robert Wuthnow, eds., *The New Christian Right: Mobilization and Legitimation.* New York: Aldine Publishing.

Harris, Joseph P. 1929. *Registration of Voters in the United States.* Washington, D.C.: Brookings Institution.

Hartmann, Susman. 1971. *Truman and the 80th Congress.* Columbia: University of Missouri Press.

Hartz, Louis. 1955. *The Liberal Tradition in America.* New York: Harcourt, Brace.

Harvard/ABC News Symposium. 1984. *Voting for Democracy.* New York: American Broadcasting Companies.

Hayduk, Ron. 1986. "Electoral Politics." Political Science Program, Graduate School and University Center of the City University of New York. Mimeo.

Hays, Samuel P. 1958. *Conservation and the Gospel of Efficiency.* Cambridge: Harvard University Press.

———. 1964. "The Politics of Reform in Municipal Government in the Progressive Era." *Pacific Northwest Quarterly* 55, 4 (October).

———. 1967. "Political Parties and the Community-Society Continuum." In William Nisbet Chambers and Walter Dean Burnham, eds., *The American Party System: Stages of Political Development.* New York: Oxford University Press.

———. 1981. "Politics and Society: Beyond the Political Party." In Paul Kleppner, eds., *The Evolution of American Electoral Systems.* Westport, Conn.: Greenwood Press.

Herbes, John. October 26, 1984. "Drive to Sign Up New Voters Brings Surge to the Polls." *New York Times*, A20.

Hibbs, Douglas A. 1977. "Political Parties and Macroeconomic Policy." *American Political Science Review* 71, 4 (December).

———. 1982. "Economic Outcomes and Political Support for British Governments Among Occupational Classes: A Dynamic Analysis." *American Political Science Review* 76, 2 (June).

Himmelstein, Jerome L. 1983. "The New Right." In Robert C. Liebman and Robert Wuthnow, eds., *The New Christian Right: Mobilization and Legitimation.* New York: Aldine Publishing.

Hofstadter, Richard. 1954. *The American Political Tradition.* New York: Random House.

———. 1955. *The Age of Reform: From Bryan to F.D.R.* New York: Alfred A. Knopf.

Huntington, Samuel. 1968. *Political Order in Changing Societies.* New Haven, Conn.: Yale University Press.

—————. 1974. "Postindustrial Politics: How Benign Will It Be?" *Comparative Politics* 6, 2 (January).

—————. 1975. "Chapter 3—The United States." In Michael Crozier, Samuel P. Huntington, and Joji Watanuki, *The Crisis of Democracy: Report on the Ungovernability of Democracies to the Trilateral Commission.* New York: New York University Press.

—————. 1985. "A New Role for the Democrats: The Visions of the Democratic Party." *Public Interest* 79 (Spring).

INTERFACE. July 10, 1985. *Expanding Voter Participation: An Assessment of 1984 Non-Partisan Voter Registration Efforts.* New York: Interface Development Project, p. 16.

Jackman, Robert W. 1987. "Political Institutions and Voter Turnout in the Industrial Democracies." *American Political Science Review* 81, 2 (June).

Jensen, Richard. 1971. *The Winning of the Midwest: Social and Political Conflict, 1888–1896.* Chicago: University of Chicago Press.

—————. 1981. "The Last Party System: Decay of Consensus, 1932–1980." In Paul Kleppner, et al., eds., *The Evolution of American Electoral Systems.* Westport, Conn.: Greenwood Press.

Johnson, Haynes, and Thomas B. Edsall. September 30, 1984. "North Carolina Sparks Registration War." *Washington Post*, A16.

Johnson, Paul. 1978. *A Shopkeeper's Millennium.* New York: Hill & Wang.

Karp, Walter. 1984. "Playing Politics: Why the Democratic Bosses Conspired with Reagan, and Do Not Care if They Lose in November." *Harper's*, July.

Katosh, John P., and Michael W. Traugott. 1979. "Response Validity in Surveys of Voting Behavior." *Public Opinion Quarterly* 43, 3 (Fall).

—————. 1981. "The Consequences of Validated and Self-Reported Voting Measures." *Public Opinion Quarterly* 45, 4 (Winter).

Katznelson, Ira. 1981. *City Trenches: Urban Politics and the Patterning of Class in the United States.* New York: Pantheon Books.

Keller, Morton. 1977. *Affairs of State: Public Life in Late Nineteenth Century America.* Cambridge: Harvard University Press.

Kelley, Stanley, Jr., Richard Ayers, and William C. Bowen. 1967. "Registration and Voting: Putting First Things First." *American Political Science Review* 61, 2 (June).

Key, V. O., Jr. 1955. "A Theory of Critical Elections." *Journal of Politics* 17, 1 (February).

—————. 1956. *American State Politics: An Introduction.* New York: Alfred A. Knopf.

—————. 1966. *The Responsible Electorate.* Cambridge: Harvard University Press.

———. 1984 [1949]. *Southern Politics in State and Nation*. New ed. New York: Alfred A. Knopf.

Kim, Jae-On, John R. Petrocik, and Stephen N. Enokson. 1975. "Voter Turnout Among the American States: Systemic and Individual Components." *American Political Science Review* 69, 1 (March).

Kirbo, Harold R. and Richard Shaffer. 1986. "Elite Recognition of Unemployment as a Working Class Issue, 1890–1940." *Sociology and Social Research* 70, 4 (July).

Kleppner, Paul. 1970. *The Cross of Culture: A Social Analysis of Midwestern Politics, 1850–1900*. New York: Free Press.

———. 1979. *The Third Electoral System, 1853–1892: Parties, Voters, and Political Cultures*. Chapel Hill: University of North Carolina Press.

———. 1981a. "Critical Realignments and Electoral Systems." In Paul Kleppner, et al., eds., *The Evolution of American Electoral Systems*. Westport, Conn.: Greenwood Press.

———. 1981b. "Partisanship and Ethnoreligious Conflict: The Third Electoral Systrem, 1853–1892." In Paul Kleppner, et al., eds., *The Evolution of American Electoral Systems*. Westport, Conn.: Greenwood Press.

———. 1982. *Who Voted? The Dynamics of Electoral Turnout, 1870–1890*. New York: Praeger.

Kleppner, Paul, and Stephen C. Baker. 1980. "The Impact of Voter Registration Requirements on Electoral Turnout, 1900–1916." *Journal of Political and Military Sociology* 8, 2 (Fall).

Kolko, Gabriel. 1977. *The Triumph of Conservatism*. New York: Free Press.

Kousser, J. Morgan. 1974. *The Shaping of Southern Politics: Suffrage Restrictions and the Establishment of the One-Party South*. New Haven, Conn.: Yale University Press.

Krieger, Joel. 1986. *Reagan, Thatcher, and the Politics of Decline*. New York: Oxford University Press.

Ladd, Everett Carll. 1985. "As the Realignment Turns: A Drama in Many Acts." *Public Opinion* 7, 6 (December/January).

———. 1997. "The 1996 Election and Postindustrial Realignment." In Regina Dougherty, Everett C. Ladd, David Wilber, and Lynn Zayachkiwsky, eds. *America at the Polls 1996: A Roper Center Databook*. Storrs: University of Connecticut: Roper Center for Public Opinion Research.

Lazarsfeld, Paul F., Bernard Berelson, and Helen Gaudet. 1948. *The People's Choice*. New York: Columbia University Press.

Lee, Eugene C. 1960. *The Politics of Nonpartisanship*. Berkeley: University of California Press.

Lefkowitz, Joel. 1999. "Winning the House: Re-election Strategies, Challenger Campaigns, and Mobilization Against Incumbents." Ph.D. diss., Graduate School, City University of New York.

Lemarchand, René. 1981. "Comparative Political Clientelism: Structure, Process and Optic." In S. N. Eisenstadt and René Lemarchand, eds., *Political Clientelism, Patronage, and Development.* Beverly Hills, Calif.: Sage Publications.

Lens, Sidney. 1959. *Crisis of American Labor.* New York: Sagamore Press.

Leuchtenberg, William E. 1963. *Franklin D. Roosevelt and the New Deal, 1932–1940.* New York: Harper & Row.

Levi, Margaret. 1987. "The Weapons of the Strong—and How the Weak Resist Them: Creating Compliance Over History." Paper presented at the Annual Meeting of the American Political Science Association, September 3–6, 1987, Chicago.

Levin, Murray. 1971. *Political Hysteria in America.* New York: Basic Books.

Lichtman, Allan J. 1979. *Prejudice and the Old Politics: The Presidential Election of 1928.* Chapel Hill: University of North Carolina Press.

———. 1987. "Analysis of Racial Distinctions in Voter Registration Rates: State of Mississippi." Report prepared for the Lawyers Committee for Civil Rights Under Law, in the matter of *Mississippi State Chapter Operation Push, et al.,* v. *William Allain, Governor of Mississippi, et al.,* Washington, D.C.

Liebman, Robert C. 1983a. "Mobilizing the Moral Majority." In Robert C. Liebman and Robert Wuthnow, eds., *The New Christian Right: Mobilization and Legitimation.* New York: Aldine Publishing.

———. 1983b. "The Making of the New Christian Right." In Robert C. Liebman and Robert Wuthnow, eds., *The New Christian Right: Mobilization and Legitimation.* New York: Aldine Publishing.

Lijphart, Arend. 1997. "Unequal Participation: Democracy's Unresolved Dilemma," *American Political Science Review* 91, 1 (March).

Lineberry, Robert L., and Edmund P. Fowler. 1967. "Reformism and Public Policies in America." *American Political Science Review* 61, 3 (September).

Lipset, Seymour Martin. 1960. *Political Man: The Social Bases of Politics.* Garden City, N.Y.: Doubleday.

———. 1985. "The Elections, the Economy, and Public Opinion: 1984." *PS: The Journal of the American Political Science Association* 18, 1 (Winter).

———. 1986. "Beyond 1984: The Anomalies of American Politics." *PS: The Journal of the American Political Science Association* 19, 2 (Spring).

Lipset, Seymour Martin, and Earl Raab. 1981. "The Election and the Evangelicals." *Commentary* 71 (March).

Livingston, Debra. April 1985. "Survey of 1984 Registrants." Washington, D.C.: Churches' Committee for Voter Registration/Education.

Lowi, Theodore. 1963. "Toward Functionalism in Political Science: The Case of Innovation in Party Systems." *American Political Science Review* 57, 3 (September).

———. 1968. "Foreword." In Harold Gosnell, *Machine Politics: Chicago Model.* Chicago: University of Chicago Press.

Mann, Arthur F. 1965. *LaGuardia Comes to Power, 1933*. Philadelphia: Lippincott.

Manza, Jeff, and Clem Brooks. 1998. "The Gender Gap in U.S. Presidential Elections: When? Why? Implications?" *American Journal of Sociology* 103, 5.

Marable, Manning. 1986. *Black American Politics: From the March on Washington to Jesse Jackson*. New York: Verso/Schocken.

Markus, Gregory B. 1982. "Political Attitudes During an Election Year: A Report on the 1980 NES Study." *American Political Science Review* 76, 3 (September).

Martin, Cathie Jo. 1994. "Business and the New Economic Activism: the Growth of Corporate Lobbies in the Sixties." *Polity* 27, 1 (Fall).

Martin, John B. 1976. *Adlai Stevenson of Illinois*. Garden City, N.Y.: Doubleday.

McCormick, Richard P. 1953. *The History of Voting in New Jersey: A Study of the Development of Election Machinery, 1664–1911*. New Brunswick, N.J.: Rutgers University Press.

———. 1960. "New Perspectives on Jacksonian Politics." *American Historical Review* 65, 2 (January).

———. 1967. "Political Development and the Second Party System." In William Nisbet Chambers and Walter Dean Burnham, eds., *The American Party Systems: Stages of Political Development*. New York: Oxford University Press.

———. 1979. "The Party Period and Public Policy: An Exploratory Hypothesis." *Journal of American History* 66, 2 (September).

———. 1981. *From Realignment to Reform: Political Change in New York State, 1893–1910*. Ithaca, N.Y.: Cornell University Press.

McDonald, Archie P. Undated. "The Texas Experience." Published for the Texas Committee for the Humanities. College Station: Texas A&M University Press.

McGerr, Michael E. 1986. *The Decline of Popular Politics: The American North, 1865–1928*. New York: Oxford University Press.

McLoughlin, William G. 1978. *Revivals, Awakenings and Reform*. Chicago: University of Chicago Press.

Menendez, Albert J. 1977. *Religion at the Polls*. Philadelphia: Westminster.

Merriam, Charles E., and Harold G. Gosnell. 1924. *Non-Voting: Causes and Methods of Control*. Chicago: University of Chicago Press.

Miller, Arthur H., and Warren E. Miller. 1977. "Partisanship and Performance: 'Rational' Choice in the 1976 Presidential Elections." Paper presented at the APSA meeting in Washington, D.C.

Miller, Arthur H., and Martin P. Wattenberg. 1985. "Throwing the Rascals Out and Performance Evaluations of Presidential Candidates, 1952–1980." *American Political Science Review* 79, 2 (June).

Miller, Warren E. August 1963. "Assessment of the Significance of State Laws Governing Citizen Participation in Elections." Ann Arbor: Survey Research Center, University of Michigan.

———. March 1987. "Party Identification Re-Examined: The Reagan Era." In

Where's the Party? An Assessment of Changes in Party Loyalty and Party Coalitions in the 1980s. Report no. 21. Washington, D.C.: Center For National Policy.

———. 1992. "The Puzzle Transformed: Explaining Declining Turnout," *Political Behavior* 14, 1.

Miller, Zane L. 1968. *Boss Cox's Cincinnati.* New York: Oxford University Press.

Mollenkopf, John. 1975. "The Post-War Politics of Urban Development." *Politics and Society* 5, 3.

———. 1985. *Contested Cities.* Princeton, N.J.: Princeton University Press.

David Montgomery. 1979. *Workers' Control in America.* New York: Cambridge University Press.

———. 1980. "Strikes in Nineteenth Century America," *Social Science History* 4, 4 (Fall).

———. 1981. *Beyond Equality: Labor and the Radical Republicans, 1862–1872.* Urbana: University of Illinois Press.

Morehouse, Ward, and David Dembo. 1986. *The Underbelly of the U.S. Economy: Joblessness and Pauperization of Working America.* Special Report no. 6. New York: Council on International and Public Affairs.

Moser, Ted. 1980. "If Jesus Were a Congressman." *Christian Century* 97 (April 16).

Mouzelis, Nicos. 1985. "On the Concept of Populism: Populist and Clientelist Modes of Incorporation in Semiperipheral Politics." *Politics and Society* 14, 3.

Myers, Gustavus. 1971. *The History of Tammany Hall.* New York: Dover Press.

Nagel, Jack H., and John E. McNulty. 1996. "Partisan Effects of Voter Turnout in Senatorial and Gubernatorial Elections." *American Political Science Review* 90, 4 (December).

National Association of Secretaries of State. Undated. "The National Voter Education Project, 1984." Mimeo.

Navarro, Vicente. 1985. "The 1980 and 1984 U.S. Elections and the New Deal: An Alternative Interpretation." *International Journal of Health Services* 15, 3 (Fall).

Nie, Norman H., and Kristi Andersen. 1974. "Mass Belief Systems Revisited: Political Change and Attitude Structure." *Journal of Politics* 36, 3 (August).

Nie, Norman H., Sidney Verba, and John H. Petrocik. 1976. *The Changing American Voter.* Cambridge: Harvard University Press.

Orren, Gary R. 1987. "Political Participation and Public Policy: The Case for Institutional Reform." In Alexander Heard and Michael Nelson, eds., *Presidential Selection.* Durham, N.C.: Duke University Press.

Osborne, David. 1985. "Registration Boomerang." *New Republic*, February 25.

Ostrogorski, M. 1964. *Democracy and the Organization of Political Parties.* 2 vols. Garden City, N.Y.: Doubleday/Anchor Books.

Palmer, John L., and Isabel V. Sawhill, eds., 1982. *The Reagan Experiment*. Washington, D.C.: Urban Institute Press.

Pendleton, William C. 1927. *Political History of Appalachian Virginia*. Dayton, Va.: Shenandoah Press.

Petrocik, John R. 1987a. "Voter Turnout and Electoral Preference: The Anomalous Reagan Elections." In Kay Schlozman, ed., *Elections in America*. London: Allen & Unwin.

———. 1987b. "Realignment: The South, New Party Coalitions and the Elections of 1984 and 1986." In *Where's the Party? An Assessment of Changes in Party Loyalty and Party Coalitions in the 1980s*. Report no. 21. Washington, D.C.: Center For National Policy.

Phillips, Kevin P. 1969. *The Emerging Republican Majority*. New Rochelle, N.Y.: Arlington House.

———. 1982. *Post-Conservative America: People, Politics, and Ideology in a Time of Crisis*. New York: Random House.

———, 1994. *Arrogant Capital*. Boston: Little, Brown.

Phillips, Kevin P., and Paul H. Blackman. 1975. *Electoral Reform and Voter Participation*. Stanford, Calif.: American Enterprise Institute and the Hoover Institution on War, Revolution, and Peace.

Piven, Frances Fox. 1974a. "The Urban Crisis: Who Got What, and Why?" In Richard A. Cloward and Frances Fox Piven, *The Politics of Turmoil: Essays on Poverty, Race, and the Urban Crisis*. New York: Pantheon Books.

———. 1974b. "The Great Society as Political Strategy." In Richard A. Cloward and Frances Fox Piven, *The Politics of Turmoil: Essays on Poverty, Race, and the Urban Crisis*. New York: Pantheon Books.

———. 1974c. "The New Urban Programs: The Strategy of Federal Intervention." In Richard A. Cloward and Frances Fox Piven, *The Politics of Turmoil: Essays on Poverty, Race, and the Urban Crisis*. New York: Pantheon Books.

———. 1984. "Federal Policy and Urban Fiscal Strain." *Yale Law and Policy Review* 2, 2 (Spring).

Piven, Frances Fox, and Richard A. Cloward. 1971. *Regulating the Poor*. New York: Vintage Books.

———. 1979. *Poor People's Movements: Why They Succeed, How They Fail*. New York: Vintage Books.

———. 1985. *The New Class War*. Revised and expanded ed. New York: Vintage Books.

Plotke, David. 1996. *Building a Democratic Political Order*. New York: Cambridge University Press.

Polakoff, Keith J. 1981. *Political Parties in American History*. New York: Alfred A. Knopf.

Pomper, Gerald. 1975. *Voter's Choice*. New York: Dodd, Mead.

————. 1977. "The Decline of the Party in American Elections." *Political Science Quarterly* 92, 1 (Spring).

Powell, G. Bingham, Jr. 1982. *Contemporary Democracies: Participation, Stability and Violence.* Cambridge: Harvard University Press.

————. 1986. "Voter Turnout in Comparative Perspective." *American Political Science Review* 80, 1 (March).

Prothro, James W., and Charles M. Grigg. 1960. "Fundamental Principles of Democracy: Bases of Agreement and Disagreement." *Journal of Politics* 22, 2 (May).

Przeworski, Adam. 1975. "Institutionalization of Voting Patterns, or Is Mobilization the Source of Decay?" *American Political Science Review* 69, 1 (March).

————. 1977. "Proletariat into a Class: The Process of Class Formation from Karl Kautsky's *The Class Struggle* to Recent Controversies." *Politics & Society* 7, 4.

————. 1985. *Capitalism and Social Democracy.* New York: Cambridge University Press.

Ranney, Austin. 1983. "Nonvoting Is Not a Social Disease." *Public Opinion* 6, 5 (October/November).

Ranney, Austin, and W. Kendall. 1956. *Democracy and the American Party System.* New York: Harcourt, Brace.

Raybeck, Joseph G. 1966. *A History of American Labor.* New York: Free Press.

Reynolds, George M. 1936. *Machine Politics in New Orleans, 1897–1926.* New York: Columbia University Press.

Riker, William H. 1965. *Democracy in the United States.* 2nd ed. New York: Macmillan.

Riker, William, and P. C. Ordeshook. 1968. "A Theory of the Calculus of Voting." *American Political Science Review* 62, 1 (March).

Riordan, William L. 1963 [1905]. *Plunkitt of Tammany Hall.* New York: E. P. Dutton.

Rogin, Michael Paul. 1967. *Intellectuals and McCarthy: The Radical Specter.* Cambridge: M.I.T. Press.

Rosenstone, Steven J., Roy L. Behr, and Edward H. Lazarus. 1984. *Third Parties in America: Citizen Response to Major Party Failures.* Princeton, N.J.: Princeton University Press.

Rosenstone, Steven J., and John Mark Hansen. 1993. *Mobilization, Participation, and Democracy in America,* New York: Macmillan.

Rossi, Alice. 1982. *Feminists in Politics: A Panel Analysis of the First National Women's Conference.* New York: Academic Press.

Rowbotham, Sheila. 1999. "The Tale That Never Ends," *Socialist Register.*

Rusk, Jerrold G. 1970. "Effect of the Australian Ballot Reform on Split-Ticket Voting, 1896–1908." *American Political Science Review* 64, 4 (December).

————. 1974. "Comment: The American Electoral Universe: Speculation and Evidence." *American Political Science Review* 68, 3 (September).

Rusk, Jerrold G., and John J. Stucker. 1978. "The Effect of the Southern System of Election Laws on Voter Participation: A Reply to V. O. Key." In Joel H. Silbey, Allan G. Bogue, and William H. Flanigan, eds., *The History of American Electoral Behavior*. Princeton, N.J.: Princeton University Press.

Salamon, Lester M. and Michael S. Lund. 1984. *The Reagan Presidency and the Governing of America*. Washington, D.C.: Urban Institute Press.

Salmans, Sandra. July 6, 1984. "Democrats Press to Sign Up Women." *New York Times*, A49.

Salmore, Stephen A., and Barbara G. Salmore. 1985. *Candidates, Parties, and Campaigns: Electoral Politics in America*. Washington, D.C.: Congressional Quarterly Press.

Sawyer, Kathy, and Robert Kaiser. June 26, 1981. "Evangelicals Flock to GOP Standards." *Washington Post*, Al.

Schaffer, Stephen D. 1981. "A Multivariate Explanation of Decreasing Turnout in Presidential Elections, 1960–1976." *American Journal of Political Science* 25, 1 (February).

Schattschneider, E. E. 1960. *The Semisovereign People*. New York: Holt, Rinehart & Winston.

Schlesinger, Arthur M., Jr. 1957. *The Age of Roosevelt*, vol. 1: *The Crisis of the Old Order, 1919–1933*. Boston: Houghton Mifflin.

———. 1960. *The Age of Roosevelt*, vol. 3: *The Politics of Upheaval, 1935–1936*. Boston: Houghton Mifflin.

Schlesinger, Arthur M., Sr., and Erik McKinley Eriksson. October 15, 1924. "The Vanishing Voter." *New Republic*.

Schneider, William. 1987. "The New Shape of American Politics." *Atlantic Monthly* (January).

Scott, James C. 1969. "Corruption, Machine Politics and Political Change." *American Political Science Review* 63, 4 (December).

Shefter, Martin. 1977. "New York City's Fiscal Crisis: The Politics of Inflation and Retrenchment." *Public Interest* 48 (Summer).

———. 1978a. "Party, Bureaucracy, and Political Change in the United States." In Louis Maisel and Joseph Cooper, eds., *Political Parties: Development and Decay*. Sage Electoral Studies Year Book, vol. 4. Beverly Hills, Calif.: Sage Publications.

———. 1978b. "The Electoral Foundations of the Political Machine: New York City, 1884–1897." In Joel H. Silbey, et al., eds., *The History of American Electoral Behavior*. Princeton, N.J.: Princeton University Press.

———. 1983. "Regional Receptivity to Reform." *Political Science Quarterly* 98, 3 (Fall).

———. 1984. "Political Parties, Political Mobilization, and Political Demobilization." In Thomas Ferguson and Joel Rogers, eds., *The Political Economy*. Armonk, N.Y.: M. E. Sharpe.

————. 1986. "Trade Unions and Political Machines: The Organization and Disorganization of the American Working Class in the Late Nineteenth Century." In Ira Katznelson and Aristede Zolberg, eds., *Working Class Formation: Nineteenth Century Patterns in Western Europe and the United States.* Princeton, N.J.: Princeton University Press.

Shienbaum, Kim Ezra. 1984. *Beyond the Electoral Connection: A Reassessment of the Role of Voting in Contemporary American Politics.* Philadelphia: University of Pennsylvania Press.

Shingles, Richard D. 1981. "Black Consciousness and Political Participation: The Missing Link." *American Political Science Review* 75, 1 (March).

Shortridge, Ray M. 1981. "Estimating Voter Participation." In Jerome M. Clubb, William H. Flanigan, and Nancy H. Zingale, eds., *Analyzing Electoral History: A Guide to the Study of American Voter Behavior.* Beverly Hills, Calif.: Sage Publication.

Shupe, Anson, and William Stacey. 1983. "The Moral Majority Constituency." In Robert C. Liebman and Robert Wuthnow, eds., *The New Christian Right: Mobilization and Legitimation.* New York: Aldine Publishing.

Simpson, John H. 1983. "Moral Issues and Status Politics." In Robert C. Liebman and Robert Wuthnow, eds., *The New Christian Right: Mobilization and Legitimation.* New York: Aldine Publishing.

Sinclair, Upton. 1951 [1906]. *The Jungle.* New York: Harper & Row.

Sitkoff, Harvey. 1974. "Years of the Locust." In Richard S. Kirkendall, ed., *The Truman Period as a Research Field: A Reappraisal, 1972.* Columbia: University of Missouri Press.

Skowronek, Stephen. 1982. *Building a New American State: The Expansion of Administrative Capacities, 1877–1920.* New York: Cambridge University Press.

Smith, David Michael. 1985. "Voter Registration on the Right: The Republican and Fundamentalist Christian Campaigns of 1984." Department of Political Science, Graduate School and University Center, City University of New York. Mimeo.

Squire, Peverill, David P. Glass, and Raymond E. Wolfinger. 1984. "Residential Mobility and Voter Turnout." Paper presented at a conference, "Where Have All the Voters Gone?," University of Chicago, April 26–28.

Squire, Peverill, Raymond E. Wolfinger, and David P. Glass. 1987. "Residential Mobility and Voter Turnout." *American Political Science Review* 81, 1 (March).

Steffen, Charles. 1984. *The Mechanics of Baltimore: Workers and Politics in the Age of Revolution, 1703–1812.* Urbana: University of Illinois Press.

Steffens, Lincoln. 1951 [1904]. *The Shame of the Cities.* New York: Harper & Row.

Stone, Alan. 1981. "State and Market: Economic Regulation and the Great Productivity Debate." In Thomas Ferguson and Joel Rogers, eds., *The Hidden Election: Politics and Economics in the 1980 Presidential Campaign.* New York: Pantheon Books.

Sundquist, James L. 1973. *Dynamics of the Party System: Alignment and Realignment of Political Parties in the United States.* Washington, D.C.: Brookings Institution.

———. 1985. "The 1984 Election: How Much Realignment?" *Brookings Review* 3, 2 (Winter).

Taft, Philip, and Philip Ross. 1969. In Hugh Davis Graham and Ted Robert Gurr, eds., *The History of Violence in America: A Report to the National Commission on the Causes and Prevention of Violence.* New York: Praeger.

Teixeira, Ruy. 1987. *Why Americans Don't Vote: Turnout Decline in the United States, 1960–1984.* Westport, Conn.: Greenwood Press.

Teixeira, Ruy. 1992. *The Disappearing American Voter.* Washington, D.C.: Brookings.

Thompson, E. P. 1963. *The Making of the English Working Class.* New York: Vintage Books.

Tilly, Charles. 1984. "Social Movements and National Politics." In Charles Bright and Susan Harding, *Statemaking and Social Movements.* Ann Arbor: University of Michigan Press.

Tilly, Charles, Louise Tilly, and Richard Tilly. 1977. *The Rebellious Century.* Cambridge: Harvard University Press.

Tindall, George Brown. 1972. *The Disruption of the Solid South.* Athens: University of Georgia Press.

Tocqueville, Alexis de. 1969 [1838]. *Democracy in America.* New York: Anchor Books.

Tufte, Edward R. 1978. *Political Control of the Economy.* Princeton, N.J.: Princeton University Press.

U.S. Bureau of the Census. 1980. *Projections of Voting Age for States, November 1980.* Current Population Reports, Series P-25, no. 870.

U.S. Federal Election Commission. 1997. *The Impact of the National Voter Registration Act of 1993 on the Administration of Elections for Federal Office, 1995–1996.* Report to the Congress.

———. 1999. *The Impact of the National Voter Registration Act of 1993 on the Administration of Elections for Federal Office, 1997–1998.* Report to the Congress.

Vaughan, Philip H. 1972. "President Truman's Committee on Civil Rights: The Urban Implications." *Missouri Historical Review* 66 (April).

Verba, Sidney and Norman H. Nie. 1972. *Participation in America.* New York, Harper & Row.

Verba, Sidney, Norman H. Nie, and Jae-On Kim. 1978. *Participation and Political Equality: A Seven-Nation Comparison.* New York: Cambridge University Press.

Verba, Sidney, Kay Lehman Schlozman, Henry Brady, and Norman H. Nie. 1993. "Citizen Activity: Who Participates? What Do They Say?" *American Political Science Review*, 87, 2 (June).

Vogel, David. 1983. "The Power of Business in America: A Reappraisal." *British Journal of Political Science* 13.

―――. 1989. *Fluctuating Fortunes: The Political Power of Business in America.* New York, Basic Books.

Voter Education Project News, vol. 3, no. 11, November 1969. Southern Regional Council, Atlanta, Georgia.

Waddell, Brian. 2000. *The War Against the New Deal: World War II's Military-Corporate Alliance and the Shaping of Modern U.S. Governance.* De Kalb: Northern Illinois University Press.

Walsh, J. Raymond. 1937. *CIO: Industrial Unionism in Action.* New York: W. W. Norton.

Weibe, Robert H. 1967. *The Search for Order.* New York: Hill & Wang.

Weinstein, James. 1968. *The Corporate Ideal in the Liberal State: 1900–1918.* Boston: Beacon Press.

―――. 1969. *The Decline of Socialism in America, 1912–1925.* New York: Vintage Books.

White, Claude R., and Mary K. White. 1937. *Relief Policies in the Depression.* New York: Social Science Research Council, Bulletin no. 38.

Wilentz, Sean. 1984. *Chants Democratic: New York City and the Rise of the Working Class, 1788–1850.* New York: Oxford University Press.

Will, George F. October 10, 1983. "In Defense of Nonvoting." *Newsweek*, p. 96.

Williams, Cynthia A. June 1987. *Litigation Contesting Barriers to Minority and Low-Income Voter Registration.* New York: A Publication of the Human SERVE Campaign.

Williamson, Chilton. 1960. *American Suffrage: From Property to Democracy, 1760–1860.* Princeton, N.J.: Princeton University Press.

Wolfe, Alan. 1981. *America's Impasse: The Rise and Fall of the Politics of Growth.* New York: Pantheon Books.

Wolfinger, Raymond E., and Steven J. Rosenstone. 1978. "The Effect of Registration Laws on Voter Turnout." *American Political Science Review* 72, 1 (March).

―――. 1980. *Who Votes?* New Haven, Conn.: Yale University Press.

Woodward, C. Vann. 1951. *Origins of the New South: 1877–1913.* Baton Rouge: Louisiana State University Press.

―――. 1968. *Burden of Southern History.* Enlarged ed. Baton Rouge: Louisiana State University Press.

Wright, Gavin. 1986. *Old South, New South: Revolutions in the Southern Economy Since the Civil War.* New York: Basic Books.

Yarnell, Ellen. 1974. *Democrats and Progressives: The 1948 Election as a Test of Postwar Liberalism.* Berkeley: University of California Press.

Zinn, Howard. 1980. *A People's History of the United States.* New York: Harper & Row.

Acknowledgments

*M*any people aided Human SERVE. We can mention only a few. Some of Human SERVE's board members played especially crucial roles. In 1983, George A. Brager, dean of the Columbia University School of Social Work, allowed the project to establish its headquarters in two university offices. George Wallerstein supported the project financially from the beginning. Juan Cartagena, board president in the late 1980s, guided Human SERVE through a period of bankruptcy, aided by an emergency financial gift from Roger Alcaly. Blair Clark, in addition to a term as board president, was a good friend and constant source of advice about Human SERVE's political strategy and fund-raising efforts.

It was never easy to raise money for voter registration reform, since most foundations favored traditional hands-on voter registration campaigns. Consequently, Human SERVE's budget was never large: $90,000 in 1983; $270,000, 1984; $460,000, 1985; $180,000, 1986; $170,000, 1987; $370,000, 1988; $380,000, 1989; $210,000, 1990; $180,000, 1991; $230,000, 1992; $230,000, 1993; $270,000, 1994; $320,000, 1995; $300,000, 1996; $160,000, 1997; $110,000, 1998; and $110,000 in 1999, the year Human SERVE closed. Of the various foundations that provided support over the years, two deserve special mention. David Hunter of the Stern Family Fund made the first grant in 1983, and the Ford Foundation funded the project for more than a decade. We would also like to acknowledge the following foundations: Carnegie, Aaron Diamond, Joyce, Rockefeller Family, and the North Shore Unitarian Universalist Veatch Program.

Human SERVE's first executive director, Hulbert James, and associate director Cynthia Williams, got the project up and running. Linda Davidoff followed James as executive director, and oriented Human SERVE toward working for congressional legislation. Jo-Anne Chasnow, who began as a state organizer in New Jersey in 1983, assumed the leadership of Human SERVE in its final years, and assisted in the preparation of this edition of this book.

Columbia University student interns made a large contribution to Human SERVE, some of whom joined our staff when they graduated. They included Michelle Billies, Jim Conley, Rebekah Evenson, Jim Ford, Kenneth Grossinger, Lyn Hogan, and Susan Kotcher. Other Human SERVE staff who are not mentioned in the text of this book include Margaret Beutler who worked in the northwest, Darryl Jordon in Ohio, Janice Kydd in New York, Wayne Thompson in the southern region, as well as John McGettrick, Jack Clark, Don Hazen, and David Plotkin in the national office. Tim Sampson provided invaluable staff training.

Finally, we want to thank the leaders of various national organizations with whom we worked, particularly Ira Glasser of American Civil Liberties Union, Lloyd Leonard of the national League of Women Voters, Gene Karpinski of the United States Public Interest Research Group, Greg Moore who ran Jesse Jackson's national voter registration program, and Jim Dickson in the disabilities community. Herb Stone of the House Subcommittee on Elections and Tom Zoeller of the Senate Rules Committee played critical roles. Not least, we wish to acknowledge our cherished friend and literary agent, Frances Goldin.

Human SERVE's files, suitably indexed, are available in the archives of the Libraries of Columbia University.

Index